Designing School Health Curricula

Planning for Good Health

Designing School Health Curricula

Planning for Good Health

Evelyn E. Ames
Western Washington University

Lucille A. Trucano
Health Education Consultant

Julia C. Wan
Bainbridge Island School District

Margo H. Harris
American Lung Association

WCB Wm. C. Brown Publishers

Book Team

Editor *Chris Rogers*
Developmental Editor *Susan McCormick*
Production Coordinator *Deborah Donner*

Wm. C. Brown Publishers

President *G. Franklin Lewis*
Vice President, Publisher *Thomas E. Doran*
Vice President, Operations and Production *Beverly Kolz*
National Sales Manager *Virginia S. Moffat*
Group Sales Manager *John Finn*
Executive Editor *Edgar J. Laube*
Director of Marketing *Kathy Law Laube*
Marketing Manager *George H. Chapin*
Managing Editor, Production *Colleen A. Yonda*
Manager of Visuals and Design *Faye M. Schilling*
Production Editorial Manager *Julie A. Kennedy*
Production Editorial Manager *Ann Fuerste*
Publishing Services Manager *Karen J. Slaght*

WCB Group

President and Chief Executive Officer *Mark C. Falb*
Chairman of the Board *Wm. C. Brown*

Cover and interior design by Kay D. Fulton
Copyedited by Nichols Murray

Library of Congress Catalog Card Number: 90–85856

ISBN 0–697–10158–4

Printed in the United States of America by Wm. C. Brown Publishers, 2460 Kerper Boulevard, Dubuque, IA 52001

10 9 8 7 6 5 4 3 2 1

Contents

Preface

Herophilus said, "To lose one's health renders science null, art inglorious, strength unavailing, wealth useless, and eloquence powerless." This may be the first time that health had been heralded as necessary for the achievement of goals. However, health may not always come about by chance; most people need knowledge, attitudes, and skills to make thoughtful decisions that translate into well-being.

This book focuses on school health education curricula. It bridges the gap between curriculum development theory and the reality of health instruction in schools. It is designed to help practitioners (i.e., health educators, teachers, curriculum coordinators, and administrators) to apply pedagogical knowledge.

Chapter 1 covers the philosophical foundations of a health education curriculum. Any group that gives leadership to the development of health education curricula needs to explore current concepts of health, health education, the educational process, the learner, and how all of these relate to the society in which the learner functions. The implications of these concepts provide the underpinnings of a curriculum that will give young people what they need to make decisions that lead them to a high level of well-being.

Chapter 2 looks at comprehensive school health education and the content areas of school health instruction. It examines the target population: young people in grades kindergarten through twelve. It then suggests ways to narrow and sequence the scope of health education into a form that can be handled realistically.

Chapter 3 is an overview of the general curriculum-planning process. It starts with a look at who influences the curriculum. Then the chapter discusses tasks such as conducting needs assessments, appointing committees, designing a curriculum delivery system, and setting timelines.

Chapter 4 gives guidance in selecting and writing learning objectives. The relationship of goals and objectives to the philosophy is stressed. An effort is made to take the mystery out of writing objectives.

Chapter 5 looks at the design of a curriculum. It presents a variety of curriculum designs, including a way to use categorical programs. The advantages and disadvantages of each are explained. The chapter also describes how teachers use the curriculum as a blueprint for delivering instruction.

Chapters 6 and 7 discuss the location and selection of resources. Steps in searching for resources are suggested in chapter 6. The wealth of resources available to curriculum developers is a highlight of this chapter. Chapter 7 elaborates on criteria that can be used in selecting resources and provides examples of forms for evaluating resources.

Chapter 8 shows the need for building bridges with community resources to assist in making school health education realistic and effective. Potential partners and their contributions are described as well as ways to form and maintain these relationships. The future role of school health services and a healthful school environment is discussed within this partnership design.

Chapter 9 gives future health educators thoughtful suggestions for ensuring successful programs. This chapter also includes a discussion of sensitive issues, the prevention of controversies, and laws relating to school health instruction.

Chapter 10 includes keys to successful implementation. Information is provided on pilot programs and the promotion of curricula, as well as on identifying the difficulties of implementation.

Chapter 11 covers the purposes of curriculum evaluation and the difficulties of evaluating health education. It also describes evaluation design, data collection, and the use of evaluation results.

Chapter 12 stresses the need for planned maintenance of curricular programs. The focus of this chapter is fine-tuning, updating, and revising.

Health is a major factor in the quality of life that everyone seek. Without health, all other goals may be unattainable. Carefully planned comprehensive health education curricula must be a responsibility of the educational system of this country. The community is responsible for committing time to participate in planning, to understand the program, and to support the curriculum philosophically and financially.

Acknowledgements

The authors wish to give special acknowledgement to Katey Roemmele, who provided us with her expertise in typing and editing the manuscript. Our appreciation is offered to Corine Olson and Beth Reis for their comments and suggestions. We would also like to thank all of our colleagues who encouraged us in this endeavor.

Introduction

Throughout history, individuals and groups have heralded health as *the* goal for people. Benjamin Franklin said, "No nation can ever be stronger or healthier or more understanding than the strength, health and understanding which it indicates in its youth" (Creswell, 1985: 17–18). In 1842, Horace Mann advocated health instruction in the schools. In 1850, the "Report of the Sanitary Commission of Massachusetts" made recommendations about public health and included a recommendation for school health instruction (Creswell, 1985). Between 1880 and 1890, laws were passed requiring instruction concerning the effects of alcohol and narcotics. Forty states said they would teach this material on a broader scale through physiology and hygiene. In 1922, Dr. Claire E. Turner directed the Malden Massachusetts Demonstration Project, which showed that health instruction impacts health behavior (Creswell, 1985: 20).

On the whole, however, schools promoted health in those early days mostly by providing nutritious lunches, testing eyesight, examining teeth, and screening students for physical defects. Some people credit the start of health education to the Child Health Organization (1918–1922) under the directorship of Sally Lucas Jean. This organization did not fault the value of providing health services to young people but felt that such services should also have an educational component so that young people could understand the necessity for visual screening and other preventive measures and thus be motivated to seek such services for themselves in their adult years.

In 1918, the Seven Cardinal Principles of Secondary Education listed health as one of the leading objectives in education. It stated that "health needs cannot be neglected during the period of secondary education without serious danger to the individual and race. The secondary school should therefore provide health instruction, inculcate health habits, organize an effective program of physical activities, regard health needs in planning work and play, and cooperate with home and community in safeguarding and promoting health interests." It went on to say that "to discharge the duties of life and benefit from leisure one must have good health. The health of the individual is essential also to the vitality of the race and to the defense of the nation. Health education is, therefore, fundamental" (*Report of the Commission of the Reorganization of Secondary Schools,* 1918).

In 1938, the Educational Policies Commission listed health education under the objective of self-realization:

Health Knowledge	The educated person understands the basic facts concerning health and disease.
Health Habits	The educated person protects his own health and that of his dependents.
Public Health	The educated person works to improve the health of the community. (Educational Policies Commission, 1938: 50)

In 1941, the Joint Committee on Health Problems in Education of the National Education Association and the American Medical Association suggested the following objectives for health education:

- Instruct children and youth so that they may conserve and improve their own health.
- Establish in them habits and principles of living which throughout their school life and in later years will aid in providing the abundant vigor and vitality which are a foundation for the greatest possible happiness and service in personal, family, and community life.
- Promote satisfactory habits and attitudes among parents and adults through parent and adult education and through the health education program for children, so that the school may become an effective agency for the advancement of the social aspects of health education in the family and in the community as well as in the school itself.
- Improve the individual and community life of the future; to insure a better second generation, and still better third generation; to build a healthier and fitter nation and race. (Joint Committee on Health Problems in Schools, 1941)

Oberteuffer (1964) said that people do not acquire a high level of well-being by chance. The only way to get the job done in anything but a haphazard way is for society to demand that its educational system teach these things.

Two significant studies identified a variety of reasons for the lack of sound school health education programs in our schools: the School Health Education Study in 1964 and the *Report of the President's Committee on Health Education* (1973). The School Health Education Study was an investigation of the health knowledge and behavior of youth. It also found that health instruction programs were in need of critical review; that health instruction was virtually nonexistent or, where it was carried out, that the "prevailing practices [could] be legitimately challenged" (Sliepcevich, 1964: 12). Out of the study came a conceptually designed comprehensive health education curriculum that stands as one of the best ever.

The *Report of the President's Committee* pointed to the need for more and better health education. It stated that "while the need and demand for health care services have been rising, health education has been neglected. . . . In many states legislation actually impedes development of effective school programs. . . . What is taught to children is not made meaningful enough to stay with them." The report also said that "this country is neglecting a vast opportunity to help people help themselves to have better health. . . . any changes or improvements in the delivery and financing of health care will be virtually nullified unless there is, at the same time, an improvement in health education programs" (*Report of the President's Committee on Health Education,* 1971: 11). National legislation in 1978 resulted in the passage of the Health Education Amendment to the Elementary and Secondary Education Act, which encouraged and supported health education programs.

During the 1980s, many reports were issued about the crisis in education in the United States. One report, *High School: A Report on Secondary Education in America,* strongly supported health education by saying, "No knowledge is more crucial than knowledge about health. Without it, no other life goal can be successfully achieved" (Boyer, 1983: 112).

In the early 1980s, the State School Health Education Task Force was convened by the Education Commission of the States (ECS) to study school health education and to develop a policy statement that would exemplify the state level of commitment to health education. The resulting recommendations were based upon the premise that "while health education is not a panacea for health problems, it can play a significant role in reducing the incidence of some problems and the severity of others" (Education Commission of the States, 1981: 19–20). In relation to the elementary level, the ECS handbook stated that "the schools have the opportunity to be a positive influence in the *development* of attitudes and behavior patterns that will enhance health. But health education at the secondary level is also critical. The stresses of adolescence and peer pressure place demands even on the healthy, well-adjusted teenager. This is a time for helping young people cope with the changes in their lives, for helping them learn how and where to seek assistance when needed, and to take responsibility for their actions" (Education Commission of the States, 1981: 20).

Code Blue is one of the latest reports concerned with the health status of youth and the need for health education to help them achieve a better level of well-being. In urging schools to play a stronger role in improving adolescent health, the National Commission on the Role of the School and the Community in Improving Adolescent Health said schools "should offer students a new type of health education that provides honest, relevant information and teaches skills and strategies to make wise decisions and develop positive values. They should assure schools are smoke free, drug free, and violence free, and promote the emotional and physical wellness of students and staff" (National Commission on the Role of the School, 1990: "Executive Summary").

Over the years, more than a hundred agencies, groups, and studies have stressed health as an objective of education. However, there is a credibility gap between what is said about education's responsibility for health and what is done about it. Although education cannot do everything, at no time in history have so many people believed that education is humankind's greatest hope. Health was among the objectives from the beginning. White House conferences on education have recognized health education, the Educational Policies Commission endorsed it (several times), and the American Association of School Administrators blessed it. According to Trucano (1969), this nation may have bought the educational objective of developing healthy people, but no one paid for it. Therefore, as with most things that are free, individuals and nations are paying for it in other ways.

The National Commission on the Role of the School and the Community in Improving Adolescent Health states that "it is abundantly clear from well-documented studies that without appropriate programs, large numbers of adolescents will fail educationally, fail as effective parents, and fail as productive members of the economy. Many will have chronic health problems. Many will die prematurely. Over time, such problems will require unacceptably high public expenditures" (p. 7). It goes on to say that

> to avoid these future costs, we must act immediately, using the abundant information now available to guide our investments. These investments, in turn, will reward us with even better programs. Our great technologies did not come into existence fully developed. The first computers did a few operations well, but visionary scientists realized that their potential was far greater. In fact, this potential was so great that public and private funds were and are extensively used to develop computers that have far exceeded our expectations. With sufficient time and investment, adolescent health programs can do the same. (National Commission on the Role of the School, 1990: 8)

Most schools have not really tested the power of education to develop in young people the ability to make wise decisions about their well-being. It is no wonder that we have an audience of adults and young people who do not listen to existing possibilities for preventing health problems and promoting healthy lifestyles. Improving this situation will take health knowledge, skills in applying this knowledge, and a desire to do so.

References

Boyer, E. L. 1983. *High school: A report on secondary education in America.* The Carnegie Foundation for the Advancement of Teaching. New York: Harper & Row.

Commission on the Reorganization of Secondary Education. 1918. *Cardinal principles of secondary education.* Washington, DC: Department of the Interior, Bureau of Education, Bulletin 1918 no. 35: 11–15.

Creswell, W. H., Newman, I. M., & Anderson, C. L. 1985. *School health practice.* St. Louis: C. B. Mosby.

Education Commission of the States. 1981. *Recommendations for school health education: A handbook for state policymakers* (March, 1981). Denver.

Educational Policies Commission. 1938. *The purposes of education in American democracy.* Washington, DC: National Education Association.

Joint Committee on Health Problems in Schools of the National Education Association and the American Medical Association. 1941. *Health education.* Washington, DC: National Education Association.

National Commission on the Role of the School and the Community in Improving Adolescent Health. 1990. *Code blue: Uniting for healthier youth.* Alexandria, Va.: National Association of State Boards of Education.

Oberteuffer, D. 1964. Vital ties between health and education. *NEA Journal* 53: 57–61.

Report of the Commission of the Reorganization of Secondary Schools. 1918. United States Bureau of Education bulletin. Washington, DC: United States Government Printing Office.

Report of the President's Committee on Health Education. 1973. Washington, DC: U.S. Government Printing Office.

Sliepcevich, E. M. 1964. *School health education study: A summary report of a nationwide study of health instruction in the public schools.* Washington, DC: School Health Education Study.

Trucano, L. May 1969. The complete human being. *Washington Education.*

Designing School Health Curricula

Planning for Good Health

1

Philosophy and Goals:
Seeking a Destination

After reading this chapter and participating in application activities, the student should be able to:

1. Identify a set of beliefs from which a health education philosophy can be developed.
2. Infer the effect of these beliefs on a health education curriculum.
3. Describe a process that a curriculum committee might use to develop a health education philosophy.
4. Relate curriculum goals to a philosophical statement.

A health education philosophy gives focus to curriculum development. The philosophy is derived from beliefs about health; about what health education is; about how to educate people to be healthy; about how people learn; and about what people need, healthwise, in a democracy to be comfortable with themselves, productive, and supportive of others.

Thus, health education curriculum planning starts with the formation of a philosophy that gives direction to the selection of health education goals, to the determination of scope and sequence, to the design of the curriculum, to the objectives, to teaching strategies, to the selection of resources, and to the kind of in-service training needed. Basing health education curriculum decisions on an identified philosophy gives everyone confidence in educational decisions.

This chapter presents the foundations of a philosophy for health education curriculum planning. It explains the implications of these foundations for that planning and suggests how curriculum planners arrive at a philosophy.

Foundations of a Philosophy and Their Implication

A philosophy that gives direction to health education curriculum planning is derived from a consensus of beliefs about (1) health, (2) health education, (3) the learner, (4) the society in which people live today and in which they will live in the future, and (5) the learning process.

Health

Health is multidimensional, comprising the physical, mental, emotional, social, and spiritual aspects of an individual. Individuals who are physically healthy have energy for life's activities; illnesses and disease seldom interfere in their lives. Mentally healthy people are comfortable with themselves and others and are optimistic about life. Mentally healthy people have self-direction. Their perception of reality includes the fact that adventures in life bring problems but that resolving or modifying these problems is possible. Emotionally healthy people recognize, accept, trust, and share their feelings and guide those feelings constructively. Socially healthy people like and trust others; they are realistic about the fact that they cannot like and trust everyone. Social health also involves feeling a sense of responsibility toward others. Spiritual health reflects a moral standard to live by—the belief in values that enhance all people's lives.

Health has been defined by the World Health Organization as a state of complete physical, emotional and social well-being, not merely the absence of disease or infirmity. The *School Health Education Study* defined health as "a quality of life involving dynamic interaction and interdependence among the individual's physical well-being, his mental and emotional reactions, and the social complex in which he exists" (School Health Education Study, 1967: 10). Health is a quality of life through which goals and dreams may be achieved.

Today's concept of health places the emphasis for health instruction on health and not disease. This does not mean that understanding diseases—their causes and treatment—has no place in the health curriculum; it just means less emphasis on disease. It means an effort to utilize the understanding of disease and its causes to help individuals make decisions that develop, maintain, or enhance well-being.

For example, emphasizing health and not disease would lead a curriculum committee to recommend that the mental health area of study for secondary schools include such topics as the following:

- Ways to achieve mental health
- Ways to maintain mental health throughout a person's lifetime
- How individuals positively affect other people's mental health
- How individuals and communities can establish environments that have a positive impact on mental health
- The possible causes of mental and emotional illnesses, their prevention, and treatment (may be included in a mental health unit or moved to a disease unit)

Another example that reflects today's concept of health would be an emphasis on maintaining proper weight, selecting appropriate exercise activities, and balancing dietary intake against caloric output when planning units on exercise and nutrition—as opposed to a heavy focus on dietary diseases, methods of losing weight, and how certain exercises damage the body.

Health Education

Health education is a process in which combinations of learning experiences guide and assist individuals in developing, maintaining, or improving their quality of life. This process involves planned, organized, and sequential instruction to influence health attitudes, knowledge, and behavior. Health education enables individuals to make informed decisions because it gives them the tools with which to promote and maintain their own well-being at the highest level. It is a process through which individuals can accept responsibility for their own health and that of their families and their communities. The real value of health education is that it provides a foundation for health choices throughout one's lifetime.

Leaders in health education have said that the goal of health education is to

> promote, maintain, and improve individual and community health *through the educational process*. . . . Health education is eminently interested in giving people the empowered role of defining their problems, setting the priorities, and creating the practical solutions by which they achieve a sense of interest in, commitment to, and ownership over the efforts used to address health issues. (National Task Force for the Preparation and Practice of Health Educators, 1985: vi)

The American Association of School Administrators' *Critical Issues Report* states that there are three concepts that provide the basis for a new type of education to promote health for the children and youth of our nation:

1. What we eat, drink, inhale, and how we use our bodies will do more to prevent

illnesses and keep us healthy than pills, wonder drugs, or the marvels of medicine.
2. We choose the kind of health we will have with the habits and behavior we choose.
3. Good health habits and behavior can be taught and learned, provided we start with students at an early age and work with them continually and consistently using the full resources available to the schools. (Pine, 1985)

In order to implement the present concept of health education, planners need to develop a comprehensive curriculum that reaches all students. A comprehensive health education curriculum allows for consideration of all essential health content at appropriate grade levels, with sufficient time for learning to take place. One school assembly does not teach about mathematics—and one assembly cannot teach about health. If schools have comprehensive health education, there is no problem of where to teach health topics. When new health topics of concern emerge, they can easily be inserted into a planned curriculum at appropriate levels. For example, when AIDS education surfaced, it could easily have been included with the topics of disease control, decision making, and responsible sexual behavior.

For health education to be meaningful to individuals, it must consider health from the standpoint of the whole person. People are not physical beings or social beings or emotional beings—they are human beings. For example, smoking education cannot deal only with the effects of smoking on the body; it must be concerned with why people smoke when we know so much about the harmful effects of tobacco. It must consider such issues as government subsidies for tobacco farmers and the fact that the government allows cigarette advertisements even while it requires cigarette packages to carry health warnings and spends millions of dollars on research to find ways to prevent and treat the health problems that cigarettes cause.

Code Blue—Uniting for Healthier Youth recommends that young people receive a new kind of health education that:

- provides honest, relevant information about disease and accident prevention, family life and sex education, drug and alcohol abuse, violence, mental health, and nutrition;
- teaches skills and strategies needed to make wise decisions, develop positive values, generate alternatives, deal with group pressure, work cooperatively, and avoid fights . . .
- includes participation in physical activity programs that foster lifelong exercise habits; and
- begins before students are pressured to experiment with risky behaviors and continues throughout adolescence. It should begin in kindergarten and continue in a planned, sequential manner through grade 12. (National Commission on the Role of the School, 1990: 36)

The Learner

A review of learners' growth and developmental characteristics, interests, and needs must be made before designing a curriculum. This review is an important part of the curriculum committee's work (see chapter 3 for needs assessments).

Growth and developmental characteristics, needs, and interests of learners guide curriculum decisions. For example, young people five to nine years old may have disturbing dreams, fears, and anxieties. Health education can help them understand why people dream, that dreams are just dreams, and it can help them talk out their fears and anxieties. This same age group wants to grow and learn.

FIGURE 1.1 Fourth graders' questions. (Permission to include information from the book *Students Speak,* © 1984 by Lucille Trucano, was granted from the Comprehensive Health Education Foundation (CHEF ©), Seattle, WA. All rights reserved.)

Fourth Graders' Questions

What are some ways you can get over being angry?

Why don't we like ourselves?

Why do we have feelings?

Why do we listen to other people when we don't want to do it?

Why do people laugh at handicapped people?

How is it possible to inherit things from distant relatives?

How do you change from a cell to a baby?

How does your brain get smarter?

How do the sperm and egg mix to make the baby?

How do you keep your family happy?

How can you help your mother and father get rid of their worries?

What would I do if my mom had a heart attack?

What do you do when an accident happens and you are not in it?

Health education can help them see the relation of growth and learning to health habits and allow them to explore activities that enhance growth and learning. See appendix 1 for selected growth and developmental characteristics, health interests, and health needs of age groups and their implications for health education planning.

To be meaningful, health education must relate to the learners' perceptions of their interests. Figure 1.1 lists selective fourth-grade student questions that reflect their interests.

An example of the kind of information about learners that a committee should review is the report *Turning Points.* The report states:

> The onset of adolescence is a critical period of biological and psychological change for the individual. Puberty is one of the most far-reaching biological upheavals in the life span. For many young adolescents, it involves drastic changes in the social environment. . . . These years are highly formative for behavior patterns in education and health that have enduring significance. Adolescence is typically characterized by exploratory behavior, much of which is developmentally appropriate and socially adaptive for most young people. However, many of these behaviors carry high risks. The adverse effects may be near-term and vivid, such as school dropout or alcohol-related accidents. Or they may be long-term, such as bad health habits that lead to heart disease and cancer. . . .
>
> The challenge for educational and related institutions is thus to help provide the building blocks of adolescent development and preparation for adult life. Yet most American junior high and middle schools do not meet the developmental needs of young adolescents. . . . (Carnegie Council on Adolescent Development, 1989:12)

Another report that a philosophy committee should review is *Code Blue—Uniting for Healthier Youth,* which discusses health needs of young people:

> Never before has one generation of American teenagers been less healthy, less cared for, and less prepared for life than their parents were at the same age. . . . *This commission finds that education and health are inextricably intertwined.* A teen who is depressed and doing poorly in school may begin relying on alcohol or drugs—and as a consequence, fall further and further behind. And a teenager with a baby is far more likely to be absent from school and eventually drop out. (The National Commission on the Role of the School, 1990: 3–4)

Another document that provides information about the health needs of learners is *Healthy People, 2000*. It discusses the nation's goals for improving Americans' health over the next decade by encouraging healthy living and preventing disease. To reach these goals, 298 objectives have been identified for improving the nation's health. These objectives develop targets in priority areas such as nutrition, physical activity and fitness, sexual behavior, HIV infection, mental and behavioral disorders, and violent and abusive behavior. For example, two of these objectives are:

- To reduce the prevalence of overweight adults to no more than 20 percent. The current rate is 26 percent.
- To reduce pregnancies to 50 per 1,000 teenagers younger than 18. The current rate is 71 per 1,000.

The important keys to remember about learners is that they are all unique and all important, and their growth and developmental characteristics play a large part in what their health needs and interests are.

Society

Basic beliefs about our society should affect what is taught and how it is taught. A democracy is characterized by freedom, responsibility, and diversity. There is freedom to choose among many choices; there is responsibility—to oneself, one's family, one's community, and one's environment; and there is diversity in beliefs and customs, points of view, and competing ideas.

Democracy demands for its citizens the chance to explore all aspects of competing ideas and the freedom to select from any belief, custom, or point of view. If a democracy allows many choices, then schools have a responsibility to assist students in making *wise* choices. To make wise choices about health, learners must have health knowledge, must be critical of that knowledge (is it reliable? is it valid?), and must be able to draw conclusions about that knowledge. Individuals in a democracy need a high level of health education.

If students have a right to make choices, then curriculum planners should write goals and objectives that reflect this. Teachers who plan lessons arising out of these goals and objectives are influenced to provide opportunities for exploring divergent points of view. As an example, if abortion is included as a topic to be studied, reliable information and quality resources both for and against abortion should be available.

A strong assertion in the philosophy that instruction should meet the needs, interests, and growth and developmental characteristics of young people helps curriculum planners address sensitive issues. For example, sexuality education is clearly a need in the intermediate grade levels as well as in middle and high school. If the planning committee is representative of the community, then the decision to include sexuality education should be acceptable, especially if it is shown that the decision is based on student growth and developmental characteristics, needs, and interests.

Learners must examine the delicate balance between freedom for the individual and an individual's responsibility to others. For example, a teenager may want the freedom of sexual experimentation—but this may result in pregnancy. Prior to sexual experimentation, teenagers should consider if they are able to provide good prenatal care from the moment of conception. The prospective parents must also consider whether or not they will be able to give the new life every opportunity to develop its potential physically, mentally, and emotionally, which requires, at the least, good nutrition and freedom from drugs from the moment of conception.

Whatever is taught in health education, it must help people see the implications of their decisions for their own health and that of their families, the community, and the nation.

FIGURE 1.2 Causal influences on student learning. (From Walberg, H. (1984). "Improving the Productivity of America's Schools," *Educational Leadership* 41, no. 8:21. Reprinted with permission of the Association for Supervision and Curriculum Development. Copyright © 1984 by ASCD. All rights reserved.)

Causal Influences on Student Learning

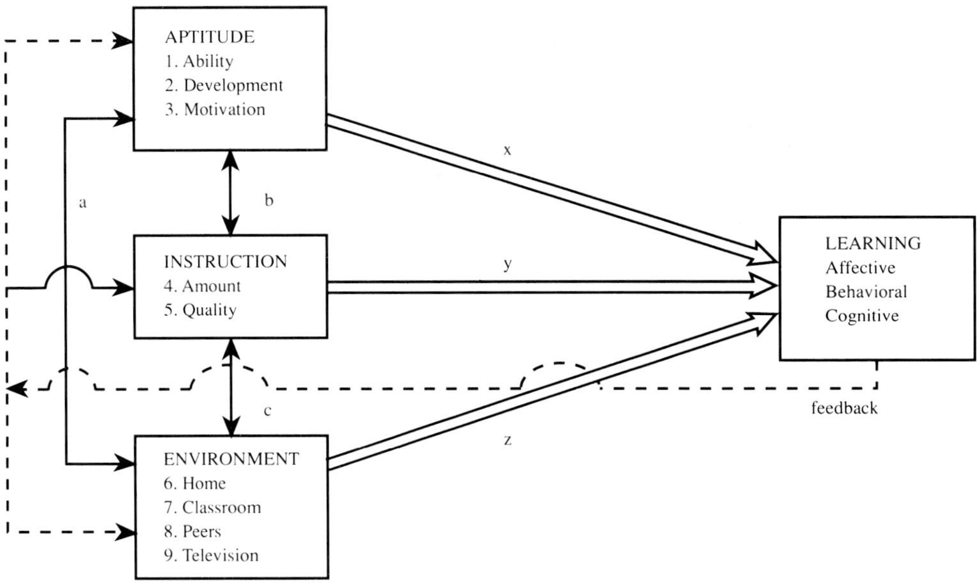

Aptitude, instruction, and the psychological environment are major direct causes of learning (shown as double arrows X, Y, and Z). They also influence one another (shown as arrows a, b, and c), and are in turn influenced by feedback on the amount of learning that takes place (shown as broken arrows).

The Learning Process

Many factors affect learning: perception of self, the health level of the learner, level of maturity, the teacher, parental involvement in and support of education, sequencing of content, amount of time allocated to health education, content selected, teaching strategies used, quantity and quality of resources, and the learning environment created within the school building and the classroom.

Walberg states that it is difficult to draw definitive conclusions about how selected factors affect learning. Since 1975 he and his colleagues have tried to analyze the power of various factors that influence learning. He says that "the prior problem, now being solved, is estimating the magnitude of effects of educational inputs on outputs, which primarily involves causal rather than value questions" (Walberg, 1984: 20). Figure 1.2 shows the interrelationships of aptitude, instruction, and environment on learning. All have direct bearing on whether or not learning takes place, but they also influence each other.

Walberg's first three factors involve the amount of instruction a student receives and the degree of ability the student has. But even if sufficient instruction and a high degree of ability exist, he feels that without motivation,

Lungs are for life. These fifth-graders blow air through straws into cows' lungs to see how lungs work. In a health curriculum project, promoted by the American Lung Association in many schools across the country, children learn to value their bodies and protect their lungs against poisons like cigarette smoke. (Reprinted with permission of the American Lung Association.)

the other two factors may not mean much. He says that factors 6 through 8 can influence learning by raising student ability, motivation, and responsiveness to instruction.

Students who come from homes with alcoholism and drug abuse, mental illness, domestic violence, or sexual abuse may have trouble learning. Health problems such as poor eyesight, malnutrition, and asthma also interfere with learning. Students with lower mental capacity must be given different learning experiences than more capable students.

A key to successful health instruction is the caliber of the teachers; their comprehension of health and health education is critical: how they plan and teach affects student learning. Because individuals learn in a variety of ways, teachers must use a variety of instructional strategies. Some individuals learn well by reading, others by role playing or debating, some through discussion, viewing, investigating, creating, simulating, observing, writing, or researching. Some may learn by repetition, by teaching others, by being tutored, by using a computer, by field activities, by visualization or contemplation, through programmed materials, or inquiry discussions, or through a combination of many of the above.

I hear—I forget;
I see—I remember;
I do—I understand.

Guild (1988) says that "the fact that people have different ways of learning, confirmed by common sense, experience and research, is now capturing the attention of educators through the study of learning styles. A relatively new term itself, *learning styles* [research] draws upon a rich history of psychology, including studies of individual differences in cognitive processes, motivation,

FIGURE 1.3 Learning style characteristics. (Used with permission, from *Marching to Different Drummers,* Association of Supervision and Curriculum Development, 1985. By Pat Guild and Steve Garger.)

Some Examples of Style Characteristics

Category	Characteristics*	Researchers
COGNITION perceiving, finding out, getting information	sensing/intuition	Jung, Myers-Briggs, Mok, Keirsey and Bates
	field dependent/field independent	Witkin
	abstract/concrete	Gregorc, Kolb and McCarthy
	visual, auditory, kinesthetic, tactile	Barbe and Swassing, Dunn and Dunn
CONCEPTUALIZATION thinking, forming ideas, processing, memory	extrovert/introvert	Jung, Myers-Briggs, Keirsey and Bates
	reflective observation/ active experimentation	Kolb and McCarthy
	random/sequential	Gregorc
AFFECT feelings, emotional response, motivation, values, judgements	feeler/thinker	Jung, Myers-Briggs, Mok, Keirsey and Bates
	effect of temperature, light, food, time of day, sound, design	Dunn and Dunn
BEHAVIOR manifestations of all the above-mentioned characteristics		

*Characteristics separated by a slash (/) indicate bipolar or opposite traits.

personality and culture. . . . Learning style describes consistent and pervasive characteristics of an individual's pattern of learning" (p. 4). Guild goes on to say that "researchers have identified and described a variety of labels [see figure 1.3] which illustrate differences in people's cognitive, conceptual, affective, and behavioral styles. The research confirms that people do bring certain consistent patterns to a learning situation which can be described as their style. But the significance of learning styles runs the risk of being diluted by too many labels and mixed messages" (p. 5). Guild feels that "teachers and administrators should study the research for the specific examples it provides, in order to increase their own awareness of the various ways people learn, but attachment to specific labels is not necessary and may be premature" (Guild, 1988: 5).

Having a variety of current and appropriate resources, helps to individualize instruction. Allowing a choice of assignments or choice in how an assignment is done also helps. Even in evaluating students, individuality should be remembered. Some students are not test-takers. There are other ways of ascertaining grades; individual projects, quality of daily assignments, and oral tests can be used to evaluate students as well as written tests.

Much of health education must begin early to be effective. The elementary schools have the potential to reach young people in their habit-forming years. Many behavioral patterns that contribute to the major diseases have their beginnings in childhood. Goethe, the German philosopher, said that the intelligent man begins with the child.

Sufficient time must be devoted to instruction for learning to occur. But Walberg feels that "it is neither the chief determinant nor a weak correlate of learning; like the other essential factors, time appears to be a necessary ingredient but insufficient by itself to produce learning" (1984). (Review figure 1.3 for the other factors.) A student needs time to exchange ideas, interact, and disagree. Time is needed to search for more meaning and to eventually weave what is learned into old ideas, to change old ideas, and/or to acquire new ones. How different this is from the one-lecture approach—one assembly or a single presentation. How reassuring it would be for learners to say no to drugs and know *why* they say no.

The learning climate an instructor sets is as important as what is taught. If the instructor conveys the message that each person is important, that people do have the right to make decisions, and that health education is important, then learning is more likely to take place. Responses from students in the survey *Students Speak* show that students are very aware of the learning environment. The students asked that teachers listen to them and not force opinions and ideas on them. One student suggested that the teacher should not be bored when teaching health education.

The values, likes, and dislikes that young people hold affect how they process information received in the classroom. Curriculum planners must provide for this. For example, the elementary student should have choices of ethnic foods when asked to make a breakfast plan from food models. Students should know that their values, likes, and dislikes, on the whole, are acquired from their families, but at certain periods of their lives, their family values may be overridden by other influences, such as peers and media. Knowing this may help them withstand adverse influences.

Learning is not a matter of knowing information; learning is the discovery of meaning in that information. Facts are important as a basis for concept formation, as a foundation in decision making, and for understanding a larger whole, but they are not ends in themselves. Thus, the learning process is multifaceted. It requires expertise to create an environment in which learning can take place. Figure 1.4 summarizes the learning process.

Arriving at a Philosophy

The committee writing the philosophy spends time together to accomplish the following:

- Become knowledgeable about the field of health education, especially current thinking about health and health education. Input from professional health educators and/or coordinators is essential at this point. If professional health educators and coordinators are not members of the philosophy committee, they should provide input in the form of presentations, research from professional journals, or excerpts from professional books.

FIGURE 1.4 The learning process

Learning Process

Master teachers know that

- Individuals learn in different ways. Choice of assignments, choice of conclusions, and choice of testing may be ways to utilize this concept.
- Creating a readiness to learn brings about greater productivity. Utilizing student interests and their growth and developmental characteristics, and involving students in planning may create a readiness.
- Feelings of success motivate individuals. Short-term goals, realistic goals, mutual setting of goals, and work geared to the maturation and ability levels of students all can help with feelings of success.
- Productive individuals strive for self-realization. Individuals must see that what is being learned will fulfill them in some way.
- Individuals are a part of their heredity, home, community, religion, and nation. Positive home environment and the freedom to make choices that do not conflict with students' values facilitate learning.
- The more a learner is involved, the more learning occurs. Learning, where possible, should be active and should involve all senses.
- What one learns may be more permanent and effective if feelings are considered. Application of the learning experience to one's interests, values, and life may make it more interesting.
- Retention of all facts is impossible. Individuals must learn where to find information to critically evaluate it and to form concepts.
- Isolated segments of information may distort conclusions. The learner must have the opportunity to look at an idea or project comprehensively.
- Learning is both a process and an outcome. Results must not be judged on facts alone (i.e., objective tests).

- Become aware of student and community health concerns and values as well as national and international health problems. Input from community health educators, health-care providers, and school health educators and coordinators can aid the committee in this endeavor.
- Explore current thinking about the learner and the learning process. Input from administrators, knowledgeable elementary teachers and health teachers, health coordinators, and teacher-training personnel is valuable here.
- Clarify their own assumptions and beliefs, so that everyone understands how each person processes the input that comes to the committee and knows where each committee member stands.

Chapter 3 emphasizes the need for community representation of diverse viewpoints on the curriculum committee; such representation aids in developing a curriculum that the community can accept and support. A successful philosophy allows for a variety of opinions and accommodates as many viewpoints as possible. For example, the philosophy probably would state that in a democracy, individuals have the right to study or have information on all pertinent topics, have access to reliable and valid materials, and have the responsibility to critically examine all sides of an issue. Such a statement allows the inclusion of topics that might otherwise be excluded because they are considered too controversial. Divergent viewpoints must be addressed, and a balance of viewpoints must be accomplished.

Once the foundations have been explored, the committee gets on with the task of writing the statement of philosophy. We have included three school districts' philosophies as examples. We feel that none of these are complete, because they do not state or imply all philosophical foundations: health, health education, the learner, the society, and the learning process.

FIGURE 1.5 Sample Philosophical Statements

Responsible citizens are called upon to make choices and decisions which will affect their community, family, and personal well-being. Health education involves an ever-changing body of information, attitudes, and skills examined in settings which stimulate the decision-making process. Such examination is dynamic in nature and needs to be constantly reviewed and validated. Health education should be provided in schools in partnership with communities, families, and individuals. (Bainbridge Island School District, WA 1988)

The objective of health education is to motivate people to help themselves and others to live healthy, happy, productive lives.

Health education is a process that bridges the gap between health information and health practices. Parents have the privilege and the primary responsibility for health of children and youth. The community, including the schools, has a vital secondary responsibility. The school, as one agency, through its health education program, can contribute to these efforts by providing students with learning experiences that help them acquire accurate information and that help them develop attitudes, values, and beliefs needed to utilize the information in making health decisions and taking sound health action.

A good health education program includes a diversity of teaching methods to accommodate different learning abilities and learning styles of students. The good health education program considers the total human being, so it includes the psychological and social as well as the physical aspects of a health topic.

A unified approach to health teaching—that is, a planned, sequential curriculum in health education throughout the school years—is necessary so that students are continuously encouraged to develop a life-style that fosters good health.

Health topics will be dealt with honestly. The intent is to complement the family's responsibility to provide values along with answers. (Sumner School District, Sumner, Wash., 1984)

All individuals are born with certain potential. One's experiences determine the realization of these potentials, and education is a big part of those experiences. The ultimate goal of health education and all education is to help individuals realize their potential. Health education can help individuals reach optimal well-being physically, socially, and emotionally, which frees them to achieve their potential.

In a democracy health education must help young people learn decision-making skills, provide them opportunities to explore information both pro and con concerning a health topic, and allow them to decide their own directions, thinking and feelings. The ultimate responsibility for health lies within oneself.

Health education must be cognizant of how individuals learn, in that:

Selected topics for learning must be meaningful to individuals and relate to their needs and interests.

Provisions for learning must allow for the different styles and levels of learning.

More than facts must be woven into learning strategies to provide enough motivation to reinforce, modify, or change behavior. (Source unknown)

The study that precedes the writing of the philosophy should lead the designers of the curriculum to see that health education must:

- Move from the concept of health as lack of disease or illness to the concept of health as optimal well-being.
- Move from memorizing and parroting facts to learning experiences involving investigation, critical thinking, and problem solving.
- Move from learning experiences that consider irrelevant health topics to experiences that relate to the health needs, interests, and developmental characteristics of learners.

FIGURE 1.6 The relation of goals and philosophy

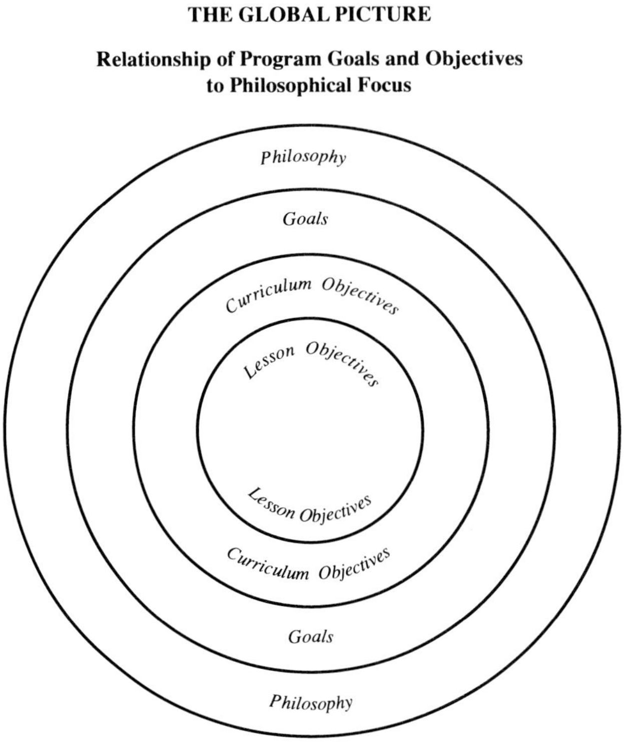

- Move from telling individuals what is right and wrong to creating opportunities for them to consider how to make wise health decisions.
- Move from employing untrained individuals to employing professional health educators.
- Move from thinking health can be "caught without being taught" to allocating specific time for health learning to take place.

Curriculum Goals Emerge from the Philosophy

As indicated in figure 1.5, goals emerge from the philosophical statement. Goals are broad statements of the final outcomes of health education.

The American Association of School Administrators' *Critical Issues Report* states that one way to find the sources of and inspiration for goals is to study the health needs and conditions of students, to explore the health needs and conditions of the community, and to search out the advice of specialists in medicine and health. The report suggests sources to consult in a systemic search for goals:

- Goals from governmental agencies
- Legal requirements on health instruction and information from advisory documents on health from the state level
- Local-level samplings of public opinion, needs-assessment studies, community advisory committee recommendations, board policy statements, faculty and administration recommendations, school

health committee proposals, data on student health needs and conditions. (Pine, 1985)

If the philosophy committee believes that health deals with the whole person, a goal might be written to say:

> A student practices behaviors that promote and maintain mental and physical health.

If the committee feels that there is a need to strengthen families, a goal might say:

> A student understands personal, social, economic, cultural, and ethnic factors that influence the type and success of family relationships.

To focus concern on accidents as one of the leading causes of death among youth, a goal may state:

> The student practices principles of safe living and is able to utilize emergency procedures in case of accidents.

If appreciation of the human organism enters into an understanding of other aspects of health studied and influences students' choice of behavior that affects their bodies, a goal could say:

> A student knows the structure and function of the human body and the patterns of healthy growth and development.

If there is need for more health care professionals, a goal may say:

> The curriculum will acquaint students with health-related careers.

If perception of self is considered important to learning, a goal may state:

> The curriculum will foster the development of self-awareness and self-esteem.

To foster responsibility to others as well as self, a goal such as the following would be written:

> Students will develop an awareness of the interdependent role of health in lives of individuals, families, and the community.

Personal responsibility for one's health might be stated in a goal as follows:

> To provide students with the knowledge and skills required to set health goals, make informed decisions, and solve health problems.

A philosophy is like a dream—what could be, what should be. Goals are influenced by this dream, but goals are more concrete. What is it that individuals should do with regard to health? How healthy will individuals be in one year, or five years, or fifty years?

Summary

What the curriculum committee, the school district, the health teachers and health coordinators, and the community believe is reflected in the philosophy that they develop. Time spent analyzing and reflecting upon the foundations that form the philosophy is crucial to curriculum planning.

This chapter discussed how beliefs about health, health education, the learner, the learning process, and a democratic society help to formulate a philosophy. It concludes with how the philosophy leads to goals.

Discussion Questions

1. How can a curriculum committee resolve the conflict over whether or not students should study about abortion?
2. What would be the rationale for including the study of mental illness in a curriculum?
3. In a philosophy, what does the statement that students learn in different ways imply to curriculum designers?
4. What statements in the Bainbridge Island School District philosophy guard against a one-hour program with no relation to scope and sequence that a self-interested community group might want taught in the health class?

Application Activities

1. If a high school health education curriculum objective is to identify five environmental influences that can affect prenatal growth and development, speculate as to what kind of a health goal this might be tied to and what health needs brought about the goal.
2. Do the same with this elementary school objective: The student describes three ways in which he or she is like others and three ways in which he or she is different from others.
3. Write a philosophical statement that reflects your feelings about health, health education, the learner, the learning process, and our society.
4. Write curriculum goals that you feel reflect your philosophical statement.

References

Bainbridge Island School District. 1988. *Health education curriculum.* Bainbridge Island, WA.

Carnegie Council on Adolescent Development. 1989. *Turning points: Preparing American youth for the 21st century. The report of the task force on education of young adolescents.* Washington, DC.

Guild, P. and Garger, S. 1985. *Marching to different drummers.* Alexandria, VA: Association of Supervision and Curriculum Development.

National Commission on the Role of the School and the Community in Improving Adolescent Health. 1990. *Code blue—Uniting for healthier youth.* Alexandria, VA: National Association of State Boards of Education.

National Task Force for the Preparation and Practice of Health Educators. 1985. *A framework for the development of competency-based curricula for entry level health educators.* New York.

Office of Superintendent of Public Instruction. 1980. *Health education framework: A resource for program planning and student learning objectives.* Olympia, WA.

Pine, P. 1985. *Critical issues report. Promoting health education in schools—problems and solutions.* Arlington, VA: American Association of School Administrators.

School health education study. 1967. *Health education: A conceptual approach to curriculum design.* 1967. St. Paul, MN: 3M Education Press.

Trucano, L. 1984. *Students speak.* Seattle, WA: Comprehensive Health Education Foundation.

Walberg, H. J. 1984. Improving the productivity of America's schools. *Educational Leadership* 41(8): 19–27.

2

Content:
Scanning the Health Horizons

After reading this chapter and participating in application activities, the student should be able to:

1. Define comprehensive school health instruction and summarize the major content areas of school health education.
2. Identify health topics and issues for each of the major content areas.
3. Utilize established criteria to narrow the scope of health education.
4. Interpret the meaning of scope and sequence as they pertain to a comprehensive school health education curriculum.

In developing health education instructional programs, curriculum planners reflect upon three main questions:

- What is the content of health education?
- Which topics are important?
- How should topics be sequenced?

The answers to these questions assist in the development of comprehensive school health education curricula.

Comprehensive School Health Education

Well-defined terms enable individuals to explain the field and process of health education to others in consistent language. In August, 1990, delegates to the Coalition of National Health Education Organizations met in Reston, Virginia to revise and update the terminology used by professional health educators. As a result of deliberations and a consensus by the delegates, the following definitions were approved:

> A *comprehensive school health program* is an organized set of policies, procedures, and activities designed to protect and promote the health and well-being of students and staff which has traditionally included health services, healthful school environment, and health education. It should also include, but not be limited to, guidance and counseling, physical education, food service, social work, psychological services, and employee health promotion.
>
> *School health education* is one component of the comprehensive school health program which includes the development, delivery, and evaluation of a planned instructional program and other activities, for students pre-school through grade 12, for parents and for school staff, and is designed to positively influence the health knowledge, attitudes, and skills of individuals.
>
> *Comprehensive school health instruction* refers to the development, delivery, and evaluation of a planned curriculum, pre-school through grade 12, with goals, objectives, content sequence, and specific classroom lessons which includes, but is not limited to the following major content areas:
>
> - Community health
> - Consumer health
> - Environmental health
> - Family life
> - Injury prevention and safety
> - Mental and emotional health
> - Nutrition
> - Personal health
> - Prevention and control of disease
> - Substance use and abuse
>
> (Association for the Advancement of Health Education, 1991)

The beauty of comprehensive school health education is that it puts perspective and balance into a curriculum. Health topics are taught at the appropriate time and with sufficient time allocated for learning to take place;

all necessary topics are included and designed to stimulate critical thinking and decision making in students.

Support for Comprehensive School Health Education

Strong support from outside the profession exists for comprehensive school health education. The American Association of School Administrators, American Medical Association, Carnegie Foundation, and Metropolitan Life Foundation issued reports during the 1980s that stressed the importance of comprehensive school health education.

The 1983 Carnegie Report entitled *High School: A Report on Secondary Education in America* stated the belief that "no knowledge is more crucial than knowledge about health. Without it, no other life goal can be successfully achieved. Therefore, all students should learn about the human body, how it changes over the life cycle, what nourishes it, and how a healthy body contributes to well-being" (Boyer, 1983: 112).

In its *Critical Issues Report—Promoting Health Education in Schools,* the American Association of School Administrators said that the defenders of the comprehensive approach "point to research indicating that children who have repeated exposures to key topics at different stages in their education form attitudes that help them avoid bad health habits when they are older. Consequently, comprehensive health education holds promise for affecting long-term behavior . . ." (Pine, 1985).

Research studies show a relationship between health-related behavior and the number of years of health education. Students exposed to three or more years of health education engaged in healthier behaviors as compared to those with two years or less, according to Louis Harris & Associates. The results of their comprehensive 1988 survey of health education in American public schools revealed a "linear trend of increase in health-related knowledge and behavior as the number of years of health classes increase for students (Harris & Associates, 1988: 4; see figure 2.1). Furthermore, the survey reported that there "seems little doubt that the best benefits for all are realized through comprehensive health education and that the greatest chance of success comes through combined and strong support from the home and the community" (Harris & Associates, 1988).

A three-year study of four health instruction programs demonstrated health education to be "an effective means of helping children improve their health knowledge and develop healthy attitudes. The study also showed that school health education can decrease the likelihood that children will adopt behaviors that are hazardous to health, such as smoking" (Department of Health and Human Services, 1989).

Establishing the Basis for Content Selection

Health education considers all dimensions of the individual—physical, mental, social, emotional, and spiritual. These dimensions are infused into health topics and issues that are studied by the target population that comprises the K–12 schools. "A *target population* means a well-defined group toward whom a health education program is focused" (Association for the Advancement of Health Education, 1991).

The first need in establishing the basis for content selection, is to look at significant preventable health problems and risk-taking behaviors among young people in our country. Research studies continue to document health problems such as accidents and violence, suicide, eating disorders, obesity, HIV and other sexually transmitted diseases, teenage pregnancy, substance abuse, chronic disease, and lack of exercise and fitness among the nation's

FIGURE 2.1 Relationship between health education experience and health-related behavior. (Prepared from the results of "Health: You've Got To Be Taught," a Metropolitan Life Foundation survey conducted by Louis Harris and Associates, Inc., 1988.) Printed with permission of Metropolitan Life, Health and Safety Division.

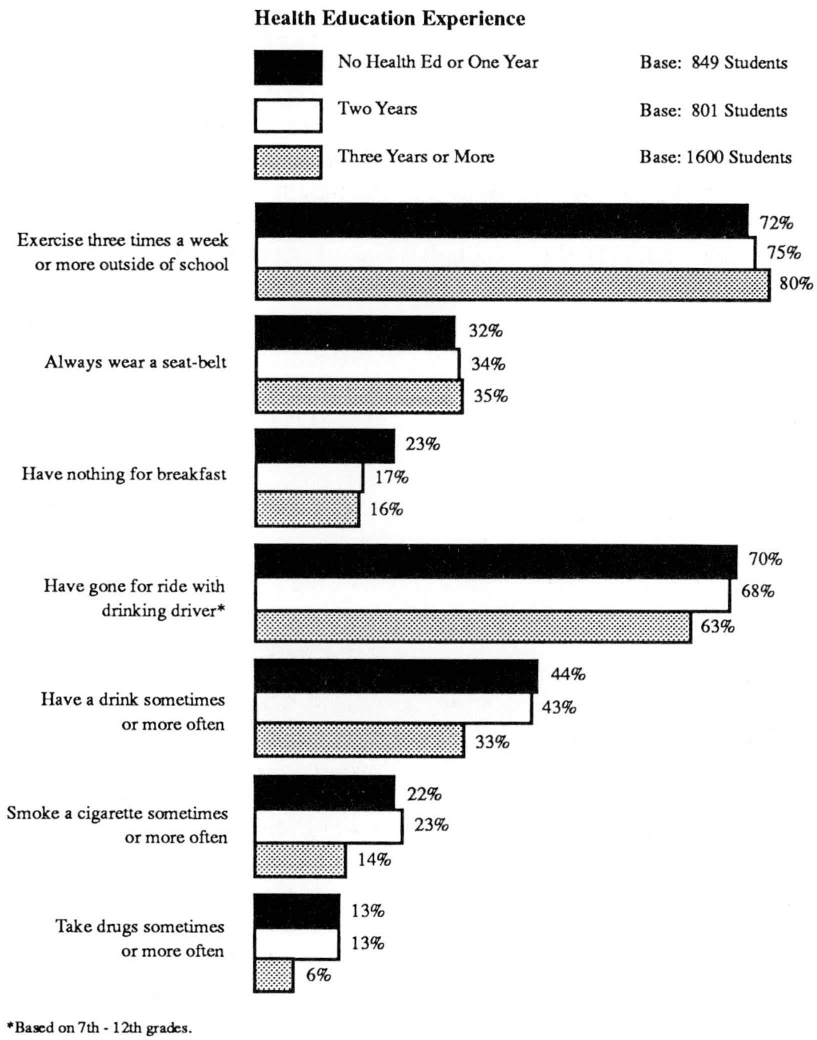

youth (American School Health Association et al., 1988; Harris & Associates, 1988). The school is a logical and natural setting to promote health for the purpose of preventing disease and promoting healthy life-styles. The variety of health topics in a comprehensive curriculum can increase health knowledge, promote healthy attitudes, and stimulate the maintenance and/or adoption of selected health behaviors (Harris & Associates, 1988; "Results of the School Health Education Evaluation," 1985).

The second need is to look at health interests of the school-age population. *Teach Us What We Want To Know* (Byler, Lewis, and

Totman, 1969) reported that over 5,000 children in Connecticut wanted to learn about health. Almost fifteen years later, Trucano surveyed over 5,000 students in Washington state. The resulting report, *Students Speak,* shows what the students' interests in health topics were at each grade level, their perceptions of the value of health education, and their comments about how they would like health education to be taught. For example, students expressed "fears and worries" at all grade levels. "There was fear of not being loved, fear about their own security, and fear about coping with the world" (Trucano, 1984). There was a high interest in drugs at all grade levels; almost all grade levels mentioned divorce. Also important was the fact that "questions voiced by students, and their request to be involved in the learning process provide a strong incentive for using the problem-solving approach to teaching. Students do not want answers given to them. They want to research out facts, evaluate the information and learn how to make the 'right' decisions" (Trucano, 1984).

In seeking information about the importance to adolescents of eleven health topics, the Harris & Associates study found students rated these health topics as being very important to them: "not taking or experimenting with drugs" (75%); "not smoking cigarettes" (68%); "not being overweight" (60%); "getting exercise for twenty minutes three or more times each week" (55%); "not drinking alcohol at all" (52%); and "eating breakfast every day" (50%). Figure 2.2 shows how important each of the eleven health topics were to the survey sample of students.

The third need is to look at student knowledge, attitudes, and behaviors. In 1987, the *National Adolescent Student Health Survey* was initiated by the Association for the Advancement of Health Education (AAHE), the American School Health Association (ASHA), and the Society for Public Health Education (SOPHE) with funding from the Office of Disease Prevention and Health Promotion, the Center for Health Promotion and Education, and the National Institute on Drug Abuse. The results of the study indicated a need for us to be concerned about teens because they are not making good health decisions. It was suggested that "America's youth are faced with difficult decisions regarding their health and if not properly informed, many of the decisions they make could put them at increased health risk (American School Health Association et al., 1988). Also, the survey suggested that the "results give us fresh insight concerning what our nation's teenagers know and how they act concerning health and sex-related issues—but they also show that too many young people, even when they know better, don't always make the right decisions" (American School Health Association et al., 1988).

A fourth area to examine relates to societal needs. Several federal documents, for example, *Healthy People; Promoting Health—Preventing Disease: Objectives for the Nation—1990;* and the *1990 Health Objectives for the Nation—A Midcourse Review* (Department of Health and Human Services, 1979, 1980, 1986) have helped set in perspective the health needs of the nation. Specific and quantifiable objectives were set forth in fifteen priority areas identified in *Healthy People: Healthy People:*

- blood pressure control
- pregnancy and infant health
- sexually transmitted diseases
- accident prevention and injury control
- surveillance and control of infectious diseases
- misuse of alcohol and drugs
- control of stress and violent behavior
- nutrition
- family planning
- immunizations
- occupational safety and health
- fluoridation and dental health
- smoking and health
- physical fitness and exercise
- toxic agent and radiation control

FIGURE 2.2 Personal importance of various health topics to students. (From "Health: You've Got To Be Taught," a Metropolitan Life Foundation survey conducted by Louis Harris and Associates, Inc., 1988.) Printed with permission of Metropolitan Life, Health and Safety Division.

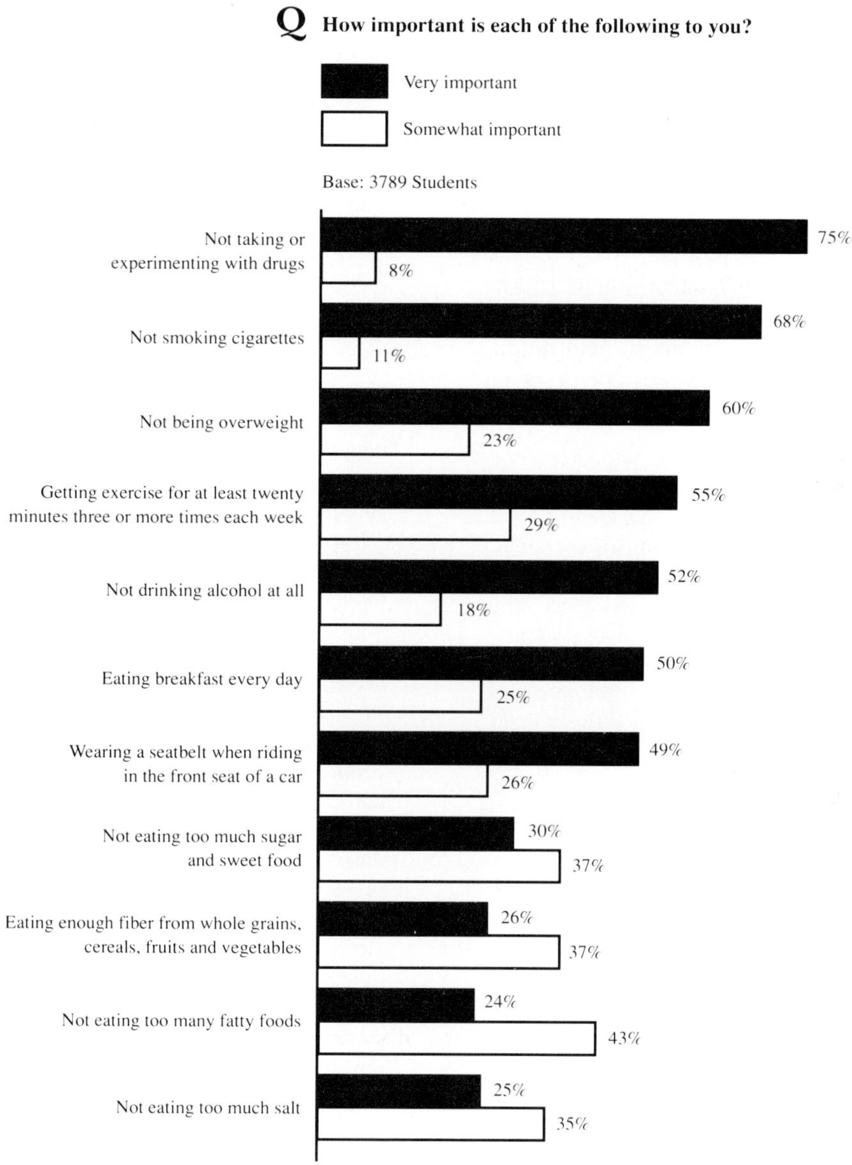

Healthy People 2000: National Health Promotion and Disease Prevention Objectives, published in September, 1990, addresses improvements in health education. Within the priority area of health education is a specific recommendation relating to school health that "there will be an increase to at least 75 percent in the proportion of the Nation's elementary and secondary schools that provide a planned and sequential kindergarten through grade 12 program of comprehensive school health education" (Dept. of Health and Human Services, 1990). Attainment of the year 2000 national health objectives relies substantially on improvements in health education. Three other objectives specific to school health are defined:

> By 2000, 80 percent of States will have systems established to monitor the percent of schools that provide a K–12 program of comprehensive school health education.
>
> By 2000, a 20 percent reduction in the prevalence of 10 priority health risk behaviors among the Nation's secondary school students (age 13–18) will be documented.
>
> By 2000, 60 percent of States will implement complementary systems to monitor the percent of secondary school students that engage in 10 priority health risk behaviors (Dept. of Health and Human Services, 1990).

Major Content Areas

To assist readers in identifying the subject matter of health that falls within school health education instruction, sections of two national documents describing health content areas have been chosen. They illustrate what comprises the minimum body of knowledge in health education.

An informative and useful report, *Recommendations for School Health Education: A Handbook for State Policymakers* (Education Commission of the States, 1981), identifies the following ten content areas and their descriptors as the minimum elements of comprehensive school health instruction.

> **Personal Health:** Physical fitness and lifetime physical activities, cardiovascular health, sleep, rest, relaxation, recreation, growth and development, nutrition, oral health, vision and hearing, prevention and control of disease, safety, body systems and their functions, aging, coping with death and dying.
>
> **Mental and Emotional Health:** Positive self-concept, personality, emotional stability, responsibility, motivation, independence, mental disorders, coping with stress, mental health services.
>
> **Prevention and Control of Disease:** Contribution of early scientists, causes of disease, preventive measures, chronic disease, degenerative disease, communicable disease, immunization, personal health practices, and community efforts.
>
> **Nutrition:** Food choices, elements in food that contribute to good nutrition, factors influencing choices, individual nutritional requirements, food groups and nutrients, food sources, weight control, effects of nutrition on growth and activity, nutritional challenges, food preparation and protection, consumer protection.
>
> **Substance Use and Abuse:** Personal goals, individual responsibility, substances beneficial to mankind, classifications of substances and their effects on the body, implications of use of substances, how habits are formed and influence health, use and misuse of tobacco, alcohol and other drugs, treatment and rehabilitation programs, respect for self and others.
>
> **Accident Prevention and Safety:** Attitudes toward safety, causes of accidents, home and school safety, traffic (auto, bicycle, school bus) safety, fire prevention, survival education, environmental hazards, accident prevention/potential hazards, first-aid and emergency health care, safety personnel, resources and agencies, individual safety precautions, recreational safety, occupational safety, safety rules, laws, regulations, legislation.

Community Health: Individual responsibility, healthful school, home, community environment, community health resources and facilities, official and nonofficial health agencies, health service careers, pollution control (clean air and water), occupational environments, safety hazards and natural disasters, community involvement—a shared responsibility (health planning).

Consumer Health: Individual responsiblity, propaganda in advertising, social and economical factors, laws for consumer protection (food labeling), protection agencies, health agencies and organizations, health insurance, selection of medical services, quackery, reliable sources of health information, evaluating health products and services, use of trained medical personnel.

Environmental Health: Environmental pollution, effect of environment on health (radiation, pollution), environmental protection agencies, population density, world health.

Family Life Education: Family composition and roles, life cycles (human growth and development), the reproductive process, heredity, marriage, selecting a compatible life partner, family relationships, parenting. (Education Commission of the States, 1981. Reprinted with permission of the Education Commission of the States, Denver, Colorado.)

In the early 1980s, leaders in national professional health organizations (specifically, the Association for the Advancement of Health Education, AAHE; American School Health Association, ASHA; School Health Education and Services Section of the American Public Health Association, SHES-S; and the Society of State Directors of Health, Physical Education, and Recreation, SSDHPER) met to establish a definition of comprehensive school health education, which was later approved by their respective organizations. Rather than ten content areas, nine were identified and described as follows.

Consumer Health: Examination of the many factors that influence the selection and use of health services, products, and information. The establishment of personal criteria for selection of health services and usage that are conducive to good health.

Environmental Health: Investigation of the causes, effects, and methods of eradication of all of the external factors (e.g., pollution, overpopulation, radiation, hunger, waste disposal) which negatively affect human health. This study is approached on both a local and worldwide basis and employs a model which examines the totality of relationships between humans and their environment.

Family Life: Investigation of the multiple roles and personal life-styles of individuals as members of larger family and societal units. Changes in the responsibilities and privileges each person encounters during the life cycle are studied in addition to the multitude of factors which influence the expression of human sexuality. The biological, sociological, and psychological variables which affect the total development of the personality and interpersonal relationships are studied.

Growth and Development: Study of the functions and structure of the human body systems, their interdependence, and how they function as a whole and contribute to health status from birth to death.

Nutritional Health: Study of the principal nutrients necessary to maintain basic body needs and how nutrients can be provided. Consideration of the essential components of a balanced diet, need for a wide variety of foods, influence of peers, family culture, media, etc., on what the individual does or does not consume.

Personal Health: Exploration of the life-style activities individuals undertake that influence their health. The focus is on problem-solving techniques, achievement of positive self-concept, and acceptance of responsibility for those personal health actions over which the individual has some control (e.g., care of teeth and gums, eyes, ears, skin, hair, as well as balance between rest and physical activity).

Prevention and Control of Diseases and Disorders: Investigation of the factors contributing to the incidence of the major chronic and communicable diseases and

FIGURE 2.3 Nutrition

Nutrition	
Understanding food groups	Food fads and quackery
Food nutrients	Food allergy
Adequate and inadequate diets	The sodium story
Pregnancy and nutrition	Fad diets
Infant and child nutrition	Promoters of fraudulent diets
Second growth period and nutrition	Artificial foods
Adult nutrition	Fast-food industry
Nutritional needs in the later years	Food-borne illnesses
Nutrition and the athlete	Food manufacturing
Food additives	Radiation and storage
Ethnic eating habits	Eating disorders
Dietary fats	Nutritional needs while breast feeding
Vitamins, minerals, and trace elements	Meal planning for diabetics
Nutrition labeling	Nutritional assessment
Nutrition and disease	Vegetarianism
Calcium and osteoporosis	Natural and artificial sweeteners
Vitamin C and colds	Irradiated foods
Interaction of drugs and food	Chemotherapy and nutrition
Food myths and fallacies	Physical activity and nutritional needs

disorders that affect individuals and communities. Study focuses on measures for the prevention, early detection, and control of such health problems.

Safety and Accident Prevention: Exploration of the methods that can be employed to reduce or eliminate hazardous conditions in all aspects of daily life. Studies of techniques for first aid and emergency care are included.

Substance Use and Abuse: Examination of the appropriate and inappropriate uses of chemical substances that are commonly used. These include those substances that are legally available such as alcohol, tobacco, or over-the-counter drugs, and those illegally available through a variety of sources. ("Comprehensive School Health Education," 1984)

Although nine or ten major content areas have been described, this does not mean that nine or ten is the magic number. Curriculum planners may wish to increase or decrease this number. Once the major subject areas of health education are established, the next step in determining content for a curriculum is to explore what health topics and issues could and should fit under each major heading; clearly various topics and issues can fall within several areas. Figures 2.3 and 2.4 are examples of suggested topics for two health areas, nutrition and community health. Note that these examples are not meant to be all-encompassing.

Narrowing the Scope

Needless to say, it is impossible to include all of the topics and issues that are identified. In deciding which topics and issues to include at each grade level, we must consider factors such

FIGURE 2.4 Community health

Community Health

Models and concepts of community health	Immigrant and migrant health
Human ecology	Voluntary health agencies
Demography	Food and water protection
Epidemiology	Immunizations and eradication of infectious diseases
Population and population control	Low-income families
Maternal and infant health	Federal/state/local programs
Aging and health needs of the elderly	Medical and dental plans
Violence control	Prevention and intervention of self-imposed risks
Recreation, fitness, and play	Safety and injury control
Communicable disease control	History of community health
County/district/state boards of health	Housing and day-care
Water and waste management	Sanitation
Control of air, noise, waste, and radiation pollution	Child and adolescent health
Religious and political influences	Isolation and quarantine
Socioeconomic influences	Health education
Social norms and health practices	Homeless individuals
Public health departments	

as the needs, interests, and maturity levels of the students, the urgency of the subject, and the need for reinforcement.

The next step is an important one—that of narrowing the scope. Scope means the range of health topics that could or should be taught at all grade levels. This is done by determining which of the topics and issues are absolutely necessary and relevant for each grade level.

The process of narrowing the scope can be accomplished through (1) the use of criteria for determining critical needs and interests of students and the needs of their families and communities, and (2) the use of a form to tabulate the levels of importance to students and society of each identified health topic. The six criteria that we have found valuable in helping to narrow the scope of health topics appear in figure 2.5.

Other factors that may play a role in determining the selection of topics and issues are legislative mandates, allocation of time within the total school curriculum, and availability of instructional resources and personnel.

By using established criteria, the curriculum-planning committee tabulates the level of importance of each topic. This is a two-step process. In step 1, the committee brainstorms and lists relevant topics under each major health area; in step 2, the committee rates the importance of the topic to students and to society (which may be family and local community). Figure 2.6 shows a sample rating form. Distinguishing among levels of importance is based upon needs-assessment data and characteristics of the learners.

Sequencing Health Topics

Earlier in this chapter, we stated that comprehensive school health education has scope and sequence. Scope refers to the range of health

FIGURE 2.5 Criteria utilized in narrowing the scope

Criteria Utilized in Narrowing the Scope

1. Are topics and skills consistent with the philosophy and goals that have been established?
   If students are called upon to make choices and decisions that affect their families and personal well-being, then the scope has to include those topics that address the continuum from health promotion to risk reduction of personal and family health problems.
2. How important is the health topic in relation to the health needs of the target population?
   Important health topics are those that epidemiological data indicate as being of major societal concern. Topics selected should reflect the identified needs of particular age groups and grades. For example, if the targeted students are fourth-graders, then the health educator will find research data that support the need for educating them about family relationships. Students in fourth grade show a high interest in and deep concern for the happiness of their families.
3. Is the topic relevant to the specific characteristics and needs of the identified population?
   The age, sex, ethnicity, geographical location, socioeconomic status, and educational levels, as well as the identified health needs of the student population, should be reflected in the topics selected to be taught. For example, the four food groups have recently included ethnic foods. Health classes have begun to help senior high students not living at home plan nutritionally balanced meals.
4. Is there relative importance and urgency of the health topic to society?
   When the crisis approach or the "disease-of-the-month club" exists, programs are not based on the sound educational planning proposed by this book. Health educators may also be influenced to change focus because of the availability of grants from government and foundation sources. Choosing health topics should be based on the urgency and importance of the topics to society, to families and individuals, and to health education. In most cases, the crisis topic will already be in a well-planned comprehensive program, sequentially treated and with time for learning to occur.
5. Is the topic of a high level of interest to the learners?
   Identifying health issues that are of greatest interest to the student population helps the curriculum planner in narrowing what should and what should not be included. For example, the effects of teen pregnancy on girls and the responsibility of boys in sharing the decision to prevent pregnancy is of high interest to tenth graders.
6. Can one distinguish between unnecessary repetition and desirable reinforcement?
   Unnecessary repetition can best be described by asking the reader to recall how many times the four food groups were covered in classes in elementary and high school. The health educator's awareness of what students have previously learned is crucial. Find out what students have learned in their primary and middle-school grades through discussion, review of elementary curricula (if available), pretests, and other similar activities. It is also important to determine when reinforcement should occur.

FIGURE 2.6 Sample form for narrowing the scope

Sample Form for Narrowing the Scope

Major Health Area	Level of Importance to Students			Level of Importance to Society		
Nutrition	High (3)	Moderate (2)	Low (1)	High (3)	Moderate (2)	Low (1)
	(circle level of importance)					
List topics in this column.						
Understanding food groups	3	2	1	3	2	1
Food nutrients	3	2	1	3	2	1
Pregnancy and nutrition	3	2	1	3	2	1
⋮						

topics, and sequence means the arrangement of those topics at various grade levels in such a way as to meet the health needs and interests of students. Only sequencing in curriculum development is discussed here.

Sequencing of health topics is important. Health topics are placed at various grade levels not only to introduce new issues, but to allow students to review and reinforce what they have previously been taught. Sequencing builds on students' prior knowledge, with selected topics remaining age-appropriate. They are tied to the developmental growth patterns of youngsters. This encourages the application of knowledge to new situations as students mature. In deciding which topics to include in each grade, curriculum planners look at growth and development traits of young people (see appendix 1) and the nature of learning (see chapter 1). Other factors, such as the district's philosophy and goals, parental and community values, and legislative mandates, also play a role. For example, when the seriousness of AIDS began to unfold, several states passed legislation mandating instruction about AIDS and HIV infection at certain grade levels.

The introduction of specific topics at certain grades is also based upon research about children's health behaviors, knowledge, and attitudes. For example, *Here's Looking At You, 2000* (Roberts, Fitzmahan & Associates, 1986) is based upon the research findings of Hawkins and Catalano, who identified childhood predictors of adolescent substance abuse. This K–12 comprehensive drug education curriculum focuses on risk factors such as family history of alcoholism, family management problems, early antisocial behavior, favorable attitudes toward drug use, and friends who use drugs. As a result of the research data, education about gateway drugs—alcohol, nicotine (cigarettes and chewing tobacco), and marijuana—is introduced two years before the average age of first use (i.e., 11 for tobacco, 12 for alcohol, and 13 for marijuana). This particular program is more comprehensive than most categorical curricula and can be easily sequenced into a school district's existing curriculum. Figure 2.7 displays the scope and sequence chart of *Here's Looking At You, 2000.*

The process of sequencing must deal with the questions of how many health topics to include at each grade level and which health topics to repeat in subsequent grades so that reinforcement and mastery can occur. To accomplish the task of sequencing, the curriculum committee can start with any one of several state frameworks for health education (e.g., Wisconsin or California). Other school districts' scope and sequence charts are also good starting points.

To illustrate the idea of sequencing, some key concepts and curriculum objectives from *Food . . . Your Choice* and *Growing Healthy* respectively, are shown in figure 2.8.

Food . . . Your Choice, from the National Dairy Council (1987), is a sequential nutrition education program. Key concepts are first introduced at preschool levels and then expanded in the following grades. Learning activities within each unit are geared to the physical, social, and intellectual development of the students.

Growing Healthy (National Center for Health Education, 1989) is a K–7 school health education program. It originated from two separate curricula, the Primary Grades Curriculum Project (PGCP) of Seattle and the Berkeley Smoking Project (grades 4–6). Curriculum objectives from the mental/emotional health content show how "emotions" can be sequenced at various grade levels.

FIGURE 2.7 K–12 Scope and Sequence Chart. (Permission to use the K–12 Scope and Sequence Chart from the *Here's Looking at You, 2000* © Teacher's Guide © 1986, Roberts, Fitzmahan & Associates and Educational Service District #121, was granted from the Comprehensive Health Education Foundation (CHEF ©), Seattle, Wash.

II. Scope and Sequence

"Here's Looking At You, 2000" presents drug-related issues in a comprehensive manner from kindergarten through twelfth grade. The curriculum was developed so that students could progress through school learning new information and skills while reviewing old ones. Thus, most of the topics are reinforced in the succeeding grades, with students' exposure to the topic becoming wider and deeper. The following chart, based on the objectives for each lesson, illustrates the scope of topics and the sequence in which they are presented.

Category	Topic	K–1	2	3	4	5	6	7–9	10–12
Information	Dangers of unknown substances	X	X						
	Drugs and their effects	X	X	X	X	X	X	X	X
	Definition of drug	X	X	X		X	X	X	X
	Chemical dependency and the individual	X	X	X		X			X
	Chemical dependency in the family	X			X		X	X	X
	Alcohol		X	X	X	X	X	X	X
	Nicotine		X	X	X	X	X	X	X
	Marijuana					X	X	X	X
	Look-alike stimulants							X	X
	Cocaine								X
	Other drugs								X
	Reasons why people use and don't use drugs			X	X			X	
	Risk factors and ways to reduce risks				X	X		X	X
	Identification and evaluation of sources of information about drugs				X		X	X	
	Drug advertisements						X	X	X
	Drugs causing problems in future as well as in present						X		X
	Factors which influence effects							X	
	Non-stereotypical description of drug users							X	
	Basic properties of cancer cells							X	
	Fetal alcohol syndrome							X	X
	Abusers hurtings others							X	X
	Driving and drugs							X	X
	Sidestream smoke								X
	Drug-related emergencies								X
	Control of substances by federal schedules								X
	Sexuality and drugs								X
	Early warning signs of drug abuse								X
	Action on drug-related issues								X
Skills	Asking someone for something	X	X						
	Abiding by Ground Rules for discussing sensitive topics in front of others	X	X	X	X	X	X	X	X
	Making decisions	X			X	X	X	X	X

FIGURE 2.7 *Continued*

II. Scope and Sequence—continued

		K–1	2	3	4	5	6	7–9	10–12
Skills continued	Asking someone to do something (assertiveness)		X						
	Keeping out of trouble (self-control)			X					
	Identifying sources of influence				X				
	Saying no to keep friends				X	X	X	X	X
	Making friends						X	X	
	Stopping enabling								X
	Intervening with friends								X
	Recognizing when to refer people to others								X
	Making referrals								X
	Teaching refusal skills								X
Bonding to School and Family	Explaining that problems are normal	X	X						
	Acknowledging feelings and dealing with them	X	X	X					
	Helping others feel included	X	X	X					
	Appreciating self as special	X	X	X	X	X	X	X	X
	Identifying ways to take care of the body			X	X				
	Identifying healthy ways to have fun			X	X	X	X	X	X
	Identifying personal strengths				X				
	Identifying others' strengths				X		X	X	
	Identifying sources of self-assessment					X			
	Assessing self					X			
	Recognizing power of saying no					X			
	Recognizing the influence of stress					X			
	Identifying stressful situations and dealing with them					X			
	Asking for advice from a trusted person					X			
	Giving positive self-talk					X		X	X
	Giving affirmations to others					X		X	X
	Identifying what is important to self						X		
	Learning what is important to others						X		
	Identifying and building relationship with someone admired						X		
	Getting feedback about personal qualities						X		
	Understanding group pressures						X		
	Discussing adolescent concerns							X	
	Identifying feelings about drugs, dependency								X
	Responding to people without using stereotypes								X
		K–1	**2**	**3**	**4**	**5**	**6**	**7–9**	**10–12**

FIGURE 2.8 Selected Key Concepts and Curriculum Objectives from Food . . . Your Choice and Growing Healthy.

Food . . . Your Choice

Grade 1 nutrition unit: *Food Helps Me Grow*

- Relationship between food and growth
- Foods categorized according to their sources—plant or animal
- Foods classified by their tastes
- Food safety

Grade 2 nutrition unit: *Food Gives Me Energy*

- Foods provide energy
- Bodies require energy to move
- Foods classified into Four Food Groups
- Foods in Four Food Groups go through many steps to get from the farm to the home

Grade 3 nutrition unit: *Food Keeps Me Healthy*

- Builds on concepts learned in first and second grades
- Explores what it means to be healthy
- Importance of each food group in maintaining good health
- Synthesis of meaning of Four Food Groups

Growing Healthy

The kindergarten student

- Explains that feelings change often and are expressed in many ways.

The first-grade student

- Describes the variety of emotions experienced in daily living.

The second-grade student

- Compares responsible with irresponsible expressions of emotions.

The seventh-grade student

- Describes the function of emotions in producing and relieving tension.

To illustrate topics and issues that have been sequenced for grades K–12, see figure 2.9 which depicts a local school district's health education scope and sequence, and figure 2.10 illustrates the concepts of scope (breadth) and sequence (depth) from a state level.

Linking Health Areas

Health issues do not exist in isolation from one another. The nation's health problems show an interdependency; none should stand as an isolated entity. We should view issues from different perspectives and address them comprehensively to acknowledge their interrelationships. Because there are many categorical curricula (e.g., AIDS/HIV, drugs) available, curriculum planners must learn how to integrate them into a comprehensive program.

Historically, the concept of linking health topics is not new. The School Health Education Study (1967) utilized the conceptual approach in curriculum planning and development. Three key concepts, *growing and developing, decision making,* and *interacting* were conceived as the unifying threads of the program. Ten concepts (indicating the scope) served as the major organizing elements. Thirty-one subconcepts, the supporting ideas, emanate from the ten concepts and serve as guides for the selection and ordering of health topics. Figure 2.11 details the ten concepts.

In the late 1960s, the New York State Education Department revised the content areas and basic objectives in its school health education program. Based upon the underlying philosophy that "the study of health affairs must be based initially upon an understanding of human ecology, the study of man in interaction with his environment" (Sincore, 1968), the Strand program was devised. The underlying theme and linkage were woven into the five strands (Physical Health, Sociological Health Problems, Mental Health, Environmental and Community Health, and Education for Survival). Figure 2.12 illustrates the New York Strand program.

Recently the State of Oregon, in reorganizing its structure for health instruction, followed a similar "Strand" format in developing comprehensive health instruction curriculum goals. Oregon's "Common Knowledge and Skills for Health Education has been organized into four content strands. These four content strands are a synthesis of the traditional health curriculum and the Health Promotion Objectives for the Nation that can be addressed in a school setting" (Oregon Department of Education, 1988). *Safe Living, Stressor/Risk-Taking Management, Physical Education,* and *Nutrition* are the four strands. Self-responsibility, consumer health, human development, and mental health are the common threads running through each of these strands.

Another way to approach linking health topics is shown in figure 2.13. The major content area of substance use and abuse is the focal point around which other major health areas are organized. Health topics within each major heading further illustrate linkage.

As you can see, there is no set pattern or format for linking health topics; the linkage can be based on concepts, strands, or major content areas. Therefore, planners do not need to reinvent the wheel when they are wondering how to interweave the various health topics and issues.

FIGURE 2.9 Bainbridge Island School District health education scope and sequence chart. (From Bainbridge Island School District, Bainbridge Island, WA, 1988.)

Bainbridge Island School District

HEALTH EDUCATION SCOPE & SEQUENCE CHART

MAJOR CONTENT AREA	HUMAN GROWTH AND DEVELOPMENT	EMOTIONAL HEALTH	NUTRITION	ENVIRONMENTAL HEALTH	FAMILY LIFE EDUCATION
Grade Level K	Major Body Parts Dental Hygiene Senses	Feelings Similarities & Differences Cooperation	Four Food Groups Healthful Eating		Family Differences Rules & Responsibilities
1	Body Systems	Decision Making Communication Skills Feelings Appreciating Self Assertiveness	Food, Growth & Health		Family Differences Loss & Grief
2	Develop Structure & Function of Teeth Dental Hygiene Senses	Feelings of Self-Worth Recognizing Self as Member of Groups Helping Others Stress Management	Healthful Eating		Family Relationships
3	Taking Care of the Body	Feelings Appreciating Self Helping Others Asking for Something (Assertiveness)	Healthful Snacks		Changing Family
4		Refusal Skills Respecting Rights & Property of Others Self-Image & Body Size	Nutritional Needs & Exercise Food Additives Food Poisoning	Water Pollution Sewage Disposal Noise Pollution	
5	Anatomy & Physiology of Body Systems	Decision Making Positive Self-Talk Asking for Advice Identifying & Dealing with Stress			
6		Making Friends Decision Making Refusal Skills Suicide Prevention			Death & Dying
7	Genetics Physiology/Body Systems Physical Fitness	Conflict Resolution		Environmental Carcinogens	
8		Refusal Skills Conflict Resolution			Caring Relationships
9–10	Physiology of Exercise Pregnancy/Fetal Development	Origin & Expression of Emotions Positive Self-Image Identifying & Managing Stress/Coping Skills Crisis/Suicide Intervention Personal Life Goals	Energy Demands & Supply Diets & Eating Disorders Prenatal Nutritional Care	Health Around the World	Interpersonal Skills
11–12					

SEX EDUCATION	DISEASES AND DISORDERS	CONSUMER HEALTH	CHEMICAL USE AND ABUSE	PERSONAL SAFETY AND FIRST AID	COMMUNITY HEALTH
	Common Childhood Diseases & Prevention Personal Hygiene		Making Choices Good/Bad Things in Body Poison	Physical & Sexual Abuse Traffic Safety Safe Behavior Fire Safety	
	Personal Hygiene Dental Hygiene		Definition of Drugs Drugs & Their Effects How Medicine Helps Dangers of Unknown Substances	Fire Safety Emergency Basics	Healthcare Providers
	Handicaps Personal Hygiene	Food Advertising	Definition of Drugs Drugs & Their Effects Chemical Dependency	Fire Safety Safe Living	Role of Dentist & Orthodontist
	Immunization		Definition of Drugs Drugs & Their Effects Tobacco Alcohol Reasons Why People Use or Don't Use Drugs	Physical & Sexual Abuse Water Safety Fire Safety	Healthcare Providers
		Identify & Evaluate Sources of Information Advertising of Health Products & Diets	Definition of a Drug Chemical Dependency Alcohol Tobacco Reasons for Not Using Drugs	First Aid	
Human Reproduction Puberty Changes	AIDS & Other Infectious Diseases	Advertising of Over the Counter Drugs & Other Health Products	Drugs & Their Effects Alcohol Tobacco Marijuana Risk Factors	Water Safety	
Love Gender Identity Sex Role Stereotyping	AIDS	Drug Advertisement Identify & Evaluate Sources of Information	Chemicals & Their Effect on the Body Chemical Dependency Legal Implications	Fire Safety Bicycle & Skateboard Safety Sexual Abuse Prevention	Understanding Physical Exams & Health Checkups
	AIDS Diseases of Digestive, Respiratory & Circulatory Systems Eating Disorders			First Aid CPR	Emergency Medical Services Health Careers
Sex Drives & Behaviors Sexual Pressures Refusal Skills Contraception	Diseases of Reproductive, Endocrine & Nervous Systems Sexually Transmitted Diseases, AIDS	Food, Drug & Cosmetic Labeling	Effects of Chemical Abuse on Body Systems	Risk Taking	Healthcare Services
Sexual Pressures Contraception Teen Pregnancy Alternative to Sexual Activities Sexual Orientation	Sexually Transmitted Diseases, AIDS Compulsive Behaviors Depression & Anxiety	Over the Counter Drugs	Classifications/ Terminology Addiction Drugs and the Law Toxicology: Intervention Chemically Dependent Family	Emergency First Aid CPR	Health Careers Healthcare Services
	AIDS				

FIGURE 2.10 Curricular progression chart. (Reprinted/excerpted from *A Guide to Curriculum Planning in Health Education* with permission from the Wisconsin Department of Public Instruction, 125 South Webster Street, Madison, WI 53702.)

MAJOR CONTENT AREA TOPICAL REFERENCES	ACCIDENT PREVENTION AND SAFETY (EMERGENCY REFERRAL)	COMMUNITY HEALTH (RESOURCES)	CONSUMER HEALTH (HEALTH ADVERTISING)	ENVIRONMENTAL HEALTH (WASTE DISPOSAL)	FAMILY LIFE EDUCATION (POSITIVE RELATIONSHIPS)
GRADE LEVEL K	•Recite the names of people who can help in case of an accident. —poison signs —protective behaviors —rules —life hazards				•Describe qualities of friends. —promoting a healthy family —similarities and differences between people
1	•Dial the emergency phone number in case of an accident. —school safety —fire drills —bus and auto safety				—groups and their importance —kinds of families —responsibilities —trust
2	—water safety —electrical safety —basic first aid —fire escape plans —accident prevention				•Recognize and value caring adults who are significant in one's life. —growth differences —human needs —abuse prevention
3	—pedestrian safety —reflective clothing —home fires —safety patrols —safety laws	—characteristics of a healthy community —problem solving —assistance with health promotion	•Identify the impact of advertising and other influences on the use of health products and services. —health products —TV ads and health	•Participate in a program aimed at reducing litter in school and within the community. —causes of air pollution —sources of environmental pollution	•Describe different kinds of friendships. •Identify trusted people who can help with personal and family problems. —families working together —life cycle —reproduction
4	•Develop a list of telephone numbers for emergency contacts. —hiking safety —first aid for bleeding —bike safety —minor injuries	•Explain the role of community health agencies in protecting and promoting the health and safety of community members. —public health workers —disease prevention	—questionable health practices —family practices, values, and emotions in choosing health products	•Describe community facilities and procedures that ensure safe water supplies and sanitary trash and sewage disposal. —water pollution —parks —recreational sites	•Realize that learning to get along with others is a process unique to each individual. —the reproductive system —puberty changes
5	—boating safety —water safety —choking symptoms	—health benefits —personal and family activities that promote health —community health issues —community health specialists	•Explain how information contained on a label can be used in selecting health products. —OTC drugs —prescription drugs —quackery versus legitimate health practice	•List sources of and methods to deal with solid waste. —land pollution —natural resources —population and land use	•List the characteristics that help maintain friendships and compare oneself to this list. —family impact on each member's development —death or divorce's impact on the family
6	•Develop a babysitter's guide of accident prevention and safety procedures. —shock —heart attack —safety attitude	•Explain how the environmental health section of a health department serves the community —community health planning —community action —volunteer health agencies	•Identify advertising techniques used in media promotion of food, tobacco, alcohol, and health-related products. —evaluation of product claims —why people select certain health products	—rodents and insects —environmental changes in the year 2000 —sanitation	•Discuss dating as one way of exploring friendships and learning new social skills. —peer pressures —family roles —decision making —dating behavior
7–9	—first aid for drug overdose —artificial respiration —first aid for choking victim	•Identify local health resources available to meet specific community health needs. —community help for the aged —health organizations —community health careers	—cost, quality, warranty, and availability of health products and services —criteria for selecting health products and services	—technology and the environment —agencies involved in environmental health —noise pollution —environmental carcinogens	•Develop the ability to resolve conflicts and formulate new friendships. •Identify the responsibilities and consequences inherent in sexual relationships. —a mother's effect on the unborn —communication with parents —the need for love and affection
10–12	—careers in safety —CPR —bandaging —splinting —safety in sports and leisure	•Demonstrate the skills for locating, evaluating, and using community health resources. —individual versus community rights —medical care trends —personal action plan	•Analyze techniques used to promote health-related products and services, including insurance. —consumer rights —governmental agencies and their regulatory powers	•Evaluate the environmental impact of toxic waste disposal. —energy sources —environmental health careers —government regulation of the environment —environmental preservation	•Analyze the interrelationships of career and family roles, responsibilities, and family harmony. —teen pregnancy —birth defects —nutrition and development —sexual assault prevention —spouse selection

MENTAL AND EMOTIONAL HEALTH (STRESS)	NUTRITION (NUTRIENTS)	PERSONAL HEALTH (FITNESS)	PREVENTION AND CONTROL OF DISEASE (COMMUNICABLE DISEASE)	SUBSTANCE USE AND ABUSE (RESOURCES)
—valuing self as unique and worthwhile —feelings and behavior —how to help others feel good about themselves —where to go for help	—breakfast —nutritious snacks —food versus non-food items —food advertisements	—personal grooming —cleanliness habits —tooth care —posture	—comparison of wellness and illness —proper dress and disease prevention —personal hygiene habits	*Explain reasons for consulting a responsible adult before using medicines and chemical substances. —medicines at home —names of medicines used or abused
—respect for others —how emotions affect the body —belonging —effort and its effect on skill development	—sensory characteristics of food —plant and animal sources of food —food forms —mealtime behavior —need to eat a variety of foods	*Recognize the relationship between physical activity and muscular development —heart health —rest and relaxation —human senses	*Discuss the relationship between germs and disease —"We are well most of the time." —medical personnel —public health efforts	—what a medicine is —how medicines are helpful or harmful —good risks versus bad risks —risks in using substances
—emotions—pleasant and unpleasant —how the environment affects feelings —appreciate consequences of behavior choices —how people express feelings	*Compare varying amounts of nutrients and energy needed throughout the life cycle. —wide varieties of food choices —dental caries —sugar —ingredient order on labels	*Recognize that the heart is a muscle that is strengthened by exercise. *Value physical well-being by practicing fitness behaviors which contribute to health. —major body organs —quiet activities	*Describe how germs cause illness. *Explain communicable disease. —immunization —effect of exercise, diet, rest or disease prevention	—recognizing names given to medicines —rules for taking medicines —avoidance of certain drugs —drug effects
*Define stress and cite examples of positive and negative stressors. *Identify positive ways of dealing with stress. —physical health and feelings —group membership —grief	*State that food supplies nutrients that are needed for growth, repair, and maintenance of cells. —food choices —sensory qualities of food —food chain —energy needs	*Cite ways to build physical activities into daily routine. —lifestyle choices —body and self image —the senses and safety, learning, and play —handicapping conditions	*Distinguish between infectious and noninfectious disease. —disease symptoms —early steps to combat illness —wellness lifestyle	*List people and places who can provide help with medicine and chemical substance use problems. —use versus abuse —effects on physical, social, and emotional well-being —caffeine —nicotine
—respect for other's feelings, rights, and property —factors that affect self-image —communication skills —personal health and esteem	*Define nutrient. *Identify the major classes of nutrients and their functions. —calories —ideal weight —reliable sources of nutrition information	—rewards for positive health behavior —"prioritizing" health activities —inherited character —mechanics of the circulatory system	—personal behavior and wellness —heredity and illness —illness and personal responsibility —family influences on health	—misuses or abuses of drugs —drug effects on body organs —misuse of OTC drugs —effects of smoking
—group decision making —peer influence —interpersonal behaviors —desirable personal qualities —risk-taking behavior	*Identify major sources of key nutrients. *Classify foods into groups based on their major nutrient contribution. —portion size and servings —diet and blood pressure —fiber —sample menu evaluation	*Identify benefits of both aerobic and anaerobic exercise. —functions of body systems —interdependence of body systems —effects of puberty on development	*Explain the process of communicable disease transmission. —avoidance of disease —motivation and health behavior	—decision making about drugs —peer and adult influences —community impact of drug abuse —laws
*Identify situations that are stress producing. —expression of feelings —decision-making strategies —significant people —fairness	*Compare nutrient density of foods. —nutrient excess —nutrient deficiencies —food economics —dietary plan for a day's energy needs	*Recognize the importance of establishing an ongoing and effective exercise plan which accommodates personal requirements and limitations. —components of a healthy lifestyle	—positive versus negative health behaviors —immune system —major killers	*Identify and utilize the names of people and organizations who can provide help concerning problems related to tobacco, alcohol, marijuana, and other drugs. —alcohol effects —confronting the pressures to use drugs
*Identify stress management techniques. —personal goals —suicide prevention —defense mechanisms —grief and coping with grief	*Identify factors affecting basic nutrient and energy requirements and compute caloric needs. —health impact of diets —nutrition and dietary careers	—adolescent health care practices —fad behaviors —skin problems and their care —interpretation of "wellness" inventories	*Identify sources, symptoms, and treatment of sexually transmitted diseases. —past, present, and future health practices —factors that enhance health or cause illness	*Identify local resources, services, and support groups that are available for substance abuse treatment and control. —alternatives to drug use —negative consequences of drug abuse —careers in drug-related areas
*Demonstrate stress management techniques. —effective communication skills —selection of a satisfying career —positive mental health plan —mental health careers	—construct a weekly diet —evaluate a diet in terms of sugar, sodium, fat, fiber, etc. —compare nutritional value of supplements and additives	*Design and implement a personal health plan adaptable to charging lifelong needs. —social forces affecting health practices —energy balance of body weight —personal health careers	*Identify agencies and referral procedures for communicable disease or chronic disorders. —disease prevention planning —disease prevention careers	*Describe how to utilize programs and facilities designed to help individuals and families with tobacco, alcohol, and other drug problems. —the right to say "no" —drugs and health status —drugs and vehicle operation —drugs and pregnancy

Curricular Progression Chart

KEY

This chart has been prepared to give a brief overview of the content to be covered to meet the student objectives identified in this curriculum guide. It is not all-inclusive, but provides an adequate review of the scope and sequence of a comprehensive K–12 health instruction program.

A specific *topical reference* has been placed in parenthesis under the title of each of the ten content areas. Sample objectives, as written in the guide, which support that specific topical reference appear in the column below the content area at the various grade levels. This demonstrates the developmental nature of the curriculum and shows how a topic can be supported by objectives and instructional units throughout the grades, K–12.

The other items in each column identify additional topics for instruction which are covered under other objectives. Once again, these topics are not all-inclusive, but provide an overview of content recommended in this guide.

NOTE

All objectives (*) in this guide are prefaced by the words, "Students will . . ."

FIGURE 2.11 School health education study concepts. (From *Health Education: A Conceptual Approach,* 1967)

Relationship of

Three Key Concepts

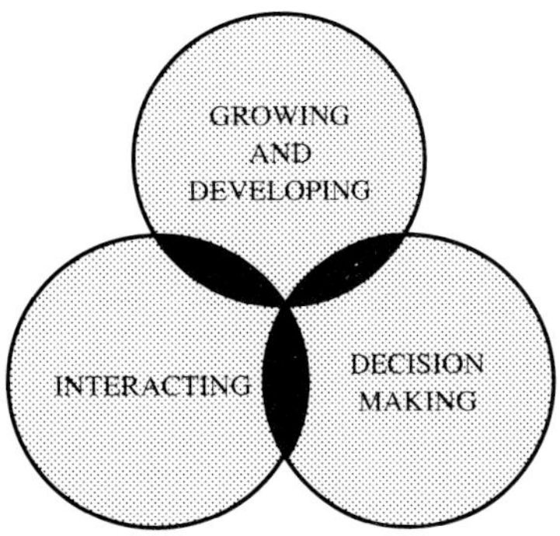

Ten Concepts

Growth and development influence and are influenced by the structure and functioning of the individual.	1
Growth and development follow a predictable sequence, yet are unique for each individual.	2
Protection and promotion of health is an individual, community, and international responsibility.	3
The potential for hazards and accidents exists, whatever the environment.	4
There are reciprocal relationships involving people, disease, and environment.	5
The family serves to perpetuate the species and to fulfill certain health needs.	6
Personal health practices are affected by a complexity of forces, often conflicting.	7
Utilization of health information, products, and services is guided by values and perceptions.	8
Use of substances that modify mood and behavior arises from a variety of motivations.	9
Food selection and eating patterns are determined by physical, social, mental, economic, and cultural factors.	10

Summary

If curriculum planners acquire an understanding of the content of comprehensive school health instruction, they have taken a major step in the process of developing an effective curriculum. Support for substantiating health needs and interests of young people and the needs of society can be obtained from research studies conducted by professional health education organizations, foundations, and governmental agencies. The selection of content is based upon looking at significant presentable health problems and risk-taking behaviors of young people; at the health interests of the school-age population as well as student knowledge, attitudes, and behaviors; and at societal needs. Utilizing needs-assessment data helps planners to narrow the scope and to sequence the subject matter to be taught. Criteria for narrowing the scope and examples of several available curricula help planners to accomplish their curriculum design tasks. Since health issues do not exist in isolation from one another, it is important for planners to explore the various approaches that can be used to link health areas.

FIGURE 2.12 Strand Program—New York. (Reprinted with permission of the National Association of Secondary Principals. Sincore, J., "New York State's Program in the Health Sciences, *NASSP Bulletin* 52(March 1986):84.)

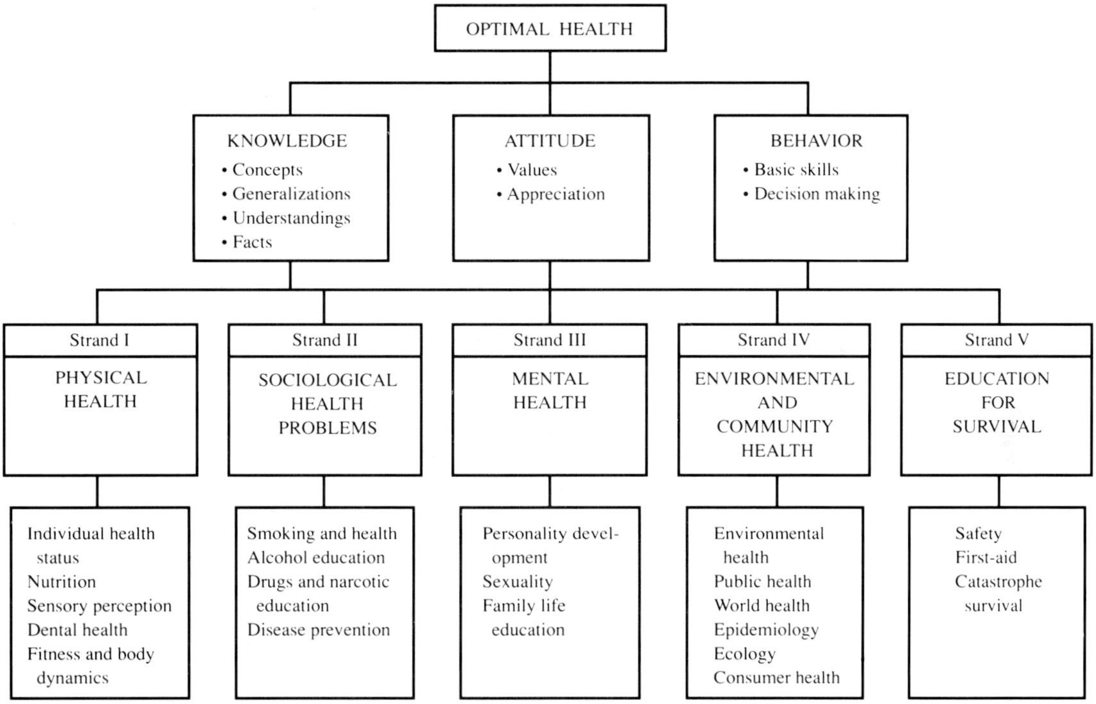

Content and Basic Aims of New York Health Education Program

Discussion Questions

1. What is the difference between a comprehensive school health program and comprehensive school health instruction? How are the two interrelated?
2. What criteria can be used to select health topics for a school's health education curriculum?
3. What resources can be used to help in the selection of essential and relevant health topics for inclusion in the scope and sequence?

Application Activities

1. Expanding the Scope of Health Education
   Part 1
   Activity: Using the Education Commission of the States' list of ten major content areas, select one content area. Expand this area by selecting all topics and issues that could possibly be included. Use personal health texts, subject matter texts, and curricula to help scan the descriptive content. Each student expands a content area and brings to the next class copies of his or her work.

FIGURE 2.13 Linking health topics to smoking/tobacco education

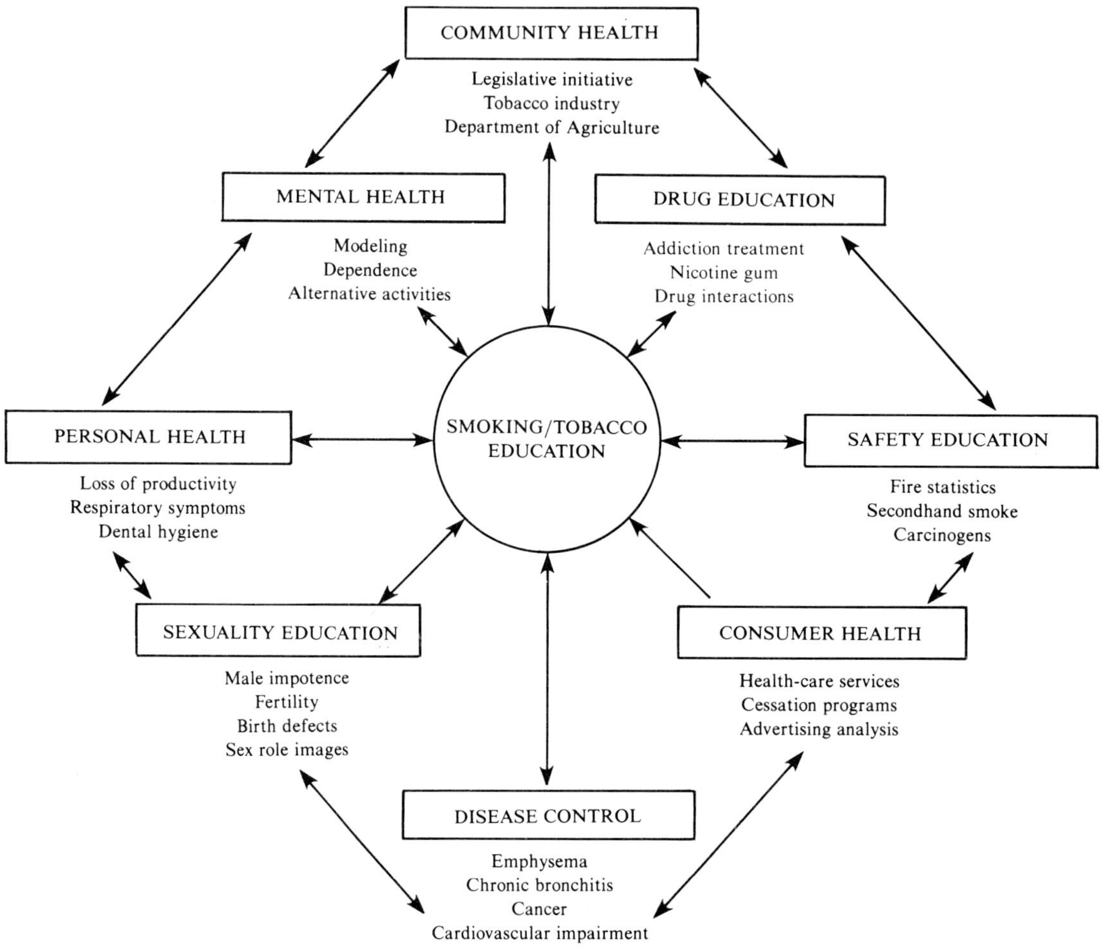

Part 2
Activity: During the following class session, as students share their assignments, classmates add to the possibilities.

2. Narrowing the Scope of Health Education
Activity: Using figures 2.5 (criteria) and 2.6 (sample form), each student narrows his or her expanded content area for a specified target population (e.g., grade 5; grade 8).
3. Linking Health Topics
Activity: Using figure 2.12, each student selects a major content, substitutes it for "Smoking/Tobacco Education," and identifies topics that can be included under the other major headings.

References

American School Health Association; Association for the Advancement of Health Education; and Society for Public Health Education, Inc. 1988. *National Adolescent Student Health Survey.* (A cooperative agreement with the American Alliance for Health, Physical Education, Recreation and Dance.) Reston, VA: Association for the Advancement of Health Education.

Association for the Advancement of Health Education. 1991. Report of the 1990 Joint Committee on Health Education Terminology. *Journal of Health Education* 22 (March/April). Reprinted with permission from the Association for the Advancement of Health Education.

Boyer, E. L. 1983. *High school: A report on secondary education in America.* The Carnegie Foundation for the Advancement of Teaching. New York: Harper & Row.

Byler, B., Lewis, G., and Totman, R. 1969. *Teach us what we want to know.* New York: Mental Health Materials Center.

Comprehensive School Health Education. 1984. *Health Education* 54 (6):6–7. (Also published under same title in *Journal of School Health* 54(8):314–315.) This article is reprinted with permission from *Health Education,* October/November, 1984, 6–7. *Health Education* is a publication of the American Alliance for Health, Physical Education, Recreation and Dance, 1900 Association Drive, Reston, VA 22091.

Department of Health and Human Services. 1979. *Healthy people: Surgeon General's report on health promotion and disease prevention.* Washington, DC: U.S. Government Printing Office.

———. 1980. *Promoting health—preventing disease: Objectives for the nation, 1990.* Washington, DC: U.S. Government Printing Office.

———. 1986. *The 1990 health objectives for the nation: A midcourse review.* Washington, DC: U.S. Government Printing Office.

———. 1989. *Promoting health—preventing disease: Year 2000 objectives for the nation.* Draft. Washington, DC: U.S. Government Printing Office.

———. 1990. *Healthy people 2000: National health promotion and disease prevention objectives.* Washington, DC: U.S. Government Printing Office.

Education Commission of the States. 1981. *Recommendations for school health education: A handbook for state policymakers.* Denver.

Harris, L. & Associates. 1988. *Health—You've got to be taught: An evaluation of comprehensive health education in American public schools.* New York: Metropolitan Life Foundation.

National Center for Health Education. 1989. *Growing healthy: Health education curricular progression chart.* New York.

National Dairy Council. 1987. *Food . . . your choice.* Rosemont, IL.

Office of Public Instruction. 1980. *Health education framework: A reference for program planning and student learning objectives.* Olympia, WA.

Oregon Department of Education. 1988. *Health education: Comprehensive curriculum goals/a model for local curriculum development.* Salem, OR.

Pine, P. 1985. *Critical issues report—promoting health education in schools: Problems and solutions.* Arlington, VA: American Association of School Administrators.

Results of the School Health Education Evaluation. 1985. *Journal of School Health* 55(8).

Roberts, Fitzmahan & Associates. 1986. *Here's looking at you, 2000.* Seattle, WA: Comprehensive Health Education Foundation.

School Health Education Study. 1967. *Health education: A conceptual approach to curriculum design.* St. Paul, MN: 3M Education Press.

Sincore, J. 1968. New York state's program in the health sciences. *The Bulletin of the National Association of Secondary School Principals* 52(326):81–87.

Trucano, L. 1984. *Students speak.* Seattle, WA: Comprehensive Health Education Foundation.

Wisconsin Department of Public Instruction. 1985. *A guide to curriculum planning in health education.* Madison, WI.

3

Curriculum Planning:
An Overview of the Process

After reading this chapter and participating in application activities, the student should be able to:

1. Identify the key people and groups in the school and community that should participate in planning a comprehensive health education curriculum.
2. Establish a timeline and an estimated budget for the planning process.
3. Identify the curricular needs of the school district.
4. Select a preferred curriculum delivery system.
5. Provide leadership or be a facilitator of a curriculum planning process.

This chapter describes the essential elements of a process that has been used successfully in developing health education curricula. To someone not intimately involved in schools, the teaching, learning, and administrative activities in schools seem natural and logical. The truth is, a great deal of time, effort, and thought must be devoted to planning and implementing school curricula and instructional activities if they are to focus on educational goals that are compatible with the desires and aspirations of the community. The planning process itself is particularly important in health education because it affects the curriculum, its implementation, and community support. The following are key steps in a curriculum-planning process:

1. Understanding who influences health education
2. Obtaining school board and administrative support
3. Establishing a budget and timeline for the planning process
4. Appointing a committee
5. Conducting a needs assessment
6. Developing a philosophy (rationale and purpose) and curriculum goals
7. Designing a delivery system
8. Writing curriculum objectives with a scope and sequence

Understanding Who Influences Health Education

Public schools are financed by public funds and are accountable to taxpayers in the local community and in the state. They are governed by elected school boards or committees who are responsive to the citizens who elect them. As a consequence, the decision-making process is often public and political—many people and factors influence curriculum decisions. Figure 3.1 visually charts the various people and organizations who have a stake in the outcome of health education.

The *school board,* or *school committee* is the governing body of a public school system and has ultimate authority to make decisions. The school board/committee determines the general educational philosophy and priorities in a school district and approves an annual budget. In some states, new curriculum and instructional materials require school board/committee approval before they can be used in the classroom.

The *school administration's* role is to provide leadership in program development, implementation, and evaluation. In large districts, the administration may include a director of curriculum and/or a health coordinator who is responsible for gathering staff and community input, providing up-to-date information, and knowing the legal requirements for health education. The administra-

FIGURE 3.1 People Who Influence Program Decisions in Public Schools

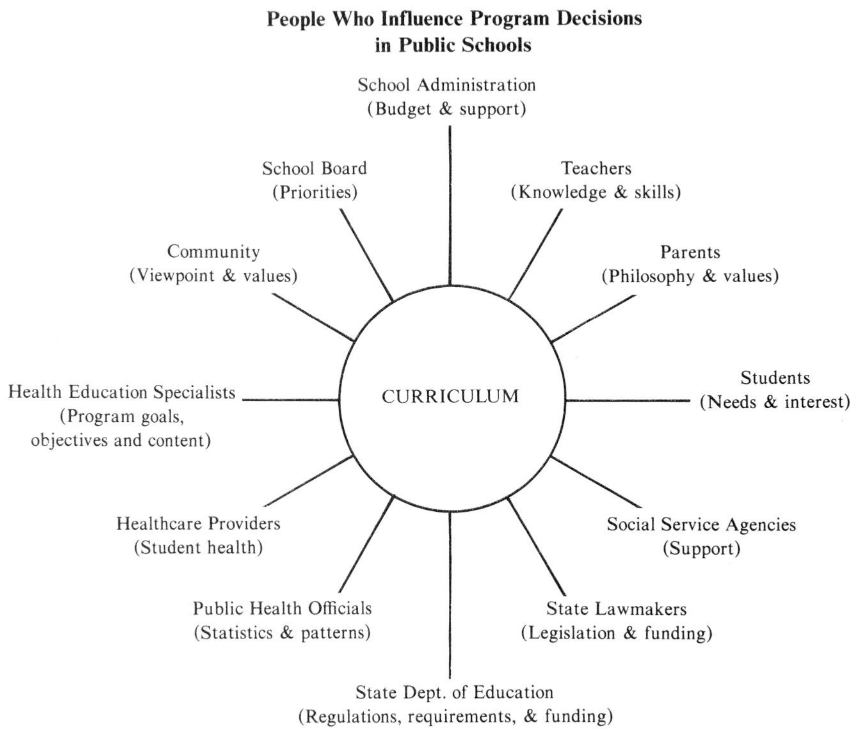

tion is also responsible for determining the necessary financial support for the program and for making funding recommendations to the school board/committee.

Teachers have two major roles that affect a program. First, teachers serving on the curriculum committee(s) are often involved in developing the curriculum and selecting accompanying materials. Second, they have control over how the curriculum is taught.

Parents can influence a curriculum by their participation or input in the curriculum development process. Their philosophy and values are usually reflected in the program adopted by the schools.

Students also have a strong influence on a curriculum, because curriculum developers are sensitive to students' health needs and interests. Teachers and/or curriculum specialists identify their needs and interests through surveys, interviews, and research studies.

Health agencies and organizations, such as hospitals and professional and voluntary health organizations, can influence school health programs in three ways: (1) they help the public and the school identify the major health needs of the community and its students, (2) many provide instructional materials and speakers to schools, and (3) they can be recruited to serve on curriculum committees.

Many *health-care providers,* such as family physicians, nurses, and dentists, have been involved in school health education by providing expert knowledge and support and serving on curriculum committees. In small communities, it is common to find dentists, for example, volunteering to teach students about dental health. Also, many state and local dental associations provide educational materials to schools at minimal or no cost.

Public health officials have a strong influence on school health education because they gather health statistics that both justify and promote health education. Without the urging of public health officials, such as the Surgeon General, education about AIDS and drug, alcohol, and tobacco use might not have become a national priority.

State lawmakers can influence school programs by passing laws that require health education and/or the teaching of specific topics such as AIDS prevention and drug and alcohol education. They can also impact schools negatively by passing legislation that is too specific or difficult to implement. Legislators, in turn, are subject to the influence of special-interest groups, and they have the authority to fund special school programs, such as drug and alcohol education.

The state department of education may establish graduation requirements, time allotment, and curriculum guidelines in health education. It may also provide technical assistance to local schools. In some states, the Department of Education screens available textbooks and instructional materials and publishes a list of approved materials from which local schools may select.

Health education specialists who have advanced degrees in health education include university faculty members, curriculum writers, supervisors, teacher trainers, and consultants. These specialists write textbooks and instructional materials, train teachers, and/or supervise health education programs in the schools. They have a great deal of influence on the philosophy, content, and quality of health education.

Community members who are not parents can also have a voice in influencing health education in public schools. Because personal values and moral issues are part of health education, the clergy is often asked by schools to serve on health advisory committees, and there are groups organized for the purpose of influencing school curriculum.

Obtaining Support

Prior to initiating the health curriculum development effort, the administrator responsible for district curriculum and the health education coordinator or specialist must obtain school board and administrative support for the project. This support normally translates into the amount of money to be budgeted for the project. As elected officials, school board/committee members are influenced by public concerns, including those of official health agencies, state Departments of Education, health-care professionals, health educators, parents, teachers, and administrators. Understanding the roles and influences of various key players and the nature of the decision process is crucial in successfully planning and implementing a health education curriculum.

Budget and Timeline for the Planning Process

The amount of time and money needed to develop and implement a program depends on whether a program already exists and how good it is. Since the curriculum development process is time-consuming, teachers often do not volunteer to be on a curriculum committee unless they are provided with release time or compensated financially for their work. It is difficult to determine in advance how much time a committee may need. Experience with different committees shows that a minimum of thirty hours is necessary. Often, a consultant or consultants need to be hired to work with the committee if the school district does not employ a health education curriculum specialist. The committee also needs to purchase some sample materials for preview because small publishers and material

FIGURE 3.2 Curriculum review procedure and timeline. (Bainbridge Island School District, Bainbridge Island, WA.)

Curriculum Review Procedure and Timeline

Tasks	Date
1. Publish notice of curriculum reviews in parent bulletins and local papers to solicit community input & patron participation	Sept
2. Establish Curriculum Committee	Sept
3. Review tasks with committee	Oct
4. Discuss plan with PTO council & solicit input	Oct
5. Contact publishers to request sample materials	Sept/Oct
6. Solicit staff input and gather student & program data	Oct
7. Review current trends & literature	Oct/Nov
8. Write point-of-view statement and program goals	Nov
9. Develop program-selection criteria	Dec
10. Submit point-of-view statement and program goals for Board review	Dec
11. Visit and/or examine exemplary programs	Dec/Feb
12. Review available programs and materials	Feb
13. Write curriculum & student learning objectives	Feb/Mar
14. Select textbooks and materials	Feb/Mar
15. Submit materials to Instructional Materials Committee (IMC) for approval	Mar/April
16. Make program recommendations to superintendent for:	
a. Education Program Committee revision	Mar/April
b. School Board approval	April/May
17. Develop implementation & inservice plan	May/June
18. Order textbooks & materials	June
19. Implement program	Sept

manufacturers do not send free examination copies. In addition, secretarial and printing costs have to be budgeted.

In the public schools, the timeline for curriculum development is closely related to the school year, which begins in September and ends in June. If curriculum implementation is targeted for the fall, recommendations and materials selection have to be completed by early spring. Ideally, more than one school year is needed to develop a comprehensive health education program, but it is possible to complete a curriculum within a school year if the committee is willing to meet frequently and the chair is experienced in and knowledgeable about committee and school district decision-making processes. A sample timeline appears in figure 3.2.

In spite of careful planning, there are often unanticipated problems that require modification of the timeline. One common situation is the existence of strong disagreement or conflict among committee members, which slows down the consensus-building process. Another potential cause of delay involves the lack of complete acceptance of the committee's recommendations by a segment of the community and/or the school board. Often a small group of parents who oppose a certain part of the curriculum can delay adoption by one or two years.

In addition to a timeline, it is often necessary to delineate the tasks and assign responsibility for each task. Certain tasks, such as setting up the committee, establishing parameters, and specifying the amount of available funds, are normal duties of administration. Therefore, it is natural to assign them to an administrator. The amount of administrative direction needed by a committee depends on the expertise and experience of the committee members. Nevertheless, it is useful for the committee to develop a task and responsibility chart such as the one shown in figure 3.3.

FIGURE 3.3 Suggested task chart for health education curriculum planning. (Courtesy of L. Trucano.)

Tasks	Needed Resources	Responsibility of	Time Line
1. Select Curriculum Committee	• Recommendations from principals, teachers' association and/or teachers	• Administration	
2. Set working dates	• School calendar • Committee members' preference	• Curriculum Committee	
3. Review health education interests and needs of students	• Washington State Health Education framework • *Student Speaks*	• Curriculum Committee	
4. Develop philosophical base	• Sample philosophies	• Curriculum Committee	
5. Determine health education goals	• District documents • Framework	• Administration • Advisory Committee • Curriculum Committee	
6. Develop scope and sequence	• Local existing curricula • Amount of time allocated to health education in grades K–6 • Where health will be taught in grades 7–12 and amount of time to be allocated • Knowledge of students' health needs, interests, and concerns	• Curriculum Committee	
7. Review (or develop) controversial issues policy	• District policy • Sample policies	• Administration and/or Curriculum Committee	
8. Determine curriculum design	• Possible examples: Objectives only Objectives/textbook Objectives/learning activities Objectives/learning activities/learning materials Objectives/learning materials	• Curriculum Committee	
9. Identify curriculum objectives related to scope and sequence	• Framework • Curriculum guides from other districts • Teachers' knowledge of students' health needs and interests	• Curriculum Committee or teacher groups	
10. Depending on Step 8 identify suggested learning activities to achieve objectives	• Curriculum guides from other districts • Teachers' own ideas • Learning resources	• Administration • Curriculum Committee • District teachers	
11. Depending on Step 8 identify suggested resources needed to help achieve objectives	• Budget available • Free materials available • Preview new materials: texts, filmstrips, posters, etc.	• Administration • Curriculum Committee • Possibly consultant • District teachers	
12. Determine how program will be presented to teachers, school board, community		• Curriculum Committee • Teachers	
13. Implement program (inservice) (orientation)	• Budget available • Timeline needed	• Administration • Curriculum Committee • Possibly consultant	

Appointing a Committee

In the public schools, a health education curriculum is often developed jointly by many people. Teachers, administrators, curriculum specialists, and school nurses are the experts involved in designing a curriculum. Community members, parents, and the school board play major roles in determining the philosophy and goals of the curriculum. Because some topics of health education, such as sexuality and drug and alcohol education, have traditionally been taught in the home and church, there is no consensus on what should be the responsibility of public schools. Many health topics are intimately related to moral values and life-styles about which there are diverse views. Each community has to decide on the role its public school should have in health education. Ideally, this decision is made jointly by health professionals, educators, and parents.

A typical committee for developing a health education program should include a health education specialist, teachers, administrators, school nurse and physician, parents, church representative, and students. The optimal size of a committee lies somewhere between twelve and sixteen members—a balance between management efficiency and participatory decision making. The committee should be large enough to accommodate different points of view, yet small enough to be manageable. A proper balance of the different categories of staff and community members is important (e.g., one-third classroom teachers, one-third administrators, and one-third parents). For a school district of small (500 students) or medium (approximately 5,000 students) size, the following composition is typical:

elementary classroom teachers	2
secondary classroom teachers (preferably with health education backgrounds)	2
principals (elementary and secondary)	2
guidance counselor	1
school nurse or physician	1
central office administrator/curriculum specialist	1
parents (with elementary- and secondary-level children)	4
representative of local church council (optional)	1
high school students (optional)	2

Since some areas of health education can be controversial, it is desirable to obtain wide community input and participation in the developmental phase. A public meeting or community survey for the purpose of obtaining comments from parents and community representatives may be useful. It is often difficult to determine what is the truly representative view of a community. Public meetings are often attended and dominated by people who are unhappy with what is being proposed. Those who support the new curriculum often stay at home, and they may be in the majority. A survey may be more representative, but surveys are costly and time-consuming to conduct. Curriculum decisions are not always rational. For example, one school district surveyed the parents and found strong support (86 percent) for sexuality education, including teaching about contraceptives to high school students. But a small group of parents was very vocal in its opposition to the curriculum and was able to persuade the school board to postpone its implementation and modify the curriculum. In general, committee recommendations have a better chance of school board approval, even when encountering opposition, than administrative recommendations.

Conducting a Needs Assessment

The assessment of needs in the schools is normally the first step taken by the committee in the curriculum development process. The purpose of such an assessment is to determine the discrepancy between the *existing* state of health education and the *desired* state of health education. The process involves gathering information about (1) the knowledge and attitudes of students, (2) the opinions of teachers and administrators about the existing program or the need for a new program, and (3) additional topics or areas of student health which need to be addressed.

Assessment methods vary in complexity. They may include the following:

- Brainstorming sessions among teachers, administrators, school nurse, and parents to generate a list of perceived needs
- Polling local health-care providers and health education experts
- Surveying students, using questionnaire or interview.

A number of needs-assessment instruments already exist. For example, the National Adolescent Student Health Survey (IOX Assessment Associates, 1987) is an instrument used to determine the health knowledge, attitudes, and behaviors of young people in eighth and tenth grades. The results of this national survey provide a basis for comparison if a school district chooses to survey its students. Another instrument that is available is a set of questionnaires developed for the survey of health interests and concerns of students in grades kindergarten through 12 (Trucano, 1984).

Opinions of teachers and administrators can be gathered through locally developed questionnaires or interviews. Four or five simple questions are often sufficient for identifying major gaps or concerns. For example:

1. Briefly describe the major health topics or units that you teach.
2. What are the major strengths of the existing program?
3. What are the major weaknesses of the existing program?
4. Do you have suggestions for change? If so, please describe.

Conducting a needs assessment does not have to be an elaborate, time-consuming process. A sampling of student knowledge and attitudes, administering a teacher questionnaire, and talking to interested parents are often sufficient to determine curriculum and program needs.

Developing Philosophy and Curriculum Goals

In order to have *continuity* (lessons build upon preceding learning experiences) and *coordination* (relationships among topics and lessons are reinforced), the most desirable approach to curriculum is to look at it from kindergarten through grade 12 (K–12), instead of separating elementary from junior high or middle school and high school. A school district that is committed to developing a grades K–12 comprehensive health education curriculum should first assemble a committee that includes teachers from various grade levels.

One of the first tasks of the committee is to write a philosophy for the health curriculum (see chapter 1). This is often the most difficult task of the committee because committee members have to come to grips with their own assumptions and beliefs and the beliefs of other committee members that differ from their own. It is also difficult to write succinctly and clearly about abstract ideas and philosophical viewpoints. Writing a philosophy statement is time-consuming, but worthwhile. It gives committee members an opportunity to articulate and discuss different viewpoints and to agree on a common philosophy of the subject. The philosophy is the foundation and unifying element of the curriculum.

The next task is writing goals or mission statements for the curriculum. Goals are broad statements outlining key concepts, skills, or attitudes. Generally, the number of goals for a comprehensive curriculum for grades K–12 ranges from six to twenty or more. Often, general topics and skills are included in the goals (see chapter 1). Some people may prefer to include the major content areas in their goal statements.

Placement and Time Allocation of Health Education

Before the committee proceeds further in developing the curriculum, it must decide how much time is to be allocated to the subject of health education at each grade level. This could be a very political decision that can only be made after consultation with principals and other subject specialists. A school is a complex system with many interrelated components, including fixed amounts of time and money. If more time is given to teaching health, time must be taken from another subject. A typical time allocation chart (figure 3.4) shows how time is divided among all the various subjects, recess, and opening/closing activities in an elementary school. The amount of time allocated to health education in elementary schools generally ranges from 60 to 120 minutes per week. At the secondary level, most junior high or middle schools require all students to take a semester of health. Unfortunately, many high schools in this country do not require students to take health; they offer health as an elective course. High schools that require students to take health traditionally place it at the eleventh or twelfth grade. The state Department of Education in Wisconsin has published time-allocation guidelines for their schools, grades K–12 (see figure 3.5).

Recommending an increase in time allocation or course requirement can cause friction among different subject specialists and secondary teachers, who often compete for students. Much lobbying and negotiation are often necessary if a committee's recommendation is to be accepted by teachers, principals, district administrators, the superintendent, and the school board. In other words, recommending that health be required at a high school where it is presently offered as an elective course is a major undertaking that requires political savvy, time, and effort from the committee.

FIGURE 3.4 Elementary school time allotment guidelines (minutes per week). (From Bainbridge Island School District, Bainbridge Island, WA.)

Elementary School Time Allotment Guidelines

(Minutes Per Week)

Activities	Grades 1–2	Grade 3	Grades 4–5
Reading	400	350	300
Language Arts	200	185	205
Penmanship	75	60	15
Spelling	75	75	75
Math	200	250	300
Social Studies	100	125	125
Science	100	100	125
Health/Safety	60	75	75
Physical Education	100	100	100
Art	55	55	55
Music	55	45	45
Library	30	30	30
Opening/Closing	75	75	75
Subtotal	1525	1525	1525
A.M. Recess	50	50	50
Lunch/Recess	300	300	300
P.M. Recess	50	50	50
Total	1925	1925	1925

It is critical that time allocation for health be decided before developing the curriculum. This is not commonly done, because many elementary schools do not have time-allocation guidelines for other subjects. If no time limit is given, curriculum developers naturally write more curriculum and/or lesson objectives than teachers can possibly teach. When there are more objectives than teachers can finish, each teacher selects what he or she likes. This results in inconsistent implementation of the curriculum.

FIGURE 3.5 Recommended time allocation guidelines, K–12. (Reprinted/excerpted from *A Guide to Curriculum Planning in Health Education* with permission from the Wisconsin Department of Public Instruction, 25 South Webster Street, Madison, WI 53702.)

Recommended Time Allocation

	Recommened Time Allocation in Minimum Number of Instructional Periods to cover the Content Areas at Specific Grade Levels*								
School Health Education Major Content Areas for Classroom Instruction	**Recommended number of periods per year One year = 34 Weeks**							**Recommended number of periods per semester**	
	K	1–2		3–4		5–6		7–8–9	10–11–12
	45 min. per wk. 1 period = 15 min.	**75 min. per wk. 1 period = 25 min.**		**100 min. per wk. 1 period = 50 min.**		**125 min. per wk. 1 period = 50 min.**		**1 course, meeting 90 periods in a semester. 1 period = 50 min.**	**1 course, meeting 90 periods in a semester. 1 period = 50 min.**
	Grade Levels								
	15-min. periods	25-min. periods			50-min. periods				
	K	1	2	3	4	5	6	7–8–9	10–11–12
I. Accident Prevention and Safety	15	12	12	15	15	6	5	5	14
II. Community Health	0	0	0	6	6	5	5	5	5
III. Consumer Health	0	0	0	6	6	5	5	10	8
IV. Environmental Health	0	0	0	6	6	5	5	10	10
V. Family Life Education	6	9	9	12	12	10	10	15	12
VI. Mental and Emotional Health	18	18	18	18	18	13	15	12	8
VII. Nutrition	18	18	18	18	18	10	10	5	5
VIII. Personal Health	18	18	18	18	18	13	12	10	9
IX. Prevention and Control of Disease	6	6	6	6	6	3	3	3	4
X. Substance Use and Abuse	6	9	9	15	15	15	15	10	10
TOTAL PERIODS	87	90	90	120	120	85	85	85	85

*The recommended periods for a year or semester *do not* necessarily mean that all instruction should be completed in that specific content area in consecutive lessons.

A desire to integrate health education into other subjects rather than allocating time for health education separately has prevented the planning and implementation of quality health education. Health education is a discipline in itself, needing intensive instruction over a long period of time. Then and only then can applicable and relevant health concepts be reinforced in other subject areas.

The integration of health into other subjects has been tried and has not been successful. This is partly because of the inadequate health background of teachers in other disciplines. Very little health education has occurred in grades K–12 during the last fifty years. Individuals going into teacher education therefore have meager health backgrounds, and many receive little or no additional training during teacher preparation. It is unfair to expect these people to incorporate health into their teaching when they have insufficient background to do so.

Another reason integration has not been successful is that leadership, time, and money to do what needs to be done are not available. Because teacher preparation trains people by discipline, on the whole, it would take someone with unusual background to give leadership to this kind of endeavor. Furthermore, the time and money needed to design the curriculum and provide in-service training for teachers would be prohibitive.

The advantages of curricular integration are the efficient use of time in the school day and the reality that every topic probably relates to other topics in the same discipline as well as topics in other disciplines.

A disadvantage of integration is that one of the subject areas usually gets detailed treatment, while the other is superficially taught. Generally, it is the health implications of a topic that are superficially taught. For example, in elementary grades, science books discuss pollutants in water and air but do not concern themselves with the health implications of these pollutants. Another disadvantage is that when objectives are divided up and taught in different classrooms (e.g., during substance-abuse education), young people have difficulty seeing relationships and transferring knowledge.

Given the present state of education, the best placement for health education is to teach it as a separate subject.

Writing Curriculum Objectives with Scope and Sequence

One of the most enjoyable aspects of curriculum development is selecting what concepts, knowledge, skills, and attitudes should be taught at each grade level. Chapter 2 describes the process for developing a scope and sequence. The factors guiding the selection of content should include the developmental readiness of the students, students' needs and interests, community and societal needs, the health experts' opinions, the school district's educational philosophy, state Department of Education guidelines, and teachers' experience. One of the best resources for this activity is the *Health Education Framework: Supplemental Materials* (Office of the Superintendent of Public Instruction, 1980), which systematically links the developmental characteristics, interests, and needs of students of various age groups to the desired health knowledge, attitudes, and behavior (see appendix 1).

Once the committee has completed the philosophy, curriculum goals, and a scope and sequence, it can divide into subcommittees to focus on elementary, middle/junior high school, and high school curricula separately. This will speed up the whole process. The work of the subcommittees should be reviewed and approved by the entire committee periodically (see figure 3.6).

Scope and sequence plus the curriculum objectives direct what knowledge, attitudes, and skills should be taught and when they should be taught. They are the most important part of a curriculum. The following chapters

FIGURE 3.6 Tasks of Health Committee and Subcommittees

Health Committee tasks:	Subcommittees' task (elementary, middle school, high school)
1. Philosophy	5. Curriculum objectives by grade level
2. Goals or missions statement	
3. Delivery system/time allocation	**Health Committee (as a whole)**
4. Scope and sequence draft	6. Refine scope and sequence and curriculum objectives

explain the remaining components of curriculum development and implementation in detail.

Summary

Developing a comprehensive health education curriculum in public schools is a complex process. Because health education deals with personal and family issues and values, there is no total agreement on what should be taught. The involvement of parents, health-care professionals, community representatives, teachers, administrators, and health education specialists in a consensus-building process has proven to be a successful approach in developing a curriculum with a broad base of support.

The key elements of the process include understanding the people, agencies, and organizations that influence health education; obtaining the support of administrators and the school board; establishing a realistic budget and practical timeline for the planning process; and appointing a committee to do the work, which includes conducting a needs assessment, developing a philosophy and curriculum goals, designing a delivery system, and writing curriculum objectives with a scope and sequence.

Discussion Questions

1. If you have been given the responsibility for developing a comprehensive health education curriculum in your school district, whom do you select to serve on the committee and why?
2. Briefly describe a school district and outline a process for developing a health curriculum. Identify some of the difficulties you may encounter.
3. How would you go about deciding what should be included in your school health curriculum?

Application Activities

1. You are given the job of convincing the school board and administration that the health curriculum in the district needs major revision and that a substantial amount of time and money are required. How do you proceed? What do you say?

References

IOX Assessment Associates. 1987. *National adolescent student health survey*. Reston, VA: Association for the Advancement of Health Education.

Office of the Superintendent of Public Instruction. 1980. *Health education framework: Supplemental material*. Olympia, WA.

Trucano, L. 1984. *Students speak*. Seattle: Comprehensive Health Education Foundation.

Wisconsin Department of Public Instruction. 1985. *A guide to curriculum planning in health education*. Madison, WI.

4

Objectives:
Signposts for Direction

After reading this chapter and participating in application activities, the student should be able to:

1. Summarize the purposes of objectives in curriculum planning.
2. Distinguish between curriculum and lesson objectives.
3. Relate lesson objectives to curriculum objectives and curriculum objectives to curriculum goals and philosophy.
4. Differentiate among cognitive, affective, and psychomotor domains of learning behaviors.
5. Write curriculum and lesson objectives.
6. Critique the use of appropriate terminology in writing curriculum and lesson objectives.
7. Appreciate the usefulness and value of curriculum and lesson objectives.

The first three chapters have set the stage for the development of objectives that young people can achieve in health education. The next step is to determine the objectives.

This chapter focuses on the purposes of objectives during the planning process and distinguishes between curriculum objectives and lesson objectives. The three learning domains of cognitive, affective, and psychomotor behaviors are differentiated. Briefly discussed are some of the difficulties encountered in their use. Helpful hints for facilitating the process of writing objectives are provided, along with a list of questions that curriculum developers need to address as they tackle the task of dealing with objectives.

Purposes of Objectives

Think of the curriculum developer as a travel agent preparing an itinerary for a client. The client wants to reach a destination in the most expedient but fulfilling manner. As the travel agent, the curriculum developer has to select the best routes by which clients (i.e., the students) will travel to reach their destinations.

If goals are the destinations, then objectives are the routes that keep people going in the right direction. Objectives keep everyone on track. If the objectives (routes) are achieved, the goals are attained. Objectives describe the subject matter in the curriculum and what the participants must do to reach the goals. And, as noted in chapter 1, both goals and objectives reflect the philosophical foundations of health education.

Objectives are an essential component of a program. They are, by definition, the *intended* outcomes of instruction (Mager, 1962). They are the steps along the way that help young people achieve the program goals of the curriculum. In general, objectives have several purposes.

First, objectives tell what the students will learn. They define the subject matter of health education; that is, they describe the nature of various health topics and issues and the distinctive properties of the subject matter as they relate to health education.

Second, objectives serve to communicate the essence of a curriculum. Dialogue among developers, administrators, parents, teachers, and school boards is enhanced when well-written objectives (and goals) are available. Ambiguity and misunderstandings among these groups are certain to be reduced when objectives exist. Teachers improve their dialogue with each other; through objectives they know what is taught in other grades and understand the sequencing of health content.

Communication between parents and teachers can be improved because "a list of skills, products, or observable actions provides a more precise means for reporting to parents what a student has mastered . . ." (Bloom, Madaus, and Hastings, 1981: 20). When objectives are written for lessons, students can study more effectively. Knowing which activities are relevant to their own learning means that students don't have to second-guess their teachers (Mager, 1962).

Third, curriculum developers use objectives to organize scope and sequence. Sequencing the curriculum ensures that age-appropriate knowledge, skills, and attitudes can be built upon as students progress from grade to grade. As a bonus, curriculum writers may find health topics that are missing or ones that are repetitive.

Fourth, curriculum objectives guide instruction. These objectives suggest rather than prescribe the methods, materials, and experiences that will help students to achieve the intended program goals.

Fifth, objectives can be the indicators for student achievement and the basis for program evaluation; they set the parameters for accountability. In other words, they specify the knowledge, skills, and attitudes to be mastered by students. They are the criteria used for determining the effectiveness of a curriculum.

Curriculum and Lesson Objectives

A variety of terms has been used to describe objectives. Many of these terms, such as *behavioral, instructional, lesson, learning,* and *performance,* are used interchangeably by different planners, and they serve essentially the same purpose. They depict what a student has learned as a result of participating in a particular learning experience or what a student has accomplished after completing a prescribed unit of instruction (Mager, 1962).

Some writers use *terminal* and *enabling* or *general* and *specific* objectives to denote curriculum and lesson objectives (Bedworth and Bedworth, 1978; Pollock, 1987; Fodor and Dalis, 1989). This variation in terminology makes the language for describing *objectives* somewhat confusing. We have chosen to explain objectives from the standpoint of use—one use is in instructional planning and the other is as indicators of students' achievements. By distinguishing between objectives written for instructional planning (i.e., curriculum objectives) and objectives written to indicate student achievement (i.e., lesson objectives), the authors believe they can simplify the process of selecting and writing objectives.

Curriculum objectives provide direction for those making decisions about what learning activities and materials are to be incorporated into a particular lesson, unit, or course of instruction. They are the starting point for planning teaching strategies. Curriculum objectives are grade-specific and may be achieved over a whole year; many lessons may be needed in order to achieve a particular curriculum objective. These objectives are not necessarily listed in a particular sequence but they do describe the intended outcomes for each grade. To assist the reader in recognizing curriculum objectives for instructional planning, examples for grade 8 are given in figure 4.1.

Lesson objectives are a subset of curriculum objectives. They are specific to a grade, to health content, and to learning activities. They define expectations about what students will know, feel, or do after completing a particular lesson or sequence of lessons. Lesson objectives are more immediate in their attainability and move students toward the curriculum objectives. These objectives are generally, but not always, written sequentially: the intended outcome of the first objective sets the stage for the accomplishment of the second,

FIGURE 4.1 Curriculum objectives for grade 8

Curriculum Objectives for Grade 8

The student will be able to do the following:

- Describe the structure, function, and importance of the endocrine system.
- Explore the effects of chemical substances on the human body.
- Interpret the interrelationship of drug use and risk-taking behaviors.
- Relate the impact of chronic diseases such as Alzheimer's and cancerous diseases on the family.
- Examine the relationship of life-style to cancerous diseases.
- Assume responsibility for prevention and control of sexually transmitted diseases.
- Explain the need for public health services in today's society.
- Develop a plan of action to favorably influence one's own personal health.
- Apply principles of refusal skills to resolving interpersonal conflicts.
- Justify the benefits of caring relationships to self and to others.
- Discuss factors involved in establishing responsible sexual behaviors.
- Recognize male and female similarities and differences in sexual drives and behavior.
- Examine the relationship between sex-role stereotyping and sexual pressures and behaviors.
- Discriminate critically between reliable and unreliable health information, labeling, and advertising.

and so on. For example, listed below are objectives for a series of four lessons on cancer education for sixth-grade youngsters:

1. The student defines cancer as many diseases of abnormal cell growth.
2. The student lists ways in which cancerous cells damage the body.
3. The student defines *carcinogen.*
4. The student recognizes cancer risks as they relate to personal health decisions.
5. The student links the incidence of skin cancer to excessive sun exposure.
6. The student describes the function of melanin.
7. The student explains racial differences in skin cancer risk.
8. The student accepts the scientific evidence of the value of using sunscreen protection.
9. The student practices behaviors that can reduce the personal risk of skin cancer. (Fred Hutchinson Cancer Research Center, 1984).

If a school district plans to end the curriculum development process after developing curriculum objectives, then the selection and writing of lesson objectives are left to the teacher. If the school district plans to give its teachers actual lesson objectives, with or without accompanying learning activities to achieve them, then the curriculum planners are the principal selectors and writers of lesson objectives.

When teachers are the writers, curriculum developers can assist teachers in writing their lesson objectives. Simply asking them what they want their students to learn as a result of a particular lesson or lessons is a good starting point. Getting teachers to verbalize what they expect of students before they sit down to write the objectives can reduce the amount of time teachers spend on this task.

As with many issues in health, rigidity is not the name of the game. Some positive outcomes of the learning process cannot be anticipated, which means that all objectives cannot be spelled out ahead of time. The unanticipated outcomes may become new lesson objectives.

Cognitive, Affective, and Psychomotor Domains

Invariably readers will find discussions in the literature about objectives falling into three domains: cognitive, affective, and psychomotor. The *cognitive* domain, associated with intellectual changes, reflects measurable increases in health knowledge and comprehension, ability to analyze and synthesize health information, and ability to apply new information in decision making. The *affective* domain is associated with feelings and attitudes that people have regarding health issues. It can include personal health concepts as well as social and environmental health concepts. This domain is characterized chiefly by changes in interests, attitudes, and values. The *psychomotor* domain is characterized by health habits and practices. It refers to health skills and actions in which there is physical application of knowledge and attitudes. To gain perspective on the three domains, consider the following example of dental health objectives for second-graders:

- The student *names* factors that contribute to dental decay (cognitive domain).
- The student *agrees* to brush and floss teeth daily (affective domain).
- The student *brushes* teeth daily using correct techniques (psychomotor domain).

The action verb (italicized) connotes the learning domain in the above example. In the preceding objectives for cancer education, numbers 1–7 are cognitive, number 8 is affective, and number 9 is in the psychomotor domain.

There is no automatic answer to the question of when to use a particular domain. The decision to include more objectives from one domain than another or to have equal amounts depends mostly on what the curriculum committee has defined as the school's philosophical focus and the health education curricular goals. Part of the decision will reflect the administration's attitude about measuring and evaluating students. If cognitive tests are stressed by the school administration at the urging of the school board, then the number of cognitive objectives will be considerably greater than the number of affective and psychomotor objectives.

Some lessons may be designed for only one domain, such as the cognitive. Related objectives in the other domains are then added to move the student toward the curriculum objectives and goals. In the previous example, naming factors that contribute to dental decay does not mean that the student will practice the skill of brushing teeth or value the habit of doing it. Thus curriculum designers, to get to where they want to go (i.e., the goal), may need to write objectives in all three of the domains. Tanner has suggested that "although the term *domain* implies a separation of spheres of activity, in effect learning these spheres [is] marked not by separation and isolation, but by continuity and interdependence" (Tanner, 1972:5).

In deciding which domain—cognitive, affective, or psychomotor—to emphasize in order to achieve the curriculum's goals, the health educator needs to choose words carefully to fit the desired outcomes. Those who desire greater detail about the cognitive and affective domains are referred to the definitive sources of Bloom (1956) and Krathwohl, Bloom, and Masia (1964).

Children practice behavior of covering their noses and mouths to prevent the spreading of germs. (Published with permission of the American Lung Association.)

Some Difficulties with Objectives

School district personnel and parents are often most concerned about cognitive outcomes (e.g., reciting anatomical parts of body systems, designing balanced meals, and listing physiological effects of drugs). Teaching about students' awareness of feelings and attitudes about the human body, balanced meals, and risks in drug-taking makes some parents and administrators uneasy. Also, some teachers feel uneasy when presenting lessons that require exploration of feelings and attitudes. In health education controversy is sometimes associated with the attainment of affective objectives. Thus, curriculum writers may omit or reduce the number of these objectives, for the following reasons:

- Parents' fear of indoctrination (Can attitudes and values be taught without the teacher espousing particular beliefs or preaching?)
- Belief that the home is the proper place for the development of feelings and values
- Fear of invasion of privacy (Should students be asked to share their beliefs about health matters?)
- Belief that affective outcomes are difficult to evaluate (Should students' health attitudes, feelings, interests, and beliefs be graded?)

At times it may be difficult to measure health objectives (i.e., assessing whether knowledge, attitudes, and behaviors have been attained). Critical thinking and evaluation skills are difficult to measure, as well as those objectives stated in the affective domain. For example, let's say one indicator of student achievement is that students value the health benefits of a balanced diet. Can *value* really be measured at the end of one lesson? It is not only difficult; it may be impossible. More than one lesson is generally needed. The overall results in health education that we want students to accomplish (healthy life-styles and health-promoting behaviors) cannot be achieved in a single lesson or unit. The outcomes may occur in a year or after several years. However, the authors encourage health educators to include objectives in the affective domain and to teach toward the general outcome of valuing a healthy life-style.

There are several solutions to the problem of assessment. Health educators can teach toward affective domain objectives but not try to evaluate them per se. If this is all the health education a student receives still may make a difference, whether or not the teacher can assess the difference. For objectives with a short timeline, well-designed tools to measure affective objectives such as checklists and attitude inventories can be used (see chapter 11 on evaluation). Students can assess their own growth in learning and may or may not share this with the teacher. The teacher, through observation of student behavior in classroom work and discussion and through informal student comments, can assess whether the student is "buying into" achieving a healthy life-style. For example, senior high student, who was engaged to be married, indicated to the authors that she had begun to eat breakfast for the first time because of information she had read and discussed in health education about the effects of nutrition on the brain development of an embryo. The student had learned in class that what a woman ate before conception might make a difference in the health of the embryo.

How Many Objectives?

Perhaps the question most frequently asked by students is "How many objectives should I write?" The answer "As many as it takes" suggests there is no magic answer to that question. There is no exact number or formula to use. It all depends on the extent and specificity of the planned program as well as the nature of the learning situations. The number of objectives is generally proportional to the amount of time allotted to the program and to its scope. That is, there will be fewer objectives for a curriculum that spans a week than for one that lasts two weeks. Programs that are complex or cover a variety of issues usually need more objectives; sometimes, one may be enough.

Selecting Appropriate Terms for Objectives

Content by itself is often meaningless unless the objective statement includes what the student is supposed to do with the content. Behavior in an objective is determined by the action verb that is chosen to specify what students' actions are to be. Action verbs are such words as *analyze, explain, formulate, classify,* and *differentiate.* Verbs such as *know, learn,* and *understand* are weak words. For example, compare *know* and *list* in the same sentence: *The student knows factors that may contribute to healthy longevity* and *The student lists factors that may contribute to healthy longevity. Knows* is too general, too abstract; *lists* is more specific, more concrete. Action-oriented verbs help determine the kinds of instructions and evaluation procedures that can be used.

The behavioral term most often used inappropriately is *discuss.* When tempted to use this term, ask yourself, "What is it the learner is going to do if he or she participates successfully in a discussion?" The answer leads to the term that should be used—*describes, reports,* or *states.*

Word lists help writers to find particular words to describe behaviors desired of the target population. They also help writers avoid being repetitive and redundant. Words such as *explains, identifies,* and *describes* tend to be overused. Even the examples of objectives from the packaged curricula illustrated in this chapter show this tendency. The word lists shown in figure 4.2 are handy references.

Continuum of Behaviors: Simple to Complex

It is important also to select the behavioral term that will indicate the simplicity or complexity of the desired behavior. Are students

FIGURE 4.2 Typical lists of words to describe desired behaviors

Typical Word Lists of Verbs

Selected list of verbs that can be used for *Cognitive behaviors:*

analyze	decide	identify
apply	deduce	imagine
appraise	design	infer
assess	detect	observe
categorize	develop	perceive
classify	differentiate	predict
compare	employ	project
comprehend	estimate	question
conclude	evaluate	recognize
consider	formulate	synthesize
contrast	hypothesize	translate

Selected list of verbs that can be used for *Affective behaviors:*

accept	feel responsible for	prefer
agree	give priority to	receive
anticipate	intend	reject
appreciate	is aware	respect
believe	is interested in	support
care about	is sensitive	sympathize
desire	is willing	tolerate
empathize	like	value

Selected list of verbs that can be used for *Psychomotor behaviors:*

acknowledge	expend
adhere	express
advocate	initiate
affirm	locate
alter	maintain a practice
articulate	modify
assist	obtain
attempt	participate
attend	practice
cease or discontinue	prepare
communicate	promote
complete	pursue
consume	reduce
contribute	refer
cooperate	refuse
decline	reject
decrease	request
discuss	seek
employ	select
examine	support

expected to *discover* and *explain* information, to *acquire* and *apply* information, or to *synthesize* and *evaluate* acquired information? In health education, we frequently talk about critical thinking and decision-making skills and the freedom to make personal health choices. The behavioral terms (i.e., action-oriented verbs) are the signposts that steer students in the direction of using scientifically based information to solve health problems and to practice health behaviors that promote high-level wellness.

A higher order of thinking, although difficult to define, means that a student with a disciplined mind "can assimilate knowledge, rather than merely recall information by rote or apply simple algorithms. The student can challenge the reliability of evidence; recognize the viewpoint or voice behind the words, pictures, or ideas presented; see relationships between ideas; and ask what-if and suppose-that questions" (Carnegie Council on Adolescent Development, 1989). Therefore, as one moves from the simple to the complex end of the continuum, the potential for critical thinking and decision-making increases. Figure 4.3 displays a progression from simple to complex behaviors.

Rules to Follow

Here are a few simple rules to follow when writing objectives. First, determine what the students should be able to do as a result of the learning experience, and use verbs that describe the desired action. Second, develop a

FIGURE 4.3 Continuum of behaviors: simple to complex

Simple ---→---→---→---→---→---→--- **Complex**

Knowledge (I remember)	**Comprehension** (I understand)	**Application** (I can use it)	**Analysis** (I can separate it into parts)	**Synthesis** (I can combine it)	**Evaluation** (I can weigh alternatives)
Experiment	Explain	Group	Differentiate	Predict	Interpret
Discover	Translate	Collect	Distinguish	Formulate	Critique
Observe	Conclude	Apply	Isolate	Assume	Infer
Demonstrate	Summarize	Order	Relate	Design	Verify
Recognize	Describe	Classify	Associate	Translate	Assess
Explain		Relate	Separate	Hypothesize	Justify

working draft of the objectives; writing the first copy of the objectives in precise terms is too time-consuming. Continue to modify and fine-tune the objectives as the curriculum is developed. Third, let simplicity be the guiding principle; nothing is gained by adding verbiage. Fourth, be cognizant of who will use the curriculum, and choose words that they will recognize. Fifth, write lesson objectives that reflect a logical sequence of events. One objective sets the stage for the next. Sixth, maintain consistency. Curriculum objectives are not as concretely written as lesson objectives. Finally, be realistic! Do not allow the writing of objectives to consume all of the curriculum-planning time. Other tasks need to be done.

Selecting Objectives from Prepared Resources

Among those who develop curricula, there is an important saying: "The wheel doesn't have to be reinvented!" It is not always necessary to write original objectives. Many educational materials include objectives. Teachers' editions of textbooks frequently contain both curriculum and lesson objectives. State curriculum guides and frameworks include curriculum objectives that can serve as guidelines for local districts in writing lesson objectives. Other sources, such as packaged curricula from voluntary health organizations, nonprofit curriculum-designing businesses, and governmental agencies, may include curriculum and/or lesson objectives.

One important item to note in the packaged programs is their frequent use of the term *goals*. Goals in many of these programs should be construed to be curriculum objectives. As described in chapter 1, goals are broad statements of the final outcome of the health education process. Since the *goals* listed in packaged curricula are in reality the outcomes intended for the specified subject matter, it is more logical to label them *curriculum objectives*. Therefore, the listed objectives in such programs are lesson objectives. To illustrate this point and to show lesson objectives in a sequential order, we use *Right Choices*. This American Cancer Society categorical curriculum is a new secondary unit of study designed to reduce the risks of cancer. The two goals in figure 4.4 should be viewed as curriculum objectives.

FIGURE 4.4 Right Choices. (Reprinted with permission from the American Cancer Society, 1990.)

Right Choices

Goal I: To increase students' understanding of cancer.

Objectives: The student will be able to:

1. cite similarities and differences between normal cell and cancer cell behavior;
2. describe types of environmental cancer causes, related means of exposure, and scientific data linking these to cancer;
3. explain how certain life-style behavior patterns influence the risk of developing cancer;
4. describe how social and economic factors impact on cancer incidence, early detection, and treatment;
5. describe self-examination and health-care provider examinations and tests for detecting cancer;
6. describe proven methods for treating cancer and the danger of unproven methods;
7. specify types of health-care resources available for cancer education, diagnosis, treatment, and rehabilitation, and how to access these resources.

Goal II: To increase students' ability to reduce their personal risk of cancer.

Objectives: The student will:

1. be able to use criteria to evaluate the scientific accuracy of information related to cancer risk reduction, early detection, and treatment;
2. be able to develop a plan of action to diminish the risk of having cancer;
3. be willing to express ideas and opinions about the impact of cancer on individuals, the family, and other groups.

If a school district's health education goals were that students should apply principles of disease prevention when possible, avoid health problems, and practice behaviors that promote and maintain physical well-being then Right Choices would most certainly fit within the scope and sequence of the health education curriculum.

When using prepared resources, curriculum planners select lesson objectives to match their curriculum objectives. Several questions must be considered, however, before selecting objectives from outside sources:

1. Is the objective desirable? That is, does it relate to the school district's philosophy?
2. Does the content of the objective fit the scope and sequence? That is, does it relate to the needs and interests of students and society?
3. Is the objective feasible? Are materials available for the learning activities? Does the content address the characteristics of the students? Can the students achieve the objective?
4. Is the teacher competent to teach the subject matter? If not, in-service training should occur.
5. Can members of the planning group as well as the teachers agree on the meaning of the objective? Consensus among interested parties is important.
6. Is the objective too restrictive? Does it limit what a teacher or student can do?

Summary

Objectives are important and necessary components of curriculum design. They define programs by explaining the complexity and diversity of subject matter in health education. They give direction and communicate the essence of a program. Objectives give focus to curriculum and guide instruction. They are the criteria by which teachers and administrators evaluate student achievement and program effectiveness. Lesson objectives differ from curriculum objectives in that they are a subset of the latter. A clue to noting which are curriculum objectives is that further, more specific objectives can be written that lead students to accomplish the intended outcomes. Not only is it important to incorporate all three domains of learning behaviors, but structuring a progression from simple to complex fosters critical thinking and decision-making skills. There are obstacles in selecting and writing objectives, such as how many are needed and the difficulty of assessing the affective domain, but these can be overcome if readers follow the suggestions given in this chapter.

Discussion Questions

1. What functions do curriculum objectives serve?
2. How do curriculum and lesson objectives relate to the goals and philosophy of a health education program?
3. What reasons can you give to support the inclusion of affective objectives in a comprehensive health education program?

Application Activities

1. Given the following curriculum objectives for a unit in environmental health for ninth-grade students, write a minimum of five lesson objectives.
   Curriculum Objectives
   - To familiarize students with the causes of various forms of environmental pollution and their effects on the human body.
   - To enable students to appreciate the complexity of solving environmental pollution problems.
2. The following objectives have been altered so that the behavior and/or the content is poorly worded. Offer your suggestions for improving the statements.

   The student will:
   - Learn the factors that govern health in the United States and in other countries around the world.
   - Demonstrate positive communication.
   - Describe various emotions.
   - Know the effects of aerobic and anaerobic exercise.
3. Obtain a school district's health education curriculum goals. Write curriculum objectives for fourth-grade and eleventh-grade health classes.

References

American Cancer Society. 1990. *Right choices.* New York.

Bedworth, D. A. and Bedworth, A. E. 1978. *Health education—A process for human effectiveness.* New York: Harper & Row.

Bloom, B. S. 1956. *Taxonomy of educational objectives: The classification of educational goals.* Handbook 1. Cognitive domain. New York: McKay.

Bloom, B. S., Madaus, G. F., and Hastings, J. T. 1981. *Evaluation to improve learning.* New York: McGraw-Hill.

Carnegie Council on Adolescent Development. 1989. *Turning points: Preparing American youth for the 21st century.* The report of the task force on education of young adolescents. Washington, DC: Carnegie Council on Adolescent Development. Task Force on Education of Young Adolescents.

Fodor, J. T. and Dalis, G. T. 1989. *Health instruction: Theory and application.* 4th ed. Philadelphia: Lea & Febiger.

Fred Hutchinson Cancer Research Center. 1984. *Project choice.* Seattle, WA: CHEF.

Krathwohl, D. R., Bloom, B. S., and Masia, B. B. 1964. *Taxonomy of educational objectives: The classification of educational goals.* Handbook 2. Affective domain. New York: McKay.

Mager, R. F. 1962. *Preparing objectives for programmed instruction.* San Francisco: Fearon.

National Center for Health Education. 1989. *Growing healthy.* New York.

Pollock, M. 1987. *Planning and implementing health education in schools.* Palo Alto: Mayfield.

Tanner, D. 1972. *Using behavioral objectives in the classroom.* New York: Macmillan.

5

The Curriculum Design:
Choosing an Approach

After reading this chapter and participating in application activities, the student should be able to:

1. Describe four ways to develop curriculum beyond scope and sequence.
2. Recognize the advantages and disadvantages of various curriculum approaches.
3. Examine factors that influence a district's decision on curriculum design.
4. Critique a curriculum.
5. Distinguish among resource unit, teaching unit, and lesson plan.

After the curriculum committee has developed its philosophy, scope and sequence, and curriculum objectives, it must decide which curriculum approach to take. Four approaches are suggested for a curriculum design. In the first approach, the district develops its own curriculum. The second approach uses texts as the curriculum. The third approach utilizes packaged categorical health curricula plus a district-developed curriculum, if necessary. The last approach is the adoption of a packaged comprehensive health curriculum. Actually any combination of the four approaches could be used. For instance, a district could select a text and also include other objectives, which they might locally develop with suggested learning activities and/or other resources and/or other categorical packaged curricula.

Choosing the Approach

The decision about which approach to pursue beyond the curriculum objectives is based on several factors. One is budget: How much money is available for planning, resources, and implementation? Another factor is a district's educational philosophy. Does the district believe in developing its own curriculum? How much specificity in the curriculum does the district want and need? Does it believe in the need for a variety of resources? Another factor is personnel. Which approach would be best for the users of the curriculum? That is, what is the health education background of the users? How much money is there to enhance the background of the teachers who are not knowledgeable in health education? Another factor is availability of resources. Are there good, up-to-date textbooks? Are there good, comprehensive programs available? How much time is there to locate and evaluate resources?

The factor that creates the most disagreement is the degree of specificity needed or desired in the curriculum. District curriculum directors may lean toward curriculum development that ends with curriculum objectives and perhaps a list of resources. The curriculum directors are used to working with subject areas whose content is more established, less apt to change, and less controversial. Even at the elementary level, most teachers have had some coursework in the more traditional subjects at teacher-training institutions. Therefore, health education coordinators who are providing leadership to health education curriculum development generally recommend that curriculum development include suggested lesson objectives with suggested learning activities and that the curriculum show which resources go with which objectives. Thus, to ensure that the kind of health education desired is accomplished, health coordinators know that untrained teachers will need more than scope and sequence and curriculum objectives.

Another consideration that influences specificity is the amount of time elementary teachers have to prepare for the many different lessons they teach each day. They need detail, but they need something that will not take too much time to use. (See chapter 10 for more discussion on the background of teachers.)

Locally Developed Curriculum

After a philosophy is developed, goals are determined, the amount of time allocated to health education decided, a scope and sequence roughly drafted, and curriculum objectives identified, the process for further local development of a curriculum is as follows.

1. Review curriculum objectives. The curriculum objectives written by a small group of master teachers or a segment of the curriculum committee are brought back to the full committee for recommendations and modifications.
2. Organize resources to see if there are some for each health objective. If not, continue the search. (See chapters 6 and 7 for a discussion of searching for resources and evaluating them.)
3. Find several good curricula that have already been developed, to give curriculum writers ideas for their own curriculum.
4. Decide on format. In addition to goals, curriculum objectives, and resources, a format can include any or all of the following components, depending upon the degree of specificity wanted by a district: lesson objectives, suggested learning activities, extensions of the lesson, content, evaluation procedures, correlation possibilities, approximate time lessons will take, resources, and teacher background information.

Figures 5.1 through 5.7 show a variety of formats. Figure 5.1 ties instructional (lesson) objectives to goals and gives the teacher suggested learning experiences with specific resources. The teacher can modify and/or select from teaching strategies they are given. The format in figure 5.1 was taken from a resource module called "Survival in the City." The curriculum included sixteen units developed to supplement a high school health education program. The curriculum was not required, but was used by those teachers who wished to enhance their own instructional program.

Figure 5.2 is a form for curriculum objectives, related to each health topic and suggested resources for the objectives.

Figure 5.3 is similar to 5.1, but does not state the goal. The curriculum objectives seem more like lesson objectives. This is a lesson format from an elementary curriculum (grade 5). Teachers are required to include the objectives in their instructional programs. The learning activities are optional.

Figure 5.4 is a format taken from the "Small School Health Curriculum Project." The format is somewhat unusual in that it was developed at a state level, where curricula generally are not too detailed. States with local district autonomy usually give general guidelines for curricula, with the local level deciding specific objectives, resources, and so forth. However, this curriculum was developed to assist small school districts that have no trained health educators in developing curricula. The idea was for the local districts to select pages from the project to form their own kindergarten curriculum, a first grade curriculum, and so forth.

Figure 5.5 is a lesson from a sexuality curriculum developed for grades 5/6. This narrative format allows for flexibility of space. It eliminates the problem of not having enough space to write what is needed in the columns. It is detailed because it is concerned with an area of health education that teachers may need specific help in teaching.

Figure 5.6 is a lesson from a K–6 nutrition curriculum developed to aid teachers in planning their own nutrition lessons. Figure 5.7 is a dated format, but it is included because it is one of the few that includes almost every detail possible.

5. Organize writing teams of teachers. Decide if the teams will work as a K–1 team or a K–3 team or whatever configuration is useful. The minimum requirement is a master teacher at each grade level. Decide when the teachers will work: Will they do this during the school year and be provided with substitutes, or will they write during the summer and be compensated? A school librarian serving as a consultant to all writing teams is very helpful.
6. Secure a facility that includes large tables, duplicating machines, and places to preview audiovisual material and microcomputer software. A typist is helpful.
7. Bring together teachers, formats, and resources. Ask teachers to use formats so writing is done uniformly. If the teachers have been on the curriculum committee and are the ones who wrote the curriculum objectives, they would be the best to help write the remainder of the curriculum. If they are not, some orientation sessions about philosophy, goals, curriculum objectives, resources, and tasks will be necessary.

   The more specific the curriculum, the more working time is needed. For a K–12 program, six weeks is the minimum time needed to write a curriculum if learning activities are to be included.
8. Allow time for editing, typing of the curriculum, and getting back the first draft to the curriculum writers for their approval. Editing is a time-consuming task because no two people write alike.
9. If possible, ask the writing team to pilot the curriculum and make changes as needed. (See the discussion of piloting curricula in chapter 10.)
10. After final editing and typing, plan a short, upbeat presentation of the curriculum to the administration and school board. School board approval to develop a curriculum is assumed by budget allocation. However, in some districts the board also reviews a curriculum before it is implemented.
11. Implement, including in-service training, and evaluate the curriculum. (See chapters 10, 11, and 12.)

The curriculum guide should include philosophy, goals, curriculum objectives, scope and sequence for all grades, the format as written, policies relating to the teaching of health education, credits to those who have worked on the program, and any necessary information about where resources are and how they can be obtained.

FIGURE 5.1 Lesson from a resource module. (From Lucille Trucano, *Project Health Choices: Survival in the City* (Seattle Public Schools, 1978).)

Mental Health Overview

GOAL

The student knows that mental health is a changing and relative condition.

INSTRUCTIONAL OBJECTIVE(S)

After participating in the following activities, the student:

Describes five characteristics of a mentally healthy person.

Approx. time involved: Two class periods

Class Organization: Full class
Small groups

Learning Experiences	Learning Resources
Note to teacher: If your class is hesitant to participate in class discussions, see learning experiences on communication, pp. 38–39 and 87–90.	
1. Ask students to give their definition of *mental health*. Lead students to consider some of the following points. Write them on the board. a. Ability to live • Within limits imposed by physical abilities. (Are these real or imagined?) • With other human beings. (All humans?) • Happily. (What is happiness?) • Productively. (What is productivity?) • Without being a nuisance. (What is a nuisance?) b. "Ability to live" does not assume a fantastic state of complete happiness or understanding at all times; it allows for sorrow, fear, hate, and tears at times as well as love and happiness. c. Heredity provides raw materials that determine who we are; environment molds the raw material.	
2. Distribute plasticized material MENTAL HEALTH, and ask students to read it. Have students add items to the list on the board. • Ask the class to estimate, without calculating, how many days an average person might expect to live, to the nearest ten thousand days. (*82 years is about 30,000 days.*) (How many thought it was longer? Shorter?) • Discuss whether people live day to day, enjoying themselves the best they can, *or* do they live more deliberately, trying to plan ahead. Discuss the *merits of each*. Do people do both? • Have students number a paper 1–10. Ask them to rank the items on the board in order of importance to them, 1 being the most important in living the "days of their lives." *Do not collect. This is the student's private world.*	Plasticized material • MENTAL HEALTH (30)
3. In groups of three or four students, read pp. 13–20 in booklet EMOTIONAL HEALTH and as a group, complete Handout IT MEANS. Go over this material in class. 4. Read the following quiz to students. Students write answers. *Do not collect the answers; this is the student's private world.* a. How do you feel a great deal of the time? (e.g., happy, relaxed, comfortable, tense, frustrated, angry, depressed, bored) b. What contributes to feeling this way? (e.g., being loved, good communication with family and friends, being alone, a put-down, disappointments) c. What gets you out of this feeling? (e.g., reading, running, friends) d. Name one thing that makes you feel good. Discuss in general terms how people may gain self-understanding from reflecting on the items in the above quiz.	Book • EMOTIONAL HEALTH (10) Handout • IT MEANS, p. 45 (Duplicate one for each group) (Continued)

FIGURE 5.1 *Continued*

Learning Experiences	Learning Resources
* SUPPLEMENTARY LEARNING ACTIVITY • Display posters and discuss. • As an assignment to be done in class or as a homework assignment, have students make posters representing ideas that help lead individuals toward good mental health. (If done as a homework assignment, it would allow students to use other objects for posters, e.g., leaves, yarn, shells, etc.)	Posters • DON'T WALK IN FRONT OF ME, etc. (1) • I LIKE YOU—YOU'RE DIFFERENT (1) • CAUTION—HUMAN BEINGS HERE—HANDLE WITH CARE (1) • FEELINGS ARE NOT LIKE FAUCETS YOU CAN TURN ON AND OFF (1) • IT'S GOOD TO BE PETTED A LITTLE, PRAISED A LITTLE, APPRECIATED A LITTLE (1)
* RELATED FILMS IN SEATTLE'S AUDIO-VISUAL DEPARTMENT *Understanding Stresses and Strains* *How Are You?*	Not in box • Poster-making Materials (construction paper, crayons or marking pens, scissors, glue)

FIGURE 5.2 Curriculum objectives related to health topics in scope and sequence and suggested resources.

Grade: ______		
Health Topic	**Curriculum Objectives**	**Suggested Resources**

FIGURE 5.3 Elementary curriculum with required objectives and suggested activities. (From J. Wan, *Health Education Resource Guide,* Federal Way School District, Federal Way, Wash., 1981–83.)

#4 **CURRICULUM OBJECTIVE:** The student is able to explain the structure and function of the skeletal system by

- Identifying selected bones of the body.
- Stating what a person can do to maintain good posture.
- Relating bone growth to body growth.

SAMPLE LEARNING ACTIVITIES

1. Students read and discuss pp. 116–157.
2. Students complete handout.
3. Students construct skeleton by cutting out tagboard patterns. Secure with brads. Obtain bones to examine formation and composition.
4. Utilize activity booklet p. 15 to develop learning activity.

LEARNING RESOURCES

1. Text: YOU AND YOUR HEALTH
2. Handout: BONES, BONES, BONES
3. Duplicate skeleton pattern on tagboard, brads
4. Activity booklet: YOU AND YOUR HEALTH
5. Related films available from ESD 121:
   I AM JOE'S SPINE
   POSTURE: THINKING TALL

FIGURE 5.4 Format developed at the state level for small school districts. (From T. Peterson, *Small School Health Curriculum Project* (State Superintendent of Schools, OSPI, Olympia, WA. 1978)

Suggested Objective Placement ______

Student Learning Objective(s) The student values the five senses for the information they communicate.

Related Area(s) Art, Reading

State Goal	4.7
District Goal	
Program Goal	1.2

Suggested Activities: Grade(s) 2–3

Extension:

Title: Sense-Art

Group Size: Entire group

Materials: Paper, crayons-drawing materials (optional)

Procedure(s)

- Students draw a picture or describe:
  - One sound they like to hear and one sound they dislike.
  - One food they like to taste and one they do not.
  - One thing they like to see and one thing they do not like to see.
  - One thing they like to smell and one thing they do not like to smell.
  - One thing they like to touch or one thing they do not like to touch.

Extension: Discuss:

- When does a sound become a noise?
- What are ways to control noise? (stress self-control)
- Students share and read pamphlet NOISE, NOISE, NOISE.

Extension: Read book DO YOU SEE WHAT I SEE? and then discuss how lines, shapes and colors make us feel (do the same with DO YOU HEAR WHAT I HEAR?)

Suggested Monitoring Procedures

The student describes one way each sense helps one feel good.

Possible Resources

Books:

--Borton. DO YOU SEE WHAT I SEE? Abelard-Schuman.

--Borton. DO YOU HEAR WHAT I HEAR? Abelard-Schuman.

Pamphlet:

--NOISE, NOISE, NOISE. Scott, Foresman.

District Resources

FIGURE 5.5 Narrative lesson format of a lesson from a sexuality curriculum. (Reprinted with permission from E. Reis, 5/6 F.L.A.S.H. Copyright © Seattle-King County Department of Public Health, 1988.)

Lesson Plan

Touch and Abstinence

STUDENT LEARNING OBJECTIVES:

To be able to . . .

1. Explain that touch is a basic human need.
2. Distinguish healthy, constructive touch from risky to destructive touch.
3. Distinguish among "nurturing," "affectionate," "sexual," "violent," and "exploitive" touch.
4. Define abstinence and list four reasons for choosing it.

TIME NEEDED: One class period without a film, or two class periods with a film.

MATERIALS NEEDED:

1. Photocopies

   One per student of:

   Position Paper: Touch and Abstinence
   Touch Reference Sheet
   Touch Worksheet 1
   Touch Worksheet 2*
   Family Homework Exercise: Touch and Abstinence*

2. AV tool and equipment (See Appendix F)*

• Optional

AGENDA

1. Explain the relevance of today's lesson and how it relates to what you have studied so far.
2. Optional: Use an AV tool.
3. Lead a discussion, using open-ended questions.
4. Have volunteers read aloud the "Touch Reference Sheet."
5. Use Touch Worksheet 1 and discuss it.
6. Have students take turns reading aloud the Position Paper: Touch and Abstinence.
7. Answer students' verbal and anonymous questions.
8. Optional: Assign homework.

. . . (activities for Day One deleted. See Agenda item #1–3)

ACTIVITIES, DAY TWO:

4. Hand out, and have volunteers read aloud the Touch Reference Sheet.
5. Have students, individually or in small groups, fill out Touch Worksheet 1. Allow five minutes. Then have each student mark the ones he/she believes are good reasons for touch with an up arrow↑ and the ones he/she believes are unhealthy or destructive with a down arrow ↓. Allow five more minutes. Collect them. Shuffle them. Read examples aloud. For those "some people consider unhealthy or destructive" ask what else the person, could do *instead* of touching, to meet the need (e.g., "In order to prove they're grown" . . . healthier ways might be to get a job, act mature, learn a new skill).
6. Hand out Position Paper: Touch and Abstinence. Have volunteers take turns reading paragraphs aloud. You should read the quotes aloud, so no student appears to be speaking for him or herself.
7. Answer students' verbal and written questions.
8. Optional: Assign home work. Possible assignments might be . . .

   A Family Homework Exercise. Touch and Abstinence (students will need to take home their copies of the Position Paper, and the Touch Reference Sheet, to complete this Family Homework.)

FIGURE 5.6 Lesson from a K–6 nutrition curriculum. (From T. Destito-Peterson *A Resource for Nutrition Education.* Tacoma Public Schools. Tacoma, Wash., 1986. Used by permission.)

UNIT: NUTRITION

TOPIC: Digestive System (Overview)

OBJECTIVE(S):

1. The student describes the part digestion plays in the utilization of food.

TEACHER INFORMATION: (CURI)

1. Food must be broken down into smaller parts that the body can use for energy, growth, and maintenance of health. This process is called *digestion.* Digestion involves five parts of the body.

   The *mouth* (part one) is used to chew food into smaller particles which the body can use. Enzymes in the saliva start changing starch to sugar.

   The *esophagus* (part two) pushes the chewed food down to the stomach.

   The *stomach* (part three) holds food and churns it into a paste-like mixture (*chyme*).

   The breakdown of food is completed in the *small intestine* (part four) and nutrients from the digested food are absorbed into the blood. These nutrients include vitamins, minerals, water, amino acids from protein, fatty acids from fats, and glucose from carbohydrates. They are then used for tissue growth and repair, energy and regulation of the body system.

   The *large intestine* (part five) reabsorbs water that was used in the digestive process and holds all of the indigestible food (such as the skins of fruits and vegetables) until elimination occurs.
2. See additional teacher information, pages 86–89.

VOCABULARY:

Digestion—The breakdown of food into smaller parts which can then be used by the body to build tissue and give us energy.

SUGGESTED LEARNING ACTIVITIES:

DIGESTION RELAY (BOOMER and NIBBLES SMORGASBORD)

Materials

Set of cut-out body parts and labels
Masking tape, felt pens, crayons, scissors
8½ by 11-inch drawing paper
Worksheet, "How Food Turns Into You"
Butcher paper (long enough to outline human body)

Teacher Preparation

In this lesson two teams compete to identify the digestive process.

Secure butcher paper, felt pens, crayons, masking tape, 8½ by 11-inch drawing paper (one for each student), scissors.

Draw or have students draw outlines of three students' bodies on butcher paper.

Duplicate "Teaching Aids One Through Three," three of each, pages 81–83. Cut out parts on pages 81–82.

Duplicate worksheet, "How Food Turns Into You," one for each student, page 84.

If desired, prepare bulletin board using "Digestive System" drawings, page 85.

Activity

Post one of the body outlines in view of students and teaching aid #3 (page 83).

Describe digestion. Illustrate concept by attaching paper body parts and labels to the outline in sequence. Ask students to assist orally.

Distribute drawing paper. Have students draw and label their own examples of the digestive system.

FIGURE 5.6 *Continued*

Introduce relay game as follows.

Relay Game:

Place the two traced bodies on the wall. Divide the class into equal teams and form two lines. Distribute one set of paper organs and labels to each team. Have students arrange themselves in the proper order. When instructor says "Go," the first student in each line goes to the traced body and places an organ or label on to the body in the correct place. Completed paper body with organs in place should be in view as a reference for students. The student then goes back to the line and tags the next person in line. This continues until all of the organs and labels have been placed on the body. Repeat students if necessary. First team to finish wins. In case of errors the team with fewer errors wins. Organs must be placed correctly to win. Place only one part on outline at one time. *Caution:* Students must walk, not run. Clear obstacles to provide safe passageway.

Distribute worksheet and direct students to complete worksheet.

OPTIONAL ACTIVITY

RELATED BOOKS AND AUDIOVISUALS

Book: *Disney's Wonderful World of Knowledge,* Danbury Press
Book: Elgin, *The Human Body: The Digestive System*
Book: Showers, *What Happens to a Hamburger*
Book: Silverstein, *The Digestive System*
Book: Ward, *Food and Digestion*
Book: Zim, *Your Stomach and Digestive Tract*
Film: "Your Food," Tacoma Film Library, seven minutes
Transparencies: "Functions of Major Body Parts and Organs," set of 14, Tacoma Film Library
Filmstrip: "Digestion and Respiration," from set, *Slim Goodbody: How Your Body Works,* Tacoma Film Library

EVALUATION

Use test at end of Health Science Book, chapter 10.

FIGURE 5.7 Example of a very detailed format. (From C. Nickerson, *Health Instruction Curriculum Guide,* Ellensburg School District, Ellensburg, Wash., 1969–70.)

Safety Education
Grade IV

CONCEPTS:

1. It is important to use safe practices when riding a bicycle.
2. It is important to learn the values and uses of the bicycle for good health.

OBJECTIVES

PRACTICES:

The Student:

Rides his bicycle in a safe manner.

ATTITUDES:

The Student:

1. Appreciates and respects the law.
2. Accepts the responsibility of good safety practices and regulations to observe when cycling.

KNOWLEDGE:

The Student:

1. Identifies the values and uses of the modern bicycle.
2. Compares the responsibility of a bicycle rider with that of a driver of an automobile.
3. Identifies the causes of bicycle accidents.
4. Lists responsibilities of a bicycle rider.

EVALUATION

PRACTICES:

The teacher observes and/or parent reports:

1. Student demonstrates and practices safe riding techniques.
2. Student takes his bicycle through Safety Inspection and licensing program.
3. Student uses good judgment in selecting a route to and from school.

ATTITUDES:

1. The teacher observes that the student shows an appreciation of and respect for the law.
2. Parents report that the student is more concerned with safe practices.
3. The student expresses an awareness of the social aspects of cycling.

KNOWLEDGE:

The teacher observes:

1. Student takes the Aetna Bicycle Quiz or the "Bicycle Quiz" from *Bikes—Boys and Girls*
   Kemper Insurance Co.
   4850 Sheridan Road
   Chicago, Illinois
2. Student takes a teacher-prepared paper & pencil quiz on materials discussed in class.

Continued

FIGURE 5.7 *Continued*

Safety Education
Grade IV

OUTLINE OF CONTENT	TEACHER NOTES
I. What are the values and uses of the modern bicycle? A. Transportation B. Recreation C. Fitness D. Social activity II. Why must bicycles be ridden safely? A. To prevent accidents B. To set an example for others III. What are the causes of bicycle accidents? A. Inattention B. Defective equipment C. Failure to understand how and where to ride safely IV. How do we report an accident? A. Information needed to give the report 1. Where accident occurred 2. How many people are involved 3. What has happened B. Whom to notify 1. Police Department 2. Ambulance if the people appear to be seriously hurt V. What are the responsibilities of being a safe bicycle rider? A. Knows parts of the bicycle B. Cares for and checks all parts of the bicycle C. Practices good judgment when riding D. Has bicycle inspected and registered during Safety Inspection program at school E. Obeys traffic rules F. Understands and appreciates the laws pertaining to bicycles and riders 1. Stays to the right of the road 2. Rides single file 3. Walks bicycle at all intersections 4. Uses a light when riding at night 5. Uses a carrier basket 6. Allows only one person at a time on a bicycle 7. Uses hand signals before making turns 8. Wears light-colored clothing at night G. Knows the shapes and meaning of traffic signs H. Knows hand signals VI. What is the correct behavior when riding? (see section 5-F)	

FIGURE 5.7 *Continued*

Safety Education
Grade IV

<table>
<tr><th>SAMPLE LEARNING EXPERIENCES</th><th>RESOURCES</th></tr>
<tr><td>
I. Discuss the various uses of the modern bicycle and safety practices:
A. Group could present discussion of
1. Transportation—U.S. & Europe
2. Recreation benefits
3. Fitness
4. Social
B. Riding to and from school
C. Analyze bicycle accidents to discover causes and to determine preventive measures.
II. Demonstrations and speakers:
A. Invite person from bicycle repair shop to demonstrate proper care and minor repairs of a bicycle.
B. Invite safety officer from the Washington State Patrol—Yakima Detachment to discuss and demonstrate:
1. Traffic laws and regulations
2. Correct riding techniques
C. Invite local Chief of Police to:
1. Explain local traffic ordinances
2. Explain what will be looked for during registration and inspection
3. Advise the children about revised regulations as they pertain to our local area
4. Conduct mechanical inspection of bicycle while at the class and point out any defects that may be present.
III. Bulletin Boards—Children
A. Original safety slogans
B. Safety posters
IV. Projects
A. Write and produce a bicycle play
B. Collect and distribute safety literature
C. Keep a scrapbook of articles pertaining to bicycles
D. Plan a bicycle trip to Craig Hill as a field trip
E. Originate slogans, stories and poems about safety (bicycle prac.)
</td><td>
Films:
Play It Safe
Bicycle Institute of America
122 East 42nd Street
New York, New York
You and Your Bicycle
Kansas City
Bicycle Safety
Bicycle Safety Skills
I'm No Fool With a Bicycle
One Got Fat
Washington State Patrol
Yakima, Washington
If Bicycles Could Talk
16 mm.—13:30 minutes
Aetna Life and Casualty
Hartford, Conn. 06115
Filmstrips:
(Available at Washington School)
Safety on Two Wheels b/w
Bicycle Safety
Teacher Resources:
Booklets:
Bicycle Safety in Action
National Commission on Safety Education
National Education Association
1201 Sixteenth Street N.W.
Washington, DC 20036
$1.00 #461–13824
Wheels to Safety
Lonnie Gilliland
Director of Safety Education
Oklahoma City Public Schools
Oklahoma City, Oklahoma
Pamphlets:
Hi, Safe Riders
Wash. State Patrol
</td></tr>
</table>

How a guide is put together for a locally developed curriculum varies. Some school districts compile all elementary grades into one binder. Some combine kindergarten through third grade into one binder and fourth through sixth grades in another binder, and some separate each grade level into a separate booklet. The advantage of combining grades is that teachers know what the students have been taught at previous grade levels and therefore see what they can build upon. However, with the mobility of students in today's world, teachers probably will have to determine for themselves where their students are. The disadvantage of combining grade levels is that it is more costly to provide each teacher with a guide. In addition, a huge binder may be formidable to teachers and less likely to be used, especially if good in-service programs and monitoring by the principal have not been required.

If a district chooses to develop its own curriculum, it will have the satisfaction of matching objectives to its students, specific needs. The time spent in development also becomes good in-service training for those working on the curriculum. It also gives the district a core of "experts"—the teachers—to help with the training of teachers who have not worked on the curriculum. A locally developed curriculum allows for a variety of teaching strategies and a variety of resources, which make a program not only good but exciting. The disadvantage of this approach is that the development takes considerable time on the part of a core of teachers who write the curriculum. This is costly. Furthermore, the district may not have qualified people to direct this type of development.

Textbooks as Curriculum

Basing a curriculum on textbooks assumes that the philosophy, goals, time allocation, and scope and sequence are in place, if not finalized, at least in rough form. Some local school districts like to write curriculum objectives before looking at textbooks; others utilize what textbook writers have developed.

1. Contact textbook companies and secure copies of the latest student texts, including teacher resource materials and supplementary student materials, if any.
2. Develop an evaluation instrument to evaluate texts. See figures 5.8 and 5.9 for examples of evaluation forms.
3. Evaluate each text. This can be done by the curriculum committee or a special group of teachers brought together for this purpose.
4. Take the best of the textbooks and match the texts to the scope and sequence.
5. Decide on one to three texts and have teachers pilot the texts for a period of time.

   If there are three texts being considered, one way to proceed is to have one or more teachers try a text and teach three different health topics from the text. Another one or more teachers use the second text and teach the same three topics, and so on. The teachers might also teach from three different texts, teaching different topics each time.

   The curriculum committee should develop some type of criteria for teachers to use in judging the texts.
6. Make the final decision on the text or combination of texts.

7. At the elementary level, resolve differences in the locally developed scope and sequence and the texts' scope and sequence. The same can be said for curriculum objectives if the district writes the objectives before selecting texts.

    - Change the district health topic to the grade level of the text health topic if it can be done, keeping in mind the criteria for selection of content.
    - *Or,* for those topics not covered by the text or not covered at the grade level determined by the district, acquire other resources to meet the district's scope and sequence.
    - *Or* utilize several different grade levels of a text in a particular grade. For example, buy for grade three several texts for the second through sixth grades. The same health topics are generally repeated at more than one grade level; thus, the locally identified topic will be found at some grade level in the different texts. Such an arrangement also helps students who read at grade levels other than the grade they are in.

8. At the secondary level, if the text does not include some topics deemed desirable by the district, other resources can be secured for the topics not covered in the text or texts.
9. Decide whether or not supplementary resources are needed to meet the needs of students who do not respond well to textbooks. Secure these resources if necessary. Although reading is important, it is not always the only or the best way for some students to learn.
10. Develop a teacher's guide to accompany the texts that gives teachers the philosophy, goals, curriculum objectives, and scope and sequence for all grades; policies of the district; and information on any supplementary resources that are available to teachers. Lesson objectives can be included in this guide or reference made to their location in material furnished by the textbook company.
11. Present the program to the administration and school board as suggested in item 10 of "Locally Developed Curriculum."
12. Implement the program, including in-service training and evaluation. (See chapters 10, 11, and 12.)

The approach of adopting a text or texts is not as time-consuming as most of the other developmental approaches; the cost is mostly for textbooks. However, without the right kind of leadership, a district may allow a text to dictate the curriculum. One disadvantage of this approach, however, is that reading textbooks may not be an exciting or productive way to learn for some students. A better instructional program might result from thinking of a text as a resource and building a curriculum around it. Another disadvantage is that textbooks may not cover all topics desired in a curriculum, or they may not cover health topics adequately. Additional resources and teaching strategies will add to the cost of this approach, but the additional effort will ensure more learning.

FIGURE 5.8 Sample evaluation form

BIBLIOGRAPHICAL DATA

Author ____________________

Title of series ____________________

Publisher ____________________

Copyright date ____________________

Supplementary materials available ____________________

____

EVALUATOR (name) ____________________

Scoring: Rate each item from 1 to 5, 5 being the best. Multiply total score for each section by weighting factor.

CRITERIA

A. *Format and construction of book*

1. Book is generally attractive ____
2. Book is durable (cover, binding) ____
3. Illustrations and content reflect contributions of minority groups and maintain sex balance ____
4. Printing is well spaced and easy to read ____

TOTAL ☐ × 1 ____

B. *Reading-level*

1. Vocabulary is appropriate to grade level ____
2. Text is at reading level ____

TOTAL ☐ × 8 ____

C. *Teaching and learning aids*

1. Chapter headings and captions convey what is being learned ____
2. New words are identified (pronunciation and definitions) ____
3. Summaries, pertinent questions, and supplemental learning activities enrich chapters ____
4. Table of contents, glossary of terms, and indices help students ____
5. Teacher's edition is useful ____

TOTAL ☐ × 2 ____

D. *Content (general)*

1. Information is current and accurate ____
2. Students are helped to form own goals and decisions ____
3. Student's thinking is challenged ____

TOTAL ☐ × 3 ____

E. *Content (specific)* How well are the following health areas covered?

	Covered in Grades				
	1	2	3	4	5
1. Mental health: self-concept, decision-making, coping skills, individual differences, emotions, respect for people and property, predicting consequences of behavior, taking risks, etc.					
2. Physical health: dental health, nutrition, cleanliness, posture, fitness, need for rest, etc.					

FIGURE 5.8 *Continued*

	Covered in Grades 1	2	3	4	5
3. Growth and development: parts of body and body systems, factors affecting growth, puberty, etc.					
4. Family life: types and functions of family, responsibilities of family, influence of family, importance of family, etc.					
5. Community and consumer health: responsible use of medicines; health careers; health workers and agencies; air, water, and noise pollution; sanitary measures, etc.					

	Covered in Grades 1	2	3	4	5
6. Safe living and first aid: pedestrian, recreation, school, home, traffic, holiday, and fire safety; prevention of poisoning; first aid, etc.					
7. Disease prevention and health problems: disease transmission, health problems from misuse of drugs, including alcohol and tobacco, handicapping conditions, etc.					

Rate how well this series covers specific health content:

☐ × 15 ______

TOTAL SCORE (add all sections): ______ (maximum 260)

Comments:

FIGURE 5.9 Sample form for evaluating health textbooks, grades 7–12. (Courtesy of L. Trucano.)

COMPLETE BIBLIOGRAPHICAL DATA FOR MATERIALS EVALUATED:

Author ____________________

Title ____________________

Publisher ____________________

Copyright date ____________________

Supplementary materials available ____________________

EVALUATOR (name) ____________________

Rating factor: Use to measure how well a textbook meets a given criterion; range from 0 to 4, 4 being the best.

Multiplication factor: Use to weight a given criterion; range from 1 to 4.

CRITERIA

	Rating Factor	×	Multiplication Factor	=	Score
A. *Format and construction of book*					
1. Readability appropriate for grade level (indicate reading level ______)			4		
2. Durability of binding			1		
3. Appeal of page layouts and book in general			1		
4. Appropriateness of illustrations (modern, ethnic balance, women in nontraditional roles)			2		
5. Adequacy of table of contents and indices (detailed, cross-referenced, well organized)			1		
B. *Content (general)*					
1. Current information			4		
2. Accuracy of information			4		
3. Interesting material to capture and hold students' attention			2		
4. Comprehensive enough for the needs of your students			4		
5. Provides for critical thinking (helps students form own goals, values, and decisions)			3		
C. *Teaching and learning aids*					
1. Sufficient study helps and supplementary activities to enrich chapters			2		
2. Useful teacher's edition (teaching suggestions, philosophy, goals of the program included, bibliographies of resource materials, and ideas for meeting the individual needs of able and slow learners)			4		
3. Chapter review and supplemental references meet needs of your students			1		
4. Provision for new words (pronunciation and definitions)			1		

FIGURE 5.9 *Continued*

	Rating Factor	×	Multi-plication Factor	=	Score
D. *Coverage of health areas* (How comprehensive is the coverage?) 1. Anatomy and physiology			2		
2. Community health (e.g., noise, chemical, water-pollution control; community resources, e.g., V.D. clinics)			3		
3. Consumer health (e.g., evaluating health products, use of medicines, components of health examinations, health-care delivery systems)			3		
4. Disease prevention (e.g., life-style and disease, emotional illness, V.D., cancer, cardiovascular, immunizations, diseases of interest to ethnic groups)			4		
5. Adult life-style (e.g., changing roles; decisions about sexual life-style, marriage, and family)			4		
6. Fitness (e.g., benefits of fitness, fitness regimen, grooming and self-concept, fatigue, balanced diets, obesity, ethnic foods)			2		
7. Growth and development (e.g., reproduction process, prenatal, tools of inheritance, birth defects, genetic counseling, effects of drugs and nutrition on developing embryo and fetus)			3		
8. Mental health (e.g., coping skills, stress, human needs and emotions, self-concept, mental illness, psychological growth and development, stereotyping)			4		
9. Safety and first aid			3		
10. Smoking, drugs, and alcohol (psychoactive drugs, medical use, prescription and over-the-counter drugs)			4		

Packaged Categorical Health Curricula

If a district wishes to use packaged programs as it's health curriculum (see also chapters 6 and 7), the same procedure is followed as for the others. The philosophy, goals, curriculum objectives, and scope and sequence are first developed. While this is being accomplished, someone would be searching for packaged categorical health curricula. These curricula develop one health topic or health area, for example, cancer, nutrition, or drugs. Each package includes lesson objectives, learning activities, and (most of the time) the learning resources needed for the learning activities. The package may or may not include goals and curriculum objectives. (See chapter 6 for ways to search for resources.)

The developmental process for this approach is as follows.

1. Review curriculum objectives.
2. Screen the available packaged curricula. Do they reflect the philosophical focus of the district? Does the content match fairly closely to scope and sequence of the district? Overall, are the instructional strategies and resources of good quality?

3. Evaluate those packages that come through the screening process. The criteria discussed in chapter 7 under "Evaluation Process" could be used to evaluate packaged programs.
4. Match selected packages to scope and sequence. For health topics that are in the locally developed scope and sequence but not included in one or more of the packages, the district would need to do one or more of the following:
   - Continue looking for categorical curricula that relate to their scope and sequence.
   - Develop the topic locally. Development would entail finding resources for the topic and determining the specificity wanted in the curriculum format (as discussed for the locally developed curriculum).
   - Change the topics in the locally developed scope and sequence. If the packaged program is good, and the locally developed scope and sequence can be changed without jeopardizing the basis on which health topics should be selected, then change is acceptable. There are more health topics related to young people's needs and interests than there is time to teach them.
5. Lesson objectives are generally a part of the categorical curricula. Carefully review these objectives for acceptance and modification, keeping in mind philosophy, scope and sequence, and curriculum objectives.
6. Develop a guide that conveys to teachers the philosophy, goals, time allocation, curriculum objectives, scope and sequence, and how to use the categorical health packages. Somehow the lesson objectives from the packages must relate to the curriculum objectives and the curriculum objectives, in turn, to the goals. Include policies relating to the teaching of health education and give credit to those who contributed to putting the program together. The guide should include some kind of chart that tells teachers which topics are developed by which categorical packages and which topics are locally developed, if any. Figure 5.10 gives an example of matching the scope of a third-grade curriculum to three categorical health education packaged curricula and shows that some of the topics are locally developed.
7. Prepare a presentation for the administration and school board to explain the curriculum.
8. Implement the curriculum, including in-service training and evaluation. (See chapters 10, 11, and 12.)

The use of categorical packaged curricula shortens development time because only part of the curriculum needs to be locally written. The more categorical curricula selected, the less time required for local development. There are many small categorical curricula, so they must be carefully woven into the scope and sequence. Many of these smaller curricula are free or inexpensive because they are developed by voluntary and nonprofit health groups; many are very well done. Categorical packaged curricula offer a variety of resources and a variety of learning activities because each package is different. The time-consuming part of this approach is tying the lesson objectives to the curriculum objectives and filling the no gaps in the curriculum.

FIGURE 5.10 Example of matching scope of third grade curriculum to three categorical health education packaged curricula.

Strand and Health Topics	Curriculum for the Health Topics
Mental Health Self-esteem Helping others Feelings Social skills	*Here's Looking At You, 2000*
Safety Play activity hazards Emergency rules Rescue breathing Selected first-aid procedures Prevention of injuries Fire prevention and escape	*Basic Aid Training* (B.A.T.)
Safe fun activities	*Here's Looking at You, 2000*
Disease & Disability Bone & muscle injuries Effects of smoking Immunity Overweight	Locally developed
Health Promotion Behavior & health Effects of sleep and rest Posture and muscles and bones	Locally developed
Body Systems Overview of body systems, parts, and functions Relationship of cells, tissues, organs, and systems Types of cells	Locally developed
Nutrition Relationship of health, energy, growing, and feeling good Food groups Foods in each food group and what they do for the body Planning nutritious meals	*Food Keeps Me Healthy*
Drug Education Recognition of drugs Effects of drugs Reasons for use Chemical dependency Use and abuse	*Here's Looking At You, 2000*

Packaged Comprehensive Health Curriculum

As with the other approaches, the philosophy, goals, time allocation, curriculum objectives, and scope and sequence would be developed while someone is searching for comprehensive packaged programs. The authors believe that curriculum objectives should be written at this time, but some curriculum developers feel that this is better done after a packaged curriculum is adopted. The process for this approach is as follows.

1. Develop criteria to evaluate comprehensive curricula. The criteria in chapter 7 under "Evaluation Process" could be used. The criteria would address whether or not the packaged curriculum is in harmony with the philosophy and how well it matches the locally developed scope and sequence and curriculum objectives. The criteria would ask if modifications of the locally developed scope and sequence are possible (as is suggested under the

packaged categorical approach). Other questions to be answered are (1) Is the curriculum age-appropriate and of interest to the intended audience? (2) Does it have sufficient content to meet objectives? (3) Is the content current and accurate? (4) Is the curriculum multiethnic, without racial, cultural, ethnic, age, disability, and sex bias? (5) Are the resources varied and of quality? (6) Is it "teacher-friendly?" (7) Is it cost effective? (8) Do the teaching strategies have instructional merit?

2. If a comprehensive curriculum cannot be found for both elementary and secondary levels, another approach will have to be chosen to develop the scope and sequence not covered by the packaged curriculum.
3. Review lesson objectives in the packaged curriculum. In light of the philosophy, scope and sequence, and curriculum objectives. Accept, reject, or modify the objectives.
4. If the curriculum is accepted and modified as needed, decide how the package will be delivered to the classroom. Chapter 10 discusses delivery systems.
5. Develop a presentation for the school board.
6. Assemble a curriculum guide that includes philosophy, goals, time allocation, and scope and sequence for all grade levels; policies related to teaching health education; and a chart to show where teachers can find the resources for their grade level. Providing a teaching guide with the comprehensive package for each teacher would be ideal, but may be too costly. In packaged curricula, the teaching guide is generally located in the container tub with all the resources.
7. Implement the curriculum, including in-service training and evaluation. (See chapters 10, 11, and 12.)

The adoption of a comprehensive packaged curriculum is probably the easiest to accomplish because a district need not do too much more beyond the scope and sequence development and in-service training. However, the problem is that not many comprehensive curricula have been developed, and most of those developed do not meet all the criteria suggested. Any comprehensive curriculum will be expensive if it includes resources; however, a district may save money in the long run because developing one's own curriculum is also expensive in terms of time and teacher compensation. As a beginning, we suggest considering the following three comprehensive programs.

Growing Healthy (National Center for Health Education, 1984) is a comprehensive program for grades K–7 with lesson objectives and learning activities for each objective. It focuses on the structure and function of various body systems, mental health, personal health, nutrition, disease prevention, family life, safety education, consumer health, drug education, and community health. It uses a variety of materials such as videos, posters, transparencies, books, puzzles, games, worksheets, and so forth. The teacher's guide and all materials needed to help students achieve objectives come with the package; no further resources are necessary. Teacher training is available. The learning activities are structured for large classroom groups and small learning-center groups; they involve "hands on" activities and meet the need for a variety of learning strategies.

Student participating in the Growing Healthy Curriculum learn about the skeletal system. (Reprinted with permission from the American Lung Association.)

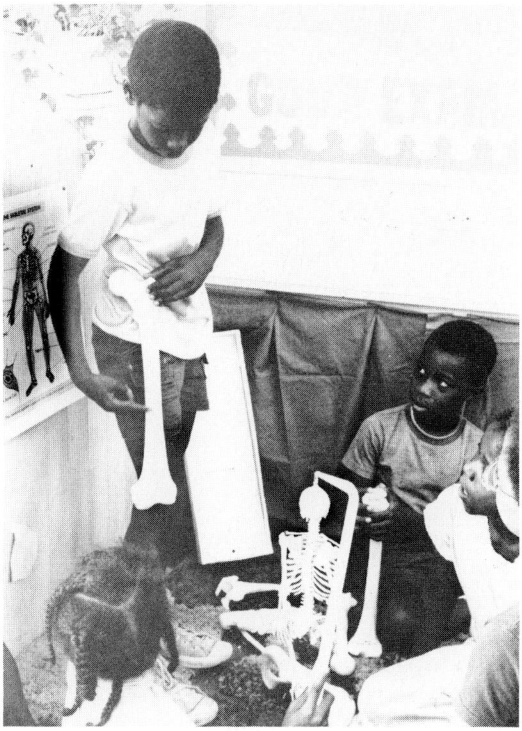

The Great Bodyshop (Children's Health Market, Inc., 1989) is a comprehensive curriculum for grades K–6. Each month of the school year, the teacher receives packets containing student issues of *The Great Bodyshop,* which are like monthly readers. The teacher receives a guide for that month's topic, complete with lesson plans, activities, and unit tests. A parents' bulletin is provided monthly. Each year the lessons are updated. School districts need to supplement this program with other resources, since this is much like selecting a text.

TABLE 5.1 BLUEPRINT FOR TEACHER PLANNING

Approach	Planning Needed
Locally developed curriculum ending with curriculum objectives	Teachers plan their own units and lessons.
Locally developed curriculum ending with suggested lesson plans	Teachers develop units if lessons are not in units and modify lessons, if desired.
Textbook as curriculum	Teachers plan units and lessons around textbooks.
Packaged categorical health curriculum	Teachers review units and lessons, modify them if allowed to, and add lessons if time permits.
Packaged comprehensive health curriculum	Teachers review units and lessons, modify them if allowed to, and add lessons if time permits.

Health Skills For Life (Terhune, 1987) is a comprehensive program but is not truly a packaged curriculum, since it includes no resources. It is a K–12 curriculum. In-service training is available. This curriculum contains seven to twelve teaching units per grade for grades K–8 and thirty-five units at the high school level. Each unit includes information to introduce the unit, required activities, health content, handouts, knowledge and skill tests, and suggestions for resources.

Curriculum Delivery—The Teacher's Role

The finished curriculum is the blueprint from which teachers do their planning. How much planning they will need to do depends upon the approach chosen. (See table 5.1.)

Teacher planning involves units and lessons. Teachers may wish to teach without tying a lesson into a unit. It is possible to teach without unit planning, but the lessons generally follow a logical and sequential pattern and fit nicely into units. If a unit is conceived of as a lesson or series of interrelated lessons, then all teacher planning is probably by unit.

The teaching unit is a way of organizing instruction around a health topic or topics. A unit organizes learning into a logical, sequential pattern and is developed for a specific class. It includes whatever will actually be used in the teaching-learning experience. Units vary in the amount of time they take to complete; they may last one day or extend to six or more weeks.

Exceptions to including in a teaching unit only what will be used may occur if a teacher decides to let students participate in the planning. The teacher would then suggest a variety of learning experiences and resources and allow students to make some decisions about how they want to move toward the lesson objectives. Another exception would involve having an alternative plan available in case the plan selected does not work.

As with curriculum formats, teaching units vary in the amount of detail they involve. In addition to the name of the unit, topics to be covered, and resources, a unit would include lesson objectives, learning experiences, and evaluation. Beyond these elements, a unit can include or not include any or all of the following: content, overview of the unit, activities to initiate the unit, optional activities, and culminating activities. Homework assignments would be considered part of the learning experiences.

There are also resource units, which differ from teaching units in that they consist of *suggested* teaching objectives, strategies, and resources organized around a health topic or topics. Other components suggested for teaching units can also be included in resource units. They are sometimes planned by a team of teachers or a group of grade-level teachers. Each teacher then makes teaching units from the resource units.

Thus, from a planned curriculum come resource units and/or teaching units. From a resource unit come teaching units, and from teaching units come lesson plans. The partial unit shown in figure 5.11 would necessitate little lesson planning.

Lesson plans are the step-by-step procedures the teacher will follow to assist students in meeting the lesson objective(s). Lessons can last 15 minutes or continue over several days. Lessons include lesson objectives (what is to be learned), generally an introductory activity (to develop interest and/or to explain what will be expected of the students), the actual learning experience (what the students will be doing to achieve the objective), resources needed, and (if a lesson is evaluated by itself rather than as part of a unit), what evaluation will be used.

The lesson is a plan the teacher will follow to facilitate the process of learning. How detailed a plan becomes depends upon the teacher. For instance, the first time a video is used, a teacher may wish to write down the questions that she will use for class discussion following the showing of the video. Another detail of a lesson plan teachers like is a section called *teacher preparation,* which reminds them of various things that they may need to do before the class begins (e.g., make a poster, order a video, schedule the library for classwork, arrange learning centers, or secure a VCR and monitor). The plan may also include the amount of time the teacher thinks the lesson will take and the content students will study. Beginning teachers will have more detail in their lesson plans than experienced teachers. Whether used by new or experienced teachers, the lesson plan tells the teacher what to do, when, and how. (Figures 5.1, 5.5–5.7 can be seen as examples of lesson plans.)

The fun of teaching is in the planning and carrying out of the lesson. After determining what the objective is (see chapter 4 for objective selection), that is, what one wants the students to learn, the teacher must determine what teaching strategy to use. The choice depends on many factors:

- Characteristics of learners. Is the strategy appropriate for the abilities and aptitude of the students?
- Is the teacher comfortable with the strategy? Is the teacher knowledgeable about it? For example, some teachers are not comfortable with role playing or may not be familiar with refusal skills.
- Will the strategy accomplish the objective?
- Is it time-effective? With all that needs to be learned, some strategies may take more time than they are worth.
- Is the teaching strategy adaptable to the facility? For instance, learning centers are excellent, especially for the elementary level. However, if a teacher has to put them up and take them down each day, the time involved may not be worth it.
- Are resources available for the strategy? Sometimes teachers ask students to discuss something, but the students have not had a learning experience (because of lack of resources) to gain information that would allow them to carry on a reasonable discussion.
- Does the teaching strategy involve the students as actively as possible?

Finally, even if lessons are ready-made, as they may be with packaged categorical health curricula or a packaged comprehensive health curriculum, each teacher must prepare to teach beyond lesson planning. The teacher must go over the lesson plan before meeting with the class to see that it is logical, sequential, and complete. He must get the classroom ready (e.g., chairs in a circle, VCR ready, learning centers ready) and should review content to be sure it is relevant to the objective, accurate, and up-to-date. The teacher must be sure that all resources needed for the lesson are on hand. If the lesson has been taught before, notes must be reviewed and changes made, as noted. The teacher needs to review what is known about the students, noting any special needs that must be kept in mind.

Teaching is like coaching; it blends emotion with objectivity. The teacher must be enthusiastic enough to give extra time to planning and to students who need it. Teaching is a creative experience—teachers must be ready to try new ideas, to risk a new approach. They must know students just as a coach must know each player. They must know the teaching game—content, teaching objectives, teaching strategies—just as the coach knows the game and develops strategies.

FIGURE 5.11 Sample teaching unit. (From Lucille Trucano, *Project Health Choices: Space Age Health*, Seattle Public Schools, 1978.)

GOAL

The student knows that modern technology influences well-being (health).

FOCUS: Introduction

INSTRUCTIONAL OBJECTIVE(S)

After participating in the following activities, the student:

Paraphrases some of the implications of future developments reviewed in class.

Approx. time involved: One and one-half class periods

Class Organization: Full class

Learning Experiences	Learning Resources
1. Introduce module by discussing the material from page 2 of the INSTRUCTOR'S RESOURCE BOOK FOR REDESIGNING MAN—SCIENCE AND HUMAN VALUES and by selecting from the plasticized materials.	Teacher reference • INSTRUCTOR'S RESOURCE BOOK FOR REDESIGNING MAN—SCIENCE AND HUMAN VALUES in the back of this notebook. Plasticized materials • BIOMEDICAL ENGINEERING FASCINATING PROFESSION (*News Article*) • SKIN GRAFT REQUIRES SKIN GIFT (*News Article*) • BIOENGINEERING IS ANOTHER BRAIN CHILD (*News Article*) • RECYCLING OF HUMAN PARTS NEAR, SAYS DOCTOR (*News Article*)
2. View film FUTURE SHOCK. (For interested students, there is a book FUTURE SHOCK by Alvin Toffler.) Discussion suggestions: • Are we victims of our own technology strength? (e.g., too much change in too short a time; too many choices?) • Is change difficult? • If, in fact, man's relationship to things is increasingly temporary, what will this do to human relationships? (e.g., children learn that nothing is permanent.) • Is freedom "a loss of a sense of belonging," as stated in the film? • Will there be "future shock" if we can "dispose" of people and parts of people as well as products? (The film says there is a potential of building modular bodies as well as modular homes.) • What do they think about manipulating skin color, intelligence, fertilization, cryonics? <u>Note to teacher:</u> *Your students may have already seen the film. They may want to look at it again in light of what is no longer "future," but "now."*	Film • FUTURE SHOCK (42 min.) (Discussion Guide is in the back of this notebook.) Not in box • 16mm film projector. (Continued)

FIGURE 5.11 *Continued*

GOAL

The student knows that modern technology influences well-being (health).

FOCUS: Transplants and Implants

INSTRUCTIONAL OBJECTIVE(S)

After participating in the following activities, the student:

1. Identifies and discusses one future development on the CHART OF THE FUTURE.
2. Discusses how the economics of life-support technology forces society to make value-testing decisions.
3. Gives three purposes of transplants and implants.
4. Explains the problem of body rejection of transplants.
5. Identifies problems with the preservation of tissue and organs.
6. Discusses two legal aspects associated with transplants.
7. Explains the Uniform Donation Act.
8. Discusses psychological and social considerations of transplantation.

Approx. time involved: Two and one-half class periods

Class organization: Full class / Small groups

Learning Experiences	Learning Resources
1. Distribute CHART OF THE FUTURE (one to each two students). a. Point out on the CHART OF THE FUTURE events related to the four areas of modern technology that the class will consider in the next few days. • Transplants and Implants: Column I—#1, 7, 15 Column II—#18 • World of the Unborn: Column I—#4, 5, 9 Column II—#17, 19 • Exploring Man's Mind: Column I—#3, 8, 10, 11, 14 Column II—#21, 22, 23, 24, 25, 29, 30 • Search for Immortality: Column II—#16, 20, 23, 26, 27 b. If there is time, discuss each item to be sure students understand it. Focus on those items that might happen by year 2,000 A.D. Note to teacher: *The polygons on the chart indicate the general range of opinions generated by the participating experts. The high point of each polygon indicates the median time of occurrence forecast by those who rated themselves "experts" or "generally familiar with" the event in question. Each development listed in the chart is keyed to the specific filmstrip in* REDESIGNING MAN *which deals with that development. Notations for doing this are FS 1 (Filmstrip 1), FS 2, etc.* *Note that almost all the developments in the chart are projected to take place during the lifetimes of today's students. (From page 4,* INSTRUCTOR'S RESOURCE BOOK FOR REDESIGNING MAN—SCIENCE AND HUMAN VALUES.*)*	Plasticized materials • CHART OF THE FUTURE (15) (See copy on p. 18)
2. Introduce the first area of modern technology to be studied with the following: a. Many lives are saved or extended in length because modern medicine is able to find replacement parts for parts which are worn out, defective, or diseased. Ask students to think about whether they would be willing to accept a *human* or *animal* transplant into their body. Would they be willing to accept a *mechanical* transplant? Why or why not? What alternatives would they prefer? b. Philip Blaiberg, the first man to receive a heart transplant, was an expensive patient. His first 115 days in the hospital cost approximately $35,000 (with all	Teacher reference • THE NEW MAN (*Reprint*) (Continued)

FIGURE 5.11 *Continued*

Learning Experiences	Learning Resources
surgical fees free). Michael Kasperak, who lived only 15 days, ran up a bill for approximately $30,000. Ask students if they believe these large expenditures should be spent to extend one person's life. Do they believe that an individual person should be responsible for paying all medical costs for transplant surgeries? Why or why not? c. People can donate specific body parts to be used for transplant or research without complicated legal procedures. A person may donate one specific body part (an eye or kidney for example) or donate one's body (cadaver) to medical school research. Ask students if they foresee any problems in securing body parts if transplant surgery becomes more common. If so, what kinds of problems? Would they be willing to be a living donor of a paired organ to a member of their family? Would they be willing to donate part of their body (an eye or kidney for example) for postmortem use? Why or why not? d. Go over vocabulary to help students understand the filmstrip. (You may wish to duplicate this list and give to students.)	Teacher reference • TRANSPLANTS AND IMPLANTS, (*Vocabulary List*) p. 19
3. Show filmstrip TRANSPLANTS AND IMPLANTS.	Filmstrip • TRANSPLANTS AND IMPLANTS (*16½ Min.*). (See filmstrip Summary and Script in INSTRUCTOR RESOURCE BOOK in back of this notebook.) Not in box • Filmstrip projector • Cassette player.
<u>*Note to teacher:*</u> *To supplement resources for the following learning activity, you may wish to schedule a day in the library so students can read current articles on transplantation and implantation. The* Reader's Guide *and encyclopedias should be utilized.* 4. Divide the class into eight groups. Assign or allow students to select an area on which to work. Give each group a STATION CARD and materials color-coded to color of STATION CARD. • Station: Psychological and Social Considerations • Station: Kidney Transplant • Station: More Applicants than Donors • Station: Rebuilt People • Station: It's the Law • Station: At Any Cost? $$$ • Station: Heart Transplant • Station: Typed, Registered, and Tattooed 5. Students give reports developed in the eight groups. (Keep reports to five minutes to avoid boredom.) 6. Homework assignment: Each student writes a one-page paper on whether or not he/she would give a healthy organ (eye, kidney, lung) to a stranger if that stranger needed it to live. She/he will: • Describe under what conditions the organ would be given. • Describe or state any legal problems associated with the donation. Describe in what specific ways, if any, one's life-style would change if such an organ were donated.	*Teacher reference* • *See copies of the STATION CARDS. Learning resources are listed on these cards, pp. 20–27.*

Summary

The decision about what a curriculum will look like in its final form is an important yet controversial one. Some teachers feel strongly that curriculum building stops with philosophy, policies, scope and sequence, and curriculum objectives. Others feel just as strongly that because many teachers responsible for teaching health lack an adequate health background, the curriculum design must give them all the help it can, including lesson objectives and learning activities. The curriculum committee must make this decision early in its deliberations. Various factors influence this decision. This chapter describes four approaches to curricular design: the district-developed curriculum, the textbook as curriculum, the packaged categorical health curriculum, and the packaged comprehensive health curriculum. Each approach has advantages and disadvantages.

Discussion Questions

1. Discuss the pros and cons of a format that includes many components.
2. Why might it be more difficult to get teachers to use a curriculum that is in a big binder? How might a district help them to use it?
3. Discuss ways to help unprepared teachers with health, other than putting content into a format.

Application Activities

1. Critique a locally developed curriculum, a textbook program, a packaged categorical health curriculum, and a packaged comprehensive curriculum. Critique selected grade levels only.
    - Are the curriculum objectives tied to the goals? Do the goals reflect the philosophy?
    - Is it clear which lesson objectives tie to curriculum objectives? to resources?
    - Is the treatment of each health topic in the scope and sequence treated adequately for learning to take place?
    - Are there health topics left out that you feel are important for the grade levels you are critiquing?
    - Do you think it is worth the cost?
    - Is the format easy to use?
    - How much in-service training would the curriculum require?
    - Are resources good? varied?
    - What would improve the curriculum?
2. Develop an evaluation instrument that might be used to help decide which curriculum to use. Review the factors that influence choice of approach before developing your instrument.

References

American Red Cross. 1987. *Basic aid training.* Washington, DC: Office of Publications.

Children's Health Market, Inc. 1989. *The great bodyshop.* Wilton, CT.

Destito-Peterson, T. 1986. *A resource for nutrition education.* Tacoma, WA: Tacoma Public Schools.

National Center for Health Education. 1984. *Growing healthy.* New York.

National Dairy Council. 1987. *Food keeps me healthy.* Rosemont, IL.

Nickerson, C. 1969–70. *Health instruction curriculum guide.* Ellensburg, WA: Ellensburg School District. (Out of print)

Peterson, T. 1978. *Small school health curriculum project.* Olympia, WA: Office of Superintendent of Public Instruction.

Reis, E. 1988. *F.L.A.S.H.: Family planning program.* Seattle, WA: Seattle-King County Department of Health.

Terhune, J. 1987. *Health skills for life.* Eugene, OR.

Trucano, L. 1978. *Project health choices.* Seattle, WA: Seattle School District. (Out of print)

Wan, J. 1981–83. *Health education resource guide.* Federal Way, WA: Federal Way School District.

6

Locating Resources:
Resources! Resources! Resources!

After reading this chapter and participating in application activities, the student should be able to:

1. Distinguish between a source and a resource.
2. Identify reputable sources of resources.
3. Identify a process for finding resources.

Two chapters about resources have been included in this book because resources are so necessary for developing and maintaining successful programs. A variety of carefully selected resources maximizes the quality of instruction by making learning experiences more effective and exciting. Furthermore, varied resources facilitate the many ways in which students learn.

Just what is a resource? It is anything that can be used to enhance learning. A resource may be a pulsating lung machine from the American Cancer Society, a video on infectious disease transmission, a local dentist who visits a class during dental health week, a health textbook selected by a school district, a health appraisal instrument, a field trip to a hospital, a poster on emotional well-being, a pamphlet on birth defects, or a puppet for role-playing social skills. This chapter reviews the many sources of resources and suggests ways to organize materials to increase their utilization and facilitate their management.

The Search

The search for resources is a challenging process. At the outset is the concern that there are few resources; at the completion of the search, inevitably the dilemma becomes how to select from the many resources located.

The search has two phases. The first occurs during curriculum development or revision, when someone is responsible for conducting an organized search for resources. This person locates and reviews resources, and brings the best of them to the committee that will evaluate them. The second phase occurs during the interim between curriculum revisions. At this time teachers, supervisors, principals, and others will be looking for resources to add to and update the curriculum.

The materials to be located in the search include pamphlets and booklets, audiovisuals (video, 16mm), textbooks, descriptions of field trips, posters, puppets, animated models, magazines, televised programs, computer software, books (fiction, nonfiction, and reference), drama, art, music, museum exhibits, and games.

The First Steps—What Already Exists/Identifying Reputable Sources

The first step in searching for resources is to consider what others have already found. Does the school district have a resource center? If so, start the search there. Is the school district a member of a cooperative or regional service center? If so, utilize their resource library and their information on resources located in nearby school districts.

From this point on, the person doing the search should be looking for reputable suppliers (sources) of quality resources. There are so many sources of materials that the searching should focus on the best—those that have a reputation for quality. Health educators in state offices of education, in public health departments, at universities, and at regional education centers can help in identifying reputable sources. Professional health educators in teaching or administrative positions in school districts also can provide information about reliable sources.

A reputable source should be around long enough to ensure that materials will be available over a period of years. Established companies sometimes have lifetime replacement policies when new editions occur or if a resource is lost or broken. This is especially important with film. Established companies ensure that the selected resources are available when implementation of the program begins. As good resources are found, the person searching starts a list of materials that the district will order for screening and evaluation.

The Next Step—Review of Materials from Community and Governmental Agencies

The next step is to review materials from reputable community and governmental agencies (local, state, and/or national). Voluntary and private nonprofit health organizations have excellent resources at little or no cost. The most expedient means of obtaining materials is to request catalogs as well as audiovisual lists from which to select resources. A visit to a chapter or state affiliate office can be highly productive. Often free-loan film libraries are included in the services provided by these agencies.

A Sampling of National Voluntary and Nonprofit Health Organizations

For addresses of selected sources and resources, please see the categorized reference lists at the end of the chapter. There are many organizations and agencies that provide resources. Some of these organizations and the categories within which they fall are:

Voluntary and non-profit organizations
American Diabetes Association
American Kidney Foundation
March of Dimes Birth Defects Foundation

Federal health information centers and clearing houses
Center for Health Promotion and Education
National Clearinghouse for Alcohol and Drug Abuse Information
National Heart, Lung and Blood Institute

Professional organizations
Association for the Advancement of Health Education
American Public Health Association
American School Health Association

A popular source that catalogs materials available from voluntary agencies is the *Coalition Index: A Wealth of Information in File Format,* which identifies and categorizes twenty-six school health topics. Each content-area folder contains a materials list by grade level, a description of the materials, the submitting organization, and the availability of the materials. Additional materials such as brochures and flyers can be placed inside the folder for easy retrieval, and each folder includes a place for comments and local contact addresses and phone numbers.

An excellent government source is the Office of Disease Prevention and Health Promotion's National Health Information Center. The Center is a referral system that helps people locate health information and resources. Its services are summarized in figure 6.1

As noted in figure 6.1, *Healthfinder* is a series of resource lists. There may be a small handling fee for each resource list requested. Specific titles of some of the publications within the *Healthfinder* series are the following:

***Healthfinder* Series**
(from National Health Information Center, 1–800–336–4797)

Adolescent Health Information
Community Health Promotion Programs
Elementary School Health Education Materials
Exercise for Older Americans
Financing Personal Health Care
Health Promotion Software
Health Risk Appraisals
Health Statistics
Herpes Information Resources
Home Health Care
Home Medical Library
Locating Audiovisual Materials
Minority Health
National Health Observances
On-Line Health Resources Information
Posters for Health Promotion
Selected Federal Health Information Clearinghouses
Stress Information Resources
Toll-Free Health Information Phone Numbers
Vitamins
Weight Control

FIGURE 6.1 Services of the Office of Disease Prevention and Health Promotions National Health Information Center

National Health Information Center

Center Components

Library
The library supports the Center's information and referral services and database development. Medical and health reference books, directories, and books on health promotion comprise the core of the collection. Files on some 800 health topics and a periodicals collection also provide current information. The library is open to the public by appointment.

Publications
The Center produces directories, resource guides, and bibliographies on various health topics and disseminates many other ODPHP publications. Center publications include:

- *Healthfinders.* A series of resource lists on current health concerns. Topics include health observances, toll-free numbers for health information, vitamins, health statistics, health risk appraisals, adolescent health, school health education, minority health, exercise for older Americans, family health, online health information, women's health, and health care financing.
- *Health Information Resources in the Federal Government.* A directory of Federal health agencies, information centers, and clearinghouses, with descriptions and contact information.
- *Locating Funds for Health Promotion Projects.* A guide to assist persons seeking health promotion funding. It includes how to seek and apply for funds, major government and private sources of funding, and resource organizations, publications, and databases.
- *Staying Healthy: A Bibliography of Health Promotion Materials.* An annotated list of pamphlets, manuals, posters, and audiovisuals produced by the U.S. Department of Health and Human Services.

For more information on available publications, write or call for a publications list.

Database
The Center maintains an online directory of more than 1,000 health-related organizations that can provide health information. They include Federal and State agencies, voluntary associations, self-help and support groups, trade associations, and professional societies. The database is accessible to the public through DIRLINE, part of the National Library of Medicine's MEDLARS system.

NICODARD
A special component, the National Information Center for Orphan Drugs and Rare Diseases (NICODARD) responds to inquiries on rare diseases (those with a prevalence in the United States of 200,000 or fewer cases) and orphan drugs (medicines not widely researched or available). The NICODARD, also a service of the ODPHP, is sponsored by the Food and Drug Administration.

FIGURE 6.2 Services of the Office of Minority Health Resource Center

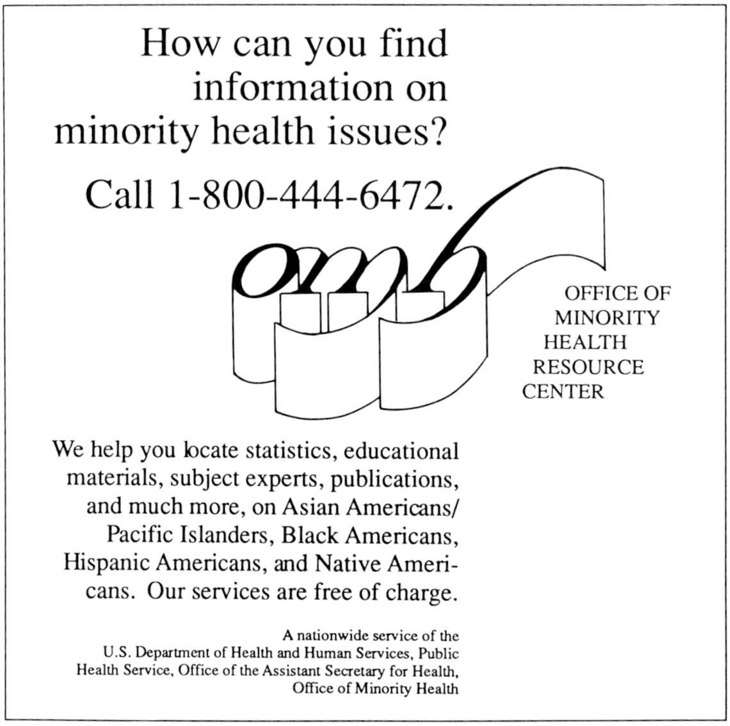

As an example, one of the Healthfinder series titled "School Health Materials, Grades K–6" (December, 1987) lists where to find health education materials primarily for grades K–6, although some items are appropriate for higher grades. It includes source information on materials for duplication, models, films, videotapes, posters, audio cassettes, coloring books, and computer software. It also includes a description of the resource, age, grade-level appropriateness, price, and source address. Neither the resource nor the source is evaluated. The series titled "Selected Federal Health Information Clearinghouses" lists information centers operated by the Federal Government.

Another valuable federal resource is the Office of Minority Health. Figure 6.2 explains its services.

The Search Continues—Other Reputable Sources

The next step is to review resource evaluations found in publications of national health education associations. Start with the *Journal of Health Education, Journal of School Health,* and *Health Education Quarterly.* Also consider other publications from organizations such as the American Academy of Family Physicians, American Academy of Pediatrics, American Dental Association, American

Nurses' Association, American Dietetic's Association and American Public Health Association.

Traditional, but good, are the textbook companies which cooperatively publish a list of all textbook companies, with their addresses and representatives. Securing this list saves time in contacting the various companies. Many textbook representatives are well versed in supplementary resources to their textbooks. For example, a suggestion from one publisher's representative is an older but very good resource, *Blood and Guts: A Working Guide to Your Own Insides.* Most teacher editions of textbooks, or materials that accompany textbooks, include listings of supplementary resources.

The next source is the television schedule, especially the one for public broadcasting stations. School districts have opportunities to pay annual membership fees to gain access to programming for grades K–12. Schools receive a monthly newsletter alerting the district to programs and events at the PBS station. Teacher workshops are offered by some PBS stations, including college credit arranged through local universities. Schools can gain access to such outstanding programs as "The Inside Story with Slim Goodbody" and "Like You, Like Me," which can be aired to district classrooms. These programs can be written into a curriculum. For example, the award-winning program "All About You" was adopted by a school district as a component of the district's first-grade health curriculum. Through membership, teachers acquire recording rights for these programs. Representatives from member districts are invited to participate in decisions about instructional programming at their local PBS stations.

Perusing audiovisual catalogs at school media centers or school purchasing departments is another way to find film, videos, and software. As quality software becomes available, the tremendous potential of computers in the health education program to deliver instruction should be utilized. Notice that the Healthfinder series includes *Health Promotion Software.* Each entry includes a brief description of the program, compatible hardware, price, review information when provided, and audience. Also included in this packet of information is a guide to evaluating software programs, software review sources, and vendors' mailing addresses. An article in *Health Education* by Paul D. Sarvela and others entitled "Applications Software Packages in the School Health Program" gives curriculum planners thoughtful suggestions on the use of software in health education.

Sources that many people overlook are the librarians in schools and public libraries, who are especially helpful if the search is for a particular kind of book. Available in all public libraries at the reference desk are various catalogs that aid in the search for materials. The following catalogs have lists of materials; all listings are annotated and indexed by author, title, and subject.

The Elementary School Library Collection: A Guide to Books and Other Media. This catalog lists books, periodicals, filmstrips, kits, video cassettes, and microcomputer programs for preschool through sixth grade. Books are both nonfiction and fiction. The catalog editors indicate that the titles reflect our multiethnic, pluralistic society.

Best Books for Children. This includes books pre-school through grade 6.

Children's Catalog, Junior High School Library Catalog, and Senior High School Library Catalog. These include fiction and nonfiction books.

The Bookfinder: *A Guide to Children's Literature about the Needs and Problems of Youth Ages 2 and Up.*

Sources not to be overlooked are curricula already developed and packaged. A school district may wish to buy a packaged curriculum that is comprehensive and modify it where needed, or it may wish to buy several categorical packaged curricula and select from each what is needed for its own scope and sequence. Chapter 5 discusses using packaged curricula in designing programs, and chapter 7 describes how packaged materials might be used.

Packaged categorical programs such as the following are well developed. Their adoption may save districts time and money when districts consider the cost of buying teacher time or paying for substitutes for teachers who are working on curricula.

Here's Looking at You, 2000 This is a K–12 drug education program which could fulfill many objectives in mental health, safety education, and drug education. It is a multimedia approach that actively involves students in learning. Each grade-level program includes objectives, vocabulary, learning activities, all resources needed, evaluation tools, and background information for teachers.

Talking about Touching This is an early childhood through fifth-grade program on personal safety. It is designed to teach young people assertiveness, decision-making skills, and effective use of community resources to reduce the risk of abuse. The three R's taught are recognize, resist, and report. The program uses a teacher's guide, story book, video, audio tape, and flannel-board characters.

Personal Safety and Decision Making For middle school, the program *Personal Safety and Decision Making* is available. It includes a teacher's guide for group discussion, story scenarios, role-play materials, and reproducible worksheets.

Second Step This is a skill-training curriculum to prevent youth violence. For grades 1–5, the curricula include lessons, background information for teachers, homework assignments, video, and laminated photos. For grades 6–8, the curriculum includes group discussion, role-play materials, and story scenarios. Also available are training videos for adults to help them respond to the problem of child sexual abuse.

Curriculum On Blood Four learning modules cover this K–12 curriculum. Each unit includes lesson plans with objectives, evaluation procedures, background information for teachers, and all multimedia materials to implement each unit. It covers information on cells, the circulatory system, blood therapy, some information on heredity, and the donation process. This material is one of the best on cells and immunity.

Supplementary Resources

Supplementary materials are generally not written into a curriculum but are acquired by teachers to enhance their programs or to fill in where there are gaps in resources. Their selection and use may or may not be a part of the formal instructional resource policy developed by a school district. If it is not, it is because there are so many resources that it is difficult to determine how to evaluate all of them. Generally, there is a statement in a policy to cover supplementary resources. For example, the policy might state that materials from voluntary health agencies may be used as supplementary materials. Other policies may include guidelines for evaluating and using supplementary materials.

Any resource can be considered for supplementary use. Those described in the following paragraphs are often found as supplements to a curriculum.

Selected commercial television programs, movies, and live theaters may be the basis for extra-credit assignments and may provide thought-provoking ideas on health topics, which can be shared through class discussions.

The private business sector has made contributions to supplementary resources. Insurance companies such as the Metropolitan Life Insurance Company, food companies such as General Mills, and pharmaceutical companies such as Pfizer, Inc. produce pamphlets, posters, and other materials that are useful in the health curriculum.

Federal, state, and local governments offer materials on health issues that can be included in a curriculum or considered as supplementary resources. On the state level, call the Department of Health or its equivalent for a list of resources. At the federal level, the *Consumer Information Catalog* identifies numerous written pamphlets, many free or at a low cost. (See figure 6.3.)

FIGURE 6.3 Consumer Information Center, a government resource.

Individual governmental agencies such as the Consumer Product Safety Commission, the Food and Drug Administration, United States Department of Agriculture, and United States Postal Service offer resources. The National Institutes of Health (e.g., National Cancer Institute and National Heart, Blood, and Lung Institute) provide important needs-assessment data as well as health education materials. The Institutes have clearinghouses that serve as information centers and provide free or inexpensive materials. City libraries may be a repository for federal materials; librarians should be able to provide addresses. The following are examples of materials available from the Office of Substance Abuse Prevention of the Alcohol, Drug Abuse, and Mental Health Administration: "Live the Dream, Say No to Alcohol and Drug Abuse" (Poster, 1989); "How to Say No" (Poster, 1989); "Saying No Isn't Tough When You Think Like McGruff" (Poster, 1989); "The Use of Steroids in Sports Can Be Dangerous" (1989); "Drug Abuse and Pregnancy" (1989).

An excellent supplementary resource is the student magazine *Current Health*. This magazine is published monthly at a relatively low cost.

Finally, for some objectives, a curriculum-planning group may actually locate no appropriate resource. In this case the teacher or students may wish to create their own. The authors have seen students develop unique resources while learning about health. Creative students have produced such products as computer software, posters, videotape programs, audio tapes, slide/sound programs, and classroom models. The teacher should also consider the possibility of creating a professional product with a sound development plan, a realistic budget, and future marketability.

Curriculum committees may wish to recommend newsletters and periodicals, district or regional resource centers, or individual school libraries for use. These help teachers keep up-to-date on health information; they provide current ideas in the health education profession, and alert teachers to resources. Some suggested newsletters are

Chemical People Newsletter
Community Intervention
Food and Nutrition News
Mayo Clinic Health Letter
School Intervention Report
Suicide Prevention
Harvard Medical School Health Letter
Nutrition Forum
NCAHF Newsletter
Health Letter
Tufts University Diet and Nutrition Letter
and *Wellness Letter*

Suggested periodicals are

Educational Leadership
Journal of Health Education
Hippocrates: Health and Medicine
Health Values
SIECUS Report
World Health
FDA Consumer
Journal of School Health
and *Family Life Educator*

Teachers, in reviewing their own magazines, may find some that offer low-cost reprints of articles. *Scientific American, Reader's Digest,* and *Consumer Reports* are three periodicals that make reprints available. Some publishers also have reprint lists.

From Chaos to Organization

As important as it is to locate resources, the development of an identification or cataloging system and a check-out system have equally high priority. Resources should be clearly and systematically cataloged. One system is by grade level and health topic; another system is by grade level and objectives. Some resources are organized through labeling and/or color coding to identify them for grade level, topic, and/or objectives. A computer system is excellent for recording and tracking resource items. This is especially important if materials are loaned out from a central depository; the cataloging and tracking system resembles a lending library. With a limited budget, misplacing or losing a film, anatomical model, or other resource can be costly.

An example of an information and tracking system is found in the office of the Health Education Director of the Puget Sound Educational Service District Center. The staff visits each school district in the region and puts the information on a "District Visitation" outline. This information is then cataloged by health programs or health education components (e.g., suicide, drug education). When a person from another district calls about a policy, a curriculum being used in another district, a program to visit, a resource, or a consultant, the regional service district is able to refer them to a source.

Like the reserve section of a library, this service center provides a professional preview library. The material in this library is not for check-out, but for individuals or curriculum committees to come in and preview. It is a mixture of current textbooks on the market, current local or national comprehensive and categorical health education curricula, books, pamphlets, videos, free and inexpensive materials, and teacher-made materials. The resources are placed in numbered tubs, with the materials in each tub having the same number, so that putting materials back where they belong is easier. This information is on data base.

This regional center also has a health resource library, from which film and materials are loaned to individual schools. This, too, is computerized.

Finally, as a way of keeping up with information, the Health Education Director utilizes professional periodicals in a unique way. Periodicals and newsletters are perused, and useful articles are labeled by health topics. The labeling is placed on the table of contents; the secretary then files the table of contents (duplicated as many times as necessary) under the labels indicated by the Health Education Director. When the director needs information for a talk or for helping to design programs or in-service training, the table of contents on file indicates which periodicals and newsletters need to be reviewed.

Another method of organizing and tracking is one used by nonprofit agencies: a centralized film-distribution service. To assist with maintenance of films and videos and to facilitate the loan process, a film-distribution service is a convenience for the lender as well as the borrower. The borrower gets information from one source about a large number of audiovisuals and the lender has a qualified person handling films loaned.

Summary

The search for resources starts with a picture of what the philosophy, goals, and objectives of the curriculum might be. As the search progresses, a list is made of promising items that will be brought into the district for a preliminary screening. Those items meeting screening criteria as outlined in chapter 7 are retained for full evaluation. The usual steps in the search process are the following:

1. Search the district's resource center, the resources of the regional educational service center, if there is one, and nearby school districts.
2. Review materials from local, state, and/or national voluntary and nonprofit health organizations and governmental agencies.
3. Locate the past year's periodicals from national professional health and educational organizations and peruse resources they have reviewed.
4. Write and ask for current editions of textbooks.
5. Review the *Healthfinder* series and federal health information clearinghouse publication lists.
6. Review film/video catalogs and utilize local libraries.
7. Review the health programs of public broadcasting stations.
8. Examine curricula already developed and packaged.
9. Finally, when all resources are selected, ordered, and in the district, organize them for easy access and for tracking.

Discussion Questions

1. Distinguish between a source and a resource.
2. What is the value of computerizing a school district's health education materials?
3. Discuss the advisability of letting students contact sources, that is, write to request materials. Suggest guidelines that teachers might provide if they do allow students to gather materials or information from sources.

Application Activities

1. Visit a school district to review its system of tracking resources. Critique the system, giving what might be the advantages and disadvantages.

2. List health-related resources reviewed in four different professional journals. Give your opinion as to which journal was the most helpful and explain why it was helpful.
3. From the possibilities suggested in this chapter, design a search process for yourself.
4. Visit a public library and summarize what is included in one or more of the following: *The Elementary School Library Collection, Children's Catalog, Junior High School Library Catalog, The Bookfinder, Senior High School Library Catalog,* and *Best Books for Children.*

References (Categorized Lists)

Voluntary and Non-profit Organizations

Alcoholics Anonymous
World Services, Inc.
P.O. Box 459
Grand Central Station
New York, NY 10163

American Anorexia/Bulimia Association
133 Cedar Lane
Teaneck, NJ 07666

American Cancer Society, Inc.
1599 Clifton Road, N.E.
Atlanta, GA 30329

American Diabetes Assoc., Inc.
1660 Duke Street
Alexandria, VA 22313

American Foundation for the Blind, Inc.
15 West 16th Street
New York, NY 10011

American Geriatrics Society, Inc.
10 Columbus Circle
New York, NY 10019

American Health Foundation
320 East 43rd Street
New York, NY 10017

American Heart Association
The National Center
7230 Greenville Avenue
Dallas, TX 75231

American Kidney Foundation
Two Park Avenue
New York, NY 10016

American Lung Association
1740 Broadway
New York, NY 10019

The American Lupus Society
23751 Madison Street
Torrance, CA 90505

American National Red Cross
Office of Publications
17th and E Streets, NW
Washington, DC 20006

Arthritis Foundation
3400 Peachtree Road, NE
Atlanta, GA 30326

Cystic Fibrosis Foundation
6000 Executive Boulevard
Rockville, MD 20852

Epilepsy Foundation of America
4351 Garden City Drive
Landover, MD 20785

Foundation for Child Development
345 East 46th Street
New York, NY 10017

Juvenile Diabetes Foundation
23 East 26th Street
New York, NY 10010

Leukemia Society of America, Inc.
733 Third Avenue
New York, NY 10017

March of Dimes Birth Defects Foundation
1275 Mamaroneck Avenue
White Plains, NY 10605

Maternity Center Association
48 East 92nd Street
New York, NY 10028

Muscular Dystrophy Association
810 Seventh Avenue
New York, NY 10019

National Association for Sickle-Cell Disease, Inc.
4221 Wilshire Blvd., Suite 360
Los Angeles, CA 90010–3503

National Child Safety Council
4065 Page Avenue
Jackson, MI 49204

National Council Against Health Fraud
P.O. Box 1276
Loma Linda, CA 92354

National Council on the Aging
600 Maryland Avenue, SW
West Wing 100
Washington, DC 20024

National Council on Alcoholism
733 Third Avenue
New York, NY 10017

National Dairy Council
6300 North River Road
Rosemont, IL 60018–4233

National Easter Seal Society
2023 West Ogden Avenue
Chicago, IL 60612

National Mental Health Association
1021 Prince Street
Arlington, VA 22314

National Safety Council
Director of Public Information
444 North Michigan Avenue
Chicago, IL 60611

National Society to Prevent Blindness
79 Madison Avenue
New York, NY 10016

Planned Parenthood Federation
of America, Inc.
810 Seventh Avenue
New York, NY 10019

Sex Information and Education Council of the
United States
130 West 42nd Street, Suite 2500
New York, NY 10036

Selected Federal Health Information Centers and Clearinghouses

Center for Health Promotion and Education
Centers for Disease Control
Building 1 South, Room SSB249
1600 Clifton Road, NE
Atlanta, GA 30333

Clearinghouse on Child Abuse and Neglect
P.O. Box 1182
Washington, DC 20013

Clearinghouse on Health Indexes
National Center for Health Statistics
Office of Analysis and Epidemiology Programs
3700 East-West Highway
Room 2–27
Hyattsville, MD 20782

Consumer Information Center
Pueblo, CO 81009

Consumer Product Safety Commission
Washington, DC 20207

Environmental Protection Agency
Public Information Center
820 Quincy Street, NW
Washington, DC 20011

Food and Drug Administration
Office of Consumer Affairs
5600 Fishers Lane, HSE-88
Rockville, MD 20857

Food and Nutrition Information Center
National Agricultural Library
Room 304
Beltsville, MD 20705

National Arthritis and Musculoskeletal and Skin
Diseases Information Clearinghouse
P.O. Box 9782
Arlington, VA 22209

National Center for the Prevention and Control of
Rape
Parklawn Bldg, Room 6C-12
5600 Fishers Lane
Rockville, MD 20857

National Cholesterol Education Program
NCEP Information Center
National Heart, Lung, and Blood Institute
Bethesda, MD 20892

National Clearinghouse on Aging
330 Independence Avenue, SW
Washington, DC 20201

National Clearinghouse for Alcohol and Drug Abuse Information
P.O. Box 416
Kensington, MD 20795

National Clearinghouse for Alcohol Information
P.O. Box 2345
Rockville, MD 20852

National Clearinghouse for Family Planning Information
P.O. Box 12921
Arlington, VA 22209

National Diabetes Information Clearinghouse
Box NDIC
Bethesda, MD 20892

National Digestive Diseases Information Clearinghouse
1255 23rd St. NW, Suite 275
Washington, DC 20037

National Health Information Center
ODPHP
P.O. Box 1133
Washington, DC 20013–1133

National Heart, Lung, and Blood Institute
120/80 National Institutes of Health
Bethesda, MD 20892

National Information Center for Handicapped Children and Youth
P.O. Box 1492
Washington, DC 20013

National Injury Information Clearinghouse
5401 Westbard Avenue
Room 625
Washington, DC 20207

National Institute on Mental Health
Public Inquiries Branch
Parklawn Building
Room 15C-05
5600 Fishers Lane
Rockville, MD 20857

National Maternal and Child Health Clearinghouse
38th and R Streets, NW
Washington, DC 20057

National Rehabilitation Information Center
4407 8th Street, NE
Washington, DC 20017

Office of Cancer Communications
National Cancer Institute
Cancer Information Service
Building 31, Room 10A-18
9000 Rockville Pike
Bethesda, MD 20892

Office of Minority Health Resource Center
U.S. Dept. of HHS, Public Health Service
Office of Minority Health
P.O. Box 37337
Washington, DC 20013

Office on Smoking and Health
Technical Information Center
Park Building, Room 1–10
5600 Fishers Lane
Rockville, MD 20857

Sudden Infant Death Syndrome Clearinghouse
8201 Greensboro Drive
Suite 600
McLean, VA 22102

Professional Organizations

American Academy of Family Physicians
1740 West 92nd Street
Kansas City, MO 64114

American Academy of Pediatrics, Inc.
1801 Hinman Avenue
P.O. Box 1034
Evanston, IL 60204

American Alliance for Health, Physical Education, Recreation, and Dance
1900 Association Drive
Reston, VA 22091

American Association for Rehabilitation Therapy, Inc.
P.O. Box 93
North Little Rock, AR 72116

American College Health Association
7910 Woodmont Avenue
Suite 300
Bethesda, MD 20814

American Dental Association
Bureau of Dental Health Education
211 East Chicago Avenue
Chicago, IL 60611

American Medical Association
Department of Health Education
535 North Dearborn Street
Chicago, IL 60610

American Nurses' Association, Inc.
2420 Pershing Road
Kansas City, MO 63141

American Optometric Association
243 N. Lindbergh Blvd.
St. Louis, MO 63141

American Osteopathic Association
212 East Ohio Street
Chicago, IL 60611

American Pediatric Society, Inc.
c/o Audrey Brown, M.D.
Dept. of Pediatrics, Box 49
SUNY Downstate Medical Center
450 Clarkson Avenue
Brooklyn, NY 11207

American Public Health Association
1015 Fifteenth St., NW
Washington, DC 20005

American School Health Association
1521 South Water Street
P.O. Box 708
Kent, OH 44240

Association for the Advancement of Health Education
1900 Association Drive
Reston, VA 22091

Association for Supervision and Curriculum Development
125 North West Street
Alexandria, VA 22314

Society for Public Health Education, Inc.
703 Market Street, Suite 535
San Francisco, CA 94103

Health-Related Literature

Chemical People Newsletter, The
WQED
4802 Fifth Avenue
Pittsburgh, PA 15213
(412) 622–1491

Community Intervention
529 South 7th Street
Suite 570
Minneapolis, MN 55415

Current Health
General Learning Corporation
60 Revere Road
Northbrook, IL 60062

Family Life Educator
ETR Associates/Network Publication
P.O. Box 1830
Santa Cruz, CA 95061–1830

Food and Nutrition News
National Livestock and Meat Board
444 North Michigan Avenue
Chicago, IL 60611

FDA Consumer
(Ten issues/year)
U.S. Food and Drug Administration
5600 Fishers Lane
Rockville, MD 20857

Harvard Medical School Health Letter
P.O. Box 10943
Des Moines, IA 50340

Health Education Quarterly
Society for Public Health Education
703 Market Street, Suite 535
San Francisco, CA 94103

Health Letter, The
North America Syndicate, Inc.
P.O. Box 19622
Irvine, CA 92713

Health Values
PNG Publications
P.O. Box 4593
Dept. D
Star City, WV 26504–4593

Hippocrates: Health and Medicine
P.O. Box 52431
Boulder, CO 80321–2431

Journal of Drug Education
Baywood Publishing Co., Inc.
26 Austin Avenue
P.O. Box 337
Amityville, NY 11701

Journal of Health Education
Association for the Advancement of Health Education
1900 Association Drive
Reston, VA 22091

Journal of Nutrition Education
Society of Nutrition Education
1700 Broadway, Suite 300
Oakland, CA 94612

Journal of School Health
American School Health Association
1521 South Water Street
P.O. Box 708
Kent, OH 44240

Nutrition Forum
210 West Washington Square
Philadelphia, PA 19106

Mayo Clinic Health Letter
Mayo Clinic
Rochester, MN 55905
(507) 284–4577

NCAHF Newsletter
National Council Against Health Fraud, Inc.
P.O. Box 1276
Loma Linda, CA 92354
(714) 824–4690

School Intervention Report
P.O. Box 1326
Holmes Beach, FL 34218
(800) 222–1525 (toll free)

Siecus Report
Sex Information and Education Council of the United States
130 West 42nd Street, Suite 2500
New York, NY 10003

Suicide Prevention
Lifeline Institute
9108 Lakewood Drive South
Tacoma, WA 98499
(206) 584–3733

Tufts University Diet and Nutrition Letter
Subscription Department
P.O. Box 57843
Boulder, CO 80321–7843

Wellness Letter
University of California—Berkeley
P.O. Box 10922
Des Moines, IA 50340

World Health Monthly
World Health Organization
Avenue Appia
1211 Geneva 27, Switzerland

Selected Health Curricula

Curriculum On Blood
Health Sciences
Center for Educational Resources
T-281 HSB SB-56
University of Washington
Seattle, WA 98195

Esteem Builders
B. L. Winch and Associates
Jalmar Press
45 Hitching Post Dr., Bldg. 2
Rolling Hills Estates, CA 90274–4297

Food . . . Your Choice
National Dairy Council
Nutrition Education Division
6300 North River Road
Rosemont, IL 60019–9922

Growing Healthy
National Center for Health Education
30 East 29th Street
New York, NY 10016

Helping Kids Handle Anger: Teaching Self-Control
The ASSIST Program
Sopris West, Inc.
1140 Boston Ave.
Longmont, CO 80501

Here's Looking at AIDS and You
CHEF
22323 Pacific Highway South
Seattle, WA 98198

Here's Looking at You, 2000
CHEF
22323 Pacific Highway South
Seattle, WA 98198

Personal Safety and Decision Making
Committee for Children
172 20th Avenue
Seattle, WA 98122

Second Step
Committee for Children
172 20th Avenue
Seattle, WA 98122

Talking about Touching
Committee for Children
172 20th Avenue
Seattle, WA 98122

Selected Health-Related Sources

Coalition Index
American School Health Association
P.O. Box 708
Kent, OH 44240

Consumer Information Catalog
Consumer Information Center
Department R.W.
Pueblo, CO 81009

Consumer Reports
256 Washington Street
Mt. Vernon, NY 10553

General Mills, Inc.
P.O. Box 5588
Stacy, MN 55079

Healthfinder
ONHIC
P.O. Box 1133
Washington, DC 20012–1133

Metropolitan Life Insurance Health and Safety Division
1 Madison Avenue
New York, NY 10010

Pfizer, Inc.
235 East Hand St.
New York, NY 10017

Puget Sound Educational Service District
Corine Olson, Health Education Director
12320 80th Avenue South
Seattle, WA 98178–4413

Reprint Editor
Reader's Digest
Box 406
Pleasantville, NY 10570

Sarvela, Paul D., Dale O. Ritzel, Marilyn J. Karaffa, and Mousa K. Naseri
"Applications Software Packages in the School Health Program"
Health Education, April/May 1989, pp. 43–49

Scientific American
P.O. Box 3187
Harlan, IA 51593

Wisconsin Clearinghouse for Alcohol and Other Drug Information
1954 E. Washington Ave.
Madison, WI 53704–5217
(608) 263–2797

7

Selecting Resources: *Choosing Wisely*

After reading this chapter and participating in application activities, the student should be able to:

1. Distinguish between screening and evaluating resources.
2. Identify criteria for evaluating health education resources.
3. Evaluate resources using identified criteria.
4. Suggest how a screening process and an evaluation process might work.
5. Critique evaluation forms.
6. Explain the process of selecting categorical curricula.

Selectively procuring, evaluating, and placing into a curriculum high-quality resources is a task intrinsically related to the success of a program. The bulk of this process is done when a curriculum is developed, but built into successful programs is some method for updating and adding to the resources.

In a successful curriculum, teachers know that resources are available for accomplishing curriculum objectives and that they can choose from various resources depending on the needs of their students. They also know how to effectively procure and utilize resources.

Using Resources Effectively

Keeping the objectives in mind, the teacher develops or chooses the best teaching strategies to help students. Part of determining what is best depends upon the nature of the students, the kinds of resources available, and the instructional time available. However, a good resource may often suggest a creative teaching activity.

Resources are intrinsically tied to learning activities. A lecture takes less time but may not imprint the learning. A teaching strategy using a thought-provoking film followed by a lively discussion may provide a better learning experience than a 50-minute film that does all the thinking for the students. An interactive exercise or simulation may be the most effective strategy for the greatest number of learners. But the interaction must be based on knowledge, which might be the result of using a high-quality resource.

Relying solely on textbooks as a resource in schools is a disadvantage to all concerned. Some health topics may be missed or poorly presented; the reading levels of the textbooks may not reach or stimulate all the reading abilities found in a classroom. A better way to use textbooks is to have available, for example, second- through sixth-grade texts for a third-grade classroom (e.g., five second-grade texts, fifteen third-grade texts, five fourth-grade texts, five fifth-grade books, and five sixth-grade books). Most texts repeat some of the same topics and information at several grade levels. The teacher then assigns reading in various texts depending on students' reading levels. This strategy, plus other resources, can result in interesting discussions of topics by the total class.

To summarize, what resource to choose for classroom use is determined by

- Teaching strategies
- The instructional objective
- The intended audience (age, background, needs, interests, cultural orientation, ethnic heritage)
- The time available
- The instructional value of the resource

It has been said we remember

- 10 percent of what we read
- 20 percent of what we hear
- 30 percent of what we see
- 50 percent of what we see and hear
- 90 percent of what we are involved in doing

The Process for Resource Selection

It is a challenge to find resources in which content is accurate, up-to-date, appropriate, and complete enough to warrant buying them. A process must be designed to aid in screening and then evaluating the resources after the screening procedures. Issues to be addressed in developing the process are who is to develop resources, the criteria to be used for screening, the criteria for evaluation, who is to evaluate the evaluation forms, the policies or laws that influence selection, and how to monitor resources brought in for screening and evaluation.

The Screening Process

The person responsible for procuring resources for eventual evaluation needs to be knowledgeable about the best *sources* of health resources. By perusing these sources, this person can carefully and selectively choose resources for each objective and order them with a minimum expenditure of time. See chapter 6 for a discussion of good sources of materials.

One of the difficulties of selecting resources for screening is that perusing sources and ordering selected items must be done several months before the curriculum objectives are finalized. This is because it takes so much time to order resources, screen them, and then evaluate those selected. Whoever is in charge of acquiring instructional resources for screening should be knowledgeable enough to anticipate the kinds of objectives commonly found in a health curriculum.

After materials are ordered, they are usually screened using two criteria. The first criterion is whether or not the resource relates to likely objectives. As mentioned, the person doing the screening must not only have a good idea of where to get good materials, but also have excellent knowledge of how the final curriculum might look. The second criterion is the overall quality of the resource. Overall quality pertains to accurate and current information, appropriateness for students, and attractiveness. Materials that are screened and found to be acceptable are then ready for the evaluation process.

The Evaluation Process

The individual who initially procures resources for evaluation quickly screens them on arrival and selects the best for evaluation. The group writing the curriculum may do the evaluation; however, a special group of people may be selected to evaluate resources. This group might consist of a health coordinator, representative parents, representative community members (e.g., church leaders, medical/dental personnel), and representative teachers.

Another organizational strategy for evaluating resources is to send them to the users: the teachers, counselors, and nurses. Evaluation forms need to be carefully filled out by the users and deadlines set for return of resources. Care must be taken not to overload the users.

Criteria for evaluating resources include some or all of the following:

1. Does the resource address a stated objective or goal?
2. Is the content current, accurate, and complete?
3. Does the resource meet the philosophical point of view?
4. Does the resource have instructional merit?
5. Would the resource be interesting to the intended audience?
6. Is the resource age-appropriate?

7. Is the resource free from cultural, ethnic, racial, age, disability, sexual-orientation, and sex bias?
8. Is the cost realistic?
9. Would there be difficulties in using the resource?

For efficient evaluation, it is best to use the first four criteria listed above. If a resource fails to meet any one of these four, time should not be spent on the other criteria.

1. *Does the resource address a stated objective or goal?* If materials are selected without objectives or goals in mind, the developed curriculum may end up with areas that lack resources. Another possibility is that the resources selected may dictate the curriculum, rather than fit into a curriculum developed around identified health needs and health interests.

   Some resources may meet objectives and be age-related but not deliver the desired message. For example, a major part of a drug education film shows a party where young people are using drugs and having a great time. The end of the film shows the same young people involved in an automobile accident on their way home. The party takes up so much of the film and looks like so much fun that the impact of the accident might be lost on the viewers.
2. *Is the content current and accurate?* One problem in determining accuracy is that some health information continually changes. At one time we thought that cocaine was nonaddictive and caused few deaths; now we know that it is highly addictive and that it does cause cardiac failure. Another problem in determining accuracy is the lack of consensus on selected information. For instance, there is no agreement on how often to have physical examinations, whether lumpectomies are sometimes better than radical mastectomies, when and how often to have mammograms, and whether oat bran lowers cholesterol levels.

   Another difficulty in evaluating resources for accuracy is that the resource may be well done overall and yet contain inaccuracies. The film *Sugar Blues* is an example. It is technically well designed and would interest most audiences, but it states that sugar can cause diabetes and impotence. There is no scientific research to verify this.

   Resources can be checked for currency by looking at such health topics as nutrition, first aid, disease, and contraception because the information in these areas changes frequently.

   Accuracy can be checked by selecting several topics (e.g., fetal alcohol syndrome, STD's such as herpes and chlamydia) and perusing this information to see if the authors or producers are knowledgeable. Better yet, physicians, public health professionals, and nutritionists in the community may be willing to review the content for approval.
3. *Does the resource meet the adopted philosophical point of view?* If the philosophy states that the curriculum helps each individual promote well-being, then resources selected should reflect health promotion more than disease understanding. If health is to be understood as a physical, emotional, and social phenomenon, then resources on, say, nutrition must consider not only the physical benefits of wise food selection but also the cultural aspects of food choices and the emotional aspects of food consumption. If a philosophy states that individuals learn in a variety of

ways, then curriculum developers must see that there is variety in the types of resources chosen.

Resources must have enough content to provide students with facts on which to base decisions if decision making is a part of a curriculum's philosophy. Resources should include alternative points of view when appropriate, so that students may be allowed choices and so that the diversity in a community is respected. Resources need to cover controversial issues if this is the intent of the program's philosophy. Resources should always be selected with the philosophy in mind, and the forms used to evaluate resources must reflect the philosophy.

4. *Does the resource have instructional merit?* The instructional contribution of a resource is very important. Evaluators should be concerned as to whether or not teaching strategies will fit the resource. As well as being useful, an acceptable resource must add something to a lesson. The question of instructional merit is related to the most effective and efficient way of presenting a topic and whether the resource can aid in this effort. For example, many films and videos are too long. They take all the instructional time and do all the thinking for the students, leaving no time for discussion or other learning activities that enhance and reinforce the facts or concepts that are to be learned.

   However, long film and video may serve the teacher who is either not knowledgeable or not comfortable with a topic but who is assigned the task of teaching the subject. Furthermore, long film and video may be the most efficient method of presenting certain topics, for example, anatomy.

5. *Would the resource be interesting to the intended audience?* Resources must not only be accurate, up-to-date, and adequate in content, they must also be of interest to the intended users. A technical presentation by an epidemiologist on sexually transmitted disease might be boring to a teenage audience, even though the topic is of interest. In addition to the format in which something is presented, cultural relatedness and ethnic diversity also may affect whether or not the topic will be perceived as interesting.

6. *Is the resource age-appropriate?* Although most resources are developed for specific age groups, some may be appropriate for and of interest to all age levels. For instance, the Disney film *How to Catch a Cold* and Disney's video *Stresses and Strains* can be used from preschool through adult levels.

   Reading levels of materials must be a concern for those selecting resources. It is difficult to find health materials with low reading levels that are interesting to teenagers. In general, reading-level formulas or instruments are not good for evaluating science and health resources. The best method of determining readability is to use good teachers to review a resource and, if possible, to ask the potential users to read and react.

   Reading level, of course, is not the only factor in age-appropriateness. A film on puberty, for example, is relevant to fourth- and fifth-graders soon to embark on the journey and sixth-graders who may be experiencing it, but not to tenth-graders, who would find it insulting.

7. *Is the resource free from cultural, ethnic, age, racial, disability, sexual-orientation, and sex bias?* Ethnic balance is achieved by portraying a variety of ethnic groups in a positive manner and as good role models. It is also achieved by relating to cultural practices. For instance, for years materials on the four food groups did not include ethnic foods, a serious oversight. Sex bias is eliminated by including men and women equally in positive role models. Racism, sexism, and stereotyping must be avoided. The following are types of questions that could be used in evaluating resources:

   - Does the material include a variety of ethnic groups, and does it leave a positive impression of ethnic groups on the student?
   - Does the content include multiethnic content appropriate to our contemporary society, e.g., folk tales versus modern situations?
   - Are both male and female members of minority groups depicted in situations that exhibit them as worthy models?
   - Is there a balance between men and women in the content/graphics?
   - In general, are contributions/achievements of various ethnic groups integrated in the content where appropriate?
   - Is the material free from ethnic, racial, or sexual stereotyping?
   - Are older people depicted as being healthy, happy and useful, or are only their problems portrayed?
   - Are people with disabilities shown to be using their capabilities?

   Figure 7.1 shows one school district's criteria for evaluating materials with regard to sexism and ethnicity.

8. *Is the cost realistic?* Is the resource cost-effective? For instance, one elementary health textbook without much content was often selected over others because of its colorful and abundant pictures. If the evaluators had used criteria that determined if there was adequate health content, the textbook series might not have been purchased. Evaluators would not expect a lot of content in a small, inexpensive pamphlet; conversely, an expensive textbook series should have substance.

   In a school setting, because textbooks are a significant budget item, some textbook evaluations might also consider general appearance, size, durability of binding, quality of paper, appeal of page layout, and instructor's resource materials.

9. *Would there be difficulties in obtaining the resource?* Resources easily available to teachers will be used; therefore, the logistics of resource location and delivery must be a part of curriculum planning. For example, teachers who set up learning centers and can leave them intact rather than dismantling them each day will accept learning-center programs more readily. Videos, transparencies, models, and other materials will be used more if the equipment is in the classroom or at least easy to procure. Packaged programs are generally well received if good in-service programs precede their use and if they are easily procured. Purchased kits that contain easily lost or breakable items generally are not well received by teachers.

FIGURE 7.1 Sample criteria for evaluating materials concerning sexism and ethnicity. (From Bainbridge Island School District, Bainbridge Island, WA.)

BAINBRIDGE ISLAND SCHOOL DISTRICT
Criteria for the Evaluation of Instructional Materials as to Their Treatment of Sexism and Ethnicity

Following is a list of criteria on which educators can evaluate most, if not all, instructional materials. While not all fifteen criteria will be applicable in every case, there are questions which should be raised in the selection of materials we use in the education of our children.

Do the instructional materials:

1. Give evidence on the part of writers, artists, and editors of a sensitivity to prejudice, to stereotypes, and to the use of offensive materials?
2. Suggest, by omission or commission, or by underemphasis or overemphasis that either women or men, or any racial, religious, or ethnic segment of our population is less or more worthy, less or more capable, less or more important in the mainstream of American life?
3. Provide abundant, but fair and well-balanced, recognition of male and female children and adults of minority groups by placing them in positions of leadership and centrality?
4. Exhibit fine and worthy examples of men and women from minority as well as majority groups in art and science, in history and literature, and in all other areas of life and culture?
5. Present a significant number of instances of fully integrated human groupings and settings to indicate equal status and nonsegregated social relationships?
6. Make clearly apparent in illustrations, the group representation of individuals—Caucasian, Black, Native American, Chinese, Japanese, Chicano, Filipino, etc.—and not seek to avoid identification by such means as smudging some color over Caucasian facial features?
7. Delineate life in contemporary urban environments, as well as in rural or suburban environments, so that today's city children can also find significant identification for themselves, their problems, and their potential for life, liberty, and the pursuit of happiness?
8. Portray men and women, racial, religious, and ethnic groups, with their similarities and differences, in such a way as to build positive images?
9. Emphasize the multicultural character of our nation as having unique and special value which we must esteem and treasure?
10. Assist students to recognize clearly and to accept the basic similarities among all members of the human race, and the uniqueness and worth of every single individual, regardless of sex, race, religion, age, or socioeconomic condition?
11. Help students appreciate the many important contributions to our civilization made by members of the various human groups, emphasizing that every human group has its list of achievers, thinkers, writers, artists, scientists, builders, and political leaders?
12. Supply an accurate and sound balance in the matter of historical perspective, making it perfectly clear that racial, religious, and ethnic groups have mixed heritages, which can well serve as sources of both group pride and group humility?
13. Clarify or present factually the historical and contemporary forces and conditions which have operated in the past, and which continue to operate to the disadvantage of minority groups and women?
14. Analyze intergroup tension and conflict fairly, frankly, objectively, and with emphasis upon resolving our social problems in a spirit of fully implementing democratic values and goals in order to achieve the American dream for all Americans?
15. Seek to motivate students to examine their own attitudes and behaviors, and to comprehend their own duties and responsibilities as citizens in a pluralistic democracy—to demand freedom and justice and equal opportunity for every individual and for every group?

FIGURE 7.2 Criteria for evaluating health education instructional materials

Criteria for Evaluating Health Education Instructional Materials

Title ______________________________

Author ______________________________

Date of publication ______________________ Cost, if known ______

Publisher ______________________________

Is material objective? _____ Yes _____ No _____ NA

Is material attractive, interesting? _____ Yes _____ No _____ NA

Is material accurate, up-to-date? _____ Yes _____ No _____ NA

Does the material:

_____ teach skills? _____ develop appreciation? _____ present a health problem?

_____ promote critical thinking? _____ present facts? _____ prompt viewer to look at own behavior?

For what audience is this material best suited? Circle all appropriate grades:

K 1 2 3 4 5 6 7 8 9 10 11 12

Is material free of sex bias? _____ Yes _____ No _____ NA

Is material free of ethnic stereotyping? _____ Yes _____ No _____ NA

Does material include contributions of minority groups? _____ Yes _____ No _____ NA

Summary of content:

Do you recommend use of this material? _____ Yes _____ No

Signature: ______________________________

School: ______________________________

Evaluation Forms

The purpose of evaluation forms is to provide the same criteria for all people evaluating materials, to save time in the previewing process, and to provide a written record of the evaluation. Forms developed for the evaluation process need specific criteria to make them effective. The simpler they are, the greater the chance that evaluators will fill them out completely. However, it is difficult to include all the information needed on an evaluation form. The one shown in figure 7.2 is designed to be concise. Evaluators do not like to fill in "summary of content," but this information is valuable months later in identifying "just what the resource was about!" A comment such as "good book" means retrieving the book to find out what it contains. Figure 7.3 shows an example of another evaluation form that is fairly concise, and figure 7.4 shows a form that requires more information.

Field Trips and Speakers

Field trips and speakers can enhance a curriculum when used appropriately. If possible, they should be identified and evaluated as the curriculum is developed.

FIGURE 7.3 Evaluation form for learning materials. (From Bainbridge Island School District, Bainbridge Island, WA.)

BAINBRIDGE ISLAND SCHOOL DISTRICT

Request for Approval of Supplementary Book and Other Learning Materials for Student Use

BIBLIOGRAPHIC INFORMATION

Type of material ______

Author ______ Hardback ______ Paperback ______

Title ______

Publisher ______ Copyright date ______

Place of publication ______ Price ______

TEACHER EVALUATION

Teacher-user name ______

School ______ Date ______

Subject area ______ Grade level ______

Course title or unit of study ______

How will this be used? ______

______

Reading level: ______ Easy ______ Average ______ Difficult

Material recommended for: ______ Classroom reference ______ Individual reading list ______ Textbook

______ Other: ______

Have you read the book? ______ Yes ______ No

Have you previewed the material? ______ Yes ______ No

Have you read a review of the materials? ______ Yes ______ No

Illustrations: ______ Excellent ______ Poor ______ Functional ______ Unrelated

Treatment of sexism and ethnicity: (see criteria)

______ Excellent ______ Good ______ Fair ______ Poor

______ In my judgment there is nothing objectionable in this material.

______ I have some concern about this material and would like the opinion of the Instructional Materials Review Committee. List those areas of concern (specific page numbers and passages).

______

______

______ Recommended by ALA or ______

______

Teacher Signature

Committee comments: ______

______

______

Recommended action: ______ Approve ______ Disapprove

If not approved, reason: ______

______

______

Date ______ ______

Signature of chairperson

FIGURE 7.4 Evaluation report for health education resources

Evaluation Report for Health Education Resources

1. Types of resource: ______ book ______ film ______ filmstrip ______ pamphlet
   ______ kit ______ speaker ______ field trip ______ other (please specify)
2. Title/name of speaker/field trip location: ______
3. Author/contact person for speaker or field trip: ______
4. Health topic with which resource deals and purpose*:
   Health topic ______
   Purpose (use numbers if desired) ______
   *For example: (1) teach skills, (2) develop appreciation, (3) modify or reinforce existing beliefs and attitudes, (4) stimulate discussion, (5) present a health problem in a social setting, (6) promote critical thinking, (7) summarize factual information, (8) correct misconceptions and misinformation, (9) inspire a sense of social responsibility, and (10) prompt the viewer to look at his own behavior and how it may affect others.
5. General rating:
   A. *Scientific accuracy* (consider date of production, source, technical consultants, content as it reflects current research)
   Excellent ______ Good ______ Fair ______ Poor ______
   B. *Teaching potential* (consider level of comprehension, continuity, casting of characters, and realistic presentation)
   Excellent ______ Good ______ Fair ______ Poor ______
   C. *Technical quality* (consider photography and sound quality)
   Excellent ______ Good ______ Fair ______ Poor ______
6. For what audience is this material best suited? Check the appropriate categories:

Elementary (6–8 years) ______	Inner city ______	Poor ______
Intermediate (9–12 years) ______	Suburban ______	Middle class ______
Junior high (13–14 years) ______	Small town ______	Affluent ______
Senior high (15–18 years) ______	Rural ______	

7. Other pertinent information (e.g., controversial, new ideas, attractive, preparation needed for field trip, teacher use only):
   ______
8. Please write a very short description which would enable others to quickly identify whether or not they can use this resource:
   ______
9. Recommend for purchase: ______ Yes ______ No

Evaluated by ______

Date ______

Consider the following criteria when selecting field trips or speakers as resources:

1. Are they cost effective? Field trips are generally very motivating, but if transportation is required, they may not be a cost-effective learning experience for students.
2. Are they worth the time needed to evaluate them? Forms can be developed to evaluate field trips and speakers; however, this is very time-consuming. An easier way is to accept a teacher's or other person's recommendation if that person has heard the speaker or has taken the field trip. Sometimes the reputation of an agency providing the speaker or field trip suffices.
3. Will the learning experience be effective? To use such resources effectively, the teacher and the speaker or the person who will be at the field trip site must communicate, but because this takes time, people may not do so. The school district and/or teacher should provide the speaker or field trip host, in writing with

- The instructional objective(s) for the activity day
- What is expected of the speaker/host
- The time and place the speaker is to appear
- Any policies, laws, or concerns that might pertain to their presentation
- The background of the students (age and knowledge).

In writing, the speaker or field trip host should provide the school district/teacher with their objectives, what the students will experience, and what preparation the students need to receive full benefit from the talk or field trip.

Packaged Curricula in Health Education

One type of resource that is gaining greater acceptance is the packaged program. Packaged curricula generally are categorical; that is, they are concerned with only one or two health topics. Most categorical packaged curricula are multimedia and involve hands-on activities. Many are educationally sound, with lesson objectives, suggested teaching strategies, and all necessary teaching resources and materials included. The criteria suggested for evaluating resources can be used with packaged curricula; however, other criteria could be developed that may be more appropriate. Figures 7.5 and 7.6, for example, present criteria for evaluating curricula on drug education and sexuality education.

Part of the process of selecting packaged curricula should be to consider how they are to be used. Once a health educator and/or the curriculum-developing committee sets up curriculum objectives, the packaged material needs to be evaluated in terms of how many objectives it addresses and how well. Sometimes when packaged materials are evaluated and found to be what a school district needs, the scope and sequence (or objectives) of a developing curriculum or developed curriculum can be modified to more effectively utilize the packaged program. The changes must be made with all the same guidelines in mind: Are the health topics of interest to the intended audience? Does the program fit into the scope and sequence, and does it relate to the philosophy?

As described in chapter 5, a school district or agency may combine a number of small packaged programs to make a comprehensive curriculum, or it may use one large packaged curriculum that needs only a few other resources to make it comprehensive.

At times a packaged curriculum may be purchased even if not all of it will be used. Because developing one's own curriculum is so time-consuming, and thus costly, purchasing a curriculum, even though all of it is not used,

FIGURE 7.5 Criteria for effective drug education curricula. (From L. D. Johnston, P. M. O'Malley, and G. G. Backman, "National Trends in Drug Use and Related . . . ," National Inst. on Drug Abuse, ADM 85-1535, National Institute on Drug Abuse, 1987.)

Criteria for Effective Drug Education Curricula

The problem of drug use and chemical dependency among our nation's young people is of crisis proportions. Alcohol-related automobile accidents alone result in the deaths of thousands of teenagers every year.

As part of a comprehensive approach to this problem, communities increasingly turn to schools. But, with so many programs available, how do you choose the one that will be most effective for your schools, your community, your children?

To help make the selection process easier, consider the following criteria for measuring the potential effectiveness of any drug education curriculum:

1. Is the curriculum based on current research about why young people use drugs? Many drug education programs are based on what the authors *think* are reasons why young people use drugs. Programs should be based on what the most *current research* says about why children use drugs. Only when a curriculum is targeted at the true causes of the problem can it be effective in reducing the problem.
2. Does the curriculum begin early, and is it ongoing? The studies of Johnston, O'Malley, and Backman (1987) have identified the average onset of drug use as ages 9–10 for nicotine, ages 10–11 for alcohol, and ages 11–12 for marijuana. An effective drug education curriculum has to begin teaching students *before* they are likely to make their first decisions about drugs, not after; and it must build on what is learned each year, adding new skills and information throughout the child's school experience.
3. Does the curriculum provide more than information? In addition to being informative, an effective drug education curriculum should include practical lessons aimed at teaching the student how to *use* new information. Helping students to master pro-social skills and to feel a stronger connection to family and school is equally important in the effort to reduce drug use.
4. Does the curriculum include parental involvement? No matter how deep a school system's commitment may be to fighting drug abuse among its students, no matter how dedicated and well-trained its teachers, the involvement of *parents* is essential to the success of any curriculum. For this reason, one of the most important criteria for judging any drug education curriculum is the strength of its parent component. Does the curriculum keep the parents informed of the nature and extent of the school's program? Does it provide parents with information, resources, and skills so they can enhance and extend the curriculum in their own homes?
5. Is the curriculum culturally sensitive? Can students from a wide variety of cultural and ethnic backgrounds learn from it?
6. Does the curriculum have a clear "no use" message? Research shows that trying drugs even "just a little" can lead to major drug problems. The curriculum you choose should clearly and unambiguously state that children of school age simply should not use drugs—at all.
7. Does the curriculum address the phenomenon of "gateway drugs?" Research shows that the early use of some drugs—nicotine, alcohol, marijuana—while harmful in itself, increases the likelihood of using other drugs later on. Therefore, an effective drug education curriculum should not be limited to the so-called "hard drugs," but at a very early stage should focus on the problems presented by gateway drugs such as nicotine, alcohol, and marijuana, in order to prevent subsequent graduation to other drugs.
8. Is the curriculum easy to use, flexible, and inclusive? Teachers are busy. They have little time to create or constantly find new teaching materials. An effective drug education curriculum should contain everything necessary for its full utilization. And, because each community is unique, a curriculum should be adaptable to local needs and conditions.
9. Is the curriculum cost-efficient? The cost of any curriculum needs to be calculated over the long run. In addition to the initial purchase price, other questions need to be asked: What is the cost of the teacher's time in preparing to teach the curriculum? What does it cost to replace materials? What is the per-pupil cost over several years?
10. Can the curriculum be easily incorporated into a total approach to health education and wellness? It isn't enough for a drug education curriculum to deal with the drug crisis as a single, isolated subject. In order to be effective, the curriculum should be easily integrated into a comprehensive health education program that includes subjects like nutrition, sexuality, physical fitness, and environmental health.
11. Is the curriculum participatory and varied in its methods? Does the curriculum offer more than assigned readings, required reports, and answers to direct questions? Is it fun, meaningful, and involving for the student? Do the lessons accommodate the varied learning styles of the students?
12. Does the curriculum include teacher training? Many teachers have a limited background in teaching not only the facts about alcohol and other drugs, but also social skills and ways to help students feel bonded to school. In addition, teachers often need to examine their own attitudes, which greatly impact their ability to teach. An effective drug education curriculum must include a training component that helps the classroom teacher use it to its maximum potential.

These criteria have been developed not only on the basis of the latest drug-use research, but also as a result of our experiences in responding to the actual needs of many communities and school systems throughout the United States. Consequently, it is intended for your use in judging the potential effectiveness of *any* drug education curriculum, as well as its appropriateness to your particular community and school system.

FIGURE 7.6 Suggested Criteria for Identifying High Quality Sexuality Curricula. (Courtesy of ASSET: The Association for Sexuality Education and Training, P.O. Box 668, Oak Harbor, WA 98277.)

DRAFT
Suggested Criteria for Identifying
High Quality Sexuality Curricula

(1) *Are sequential,* kindergarten through grade 12. They provide knowledge and skills that build logically on earlier learning.

(2) *Are educationally sound in form.* They reflect what is known about: intellectual/academic development (including reading level and reasoning ability), visual appeal (print size, illustrations, layout), and learning style (with interactive, varied teaching methods that will be effective for kinesthetic, visual, and aural learners, right and left-brain thinkers).

(3) *Are age-appropriate in content.* They reflect what is known about child and adolescent psychosocial and sexual development, behavior and experience. They should be anticipatory (e.g., learning about puberty should begin at least a year before young people begin puberty—by age 8 at the latest).

(4) *Are medically/scientifically/legally accurate.* They contain demonstrable facts. Hypotheses and theories are identified as such, and emphasized only if shared by most experts in a field.

(5) *Are comprehensive.* Taking number 3 (above) into account, they cover, in the course of thirteen years' schooling:

(a) *sexual anatomy and physiology,* i.e.:
- the male and female endocrine and reproductive systems including the physiology of menstruation,
- physical changes of puberty,
- sexual development from conception to death,
- physiology of pregnancy and fetal development,
- the sexual response system including the physiology of erection and ejaculation.

(b) *sexual health and safety,* i.e.,
- acne
- sexual exploitation
- sexually transmissible diseases including HIV/AIDS
- cancers of the breast and reproductive system
- birth defects/miscarriage/prematurity/low birthweight
- teen and unplanned pregnancy
- hygiene
- dysmennorhea
- gynecomastia
- sexual dysfunction
- infertility
- testicular torsion

the meaning and consequences of each of the above, and the prevention, detection, treatment, coping/survival/recovery, and accessing resources for each.

(c) *sexual aspects of social and emotional health,* i.e.,
- family
- body image
- loving
- monogamy
- sexual and dating values
- sexual orientation
- sexual decision-making
- communication, including how to say no and how to take no for an answer.
- friendship
- touch
- affection
- fantasy
- values
- self-esteem
- marriage
- dating
- prostitution
- infatuation
- abstinence
- attraction
- pornography
- peer and media pressure
- law and policy re: sexual issues
- sexual stereotyping and prejudice
- sexual identity
- liking
- commitment
- sex roles

(6) *Teach relatively universal values.* Specifically, they:

(a) encourage/enhance family communication.

(b) are tasteful/tactful.

(c) are respectful of learners (not condescending or patronizing).

(d) promote intimacy, tenderness, caring, and honesty within all relationships (parent-child friends, boyfriend-girlfriend, spouses).

(e) foster thoughtful, sober decisions about sex, taking care not to foster fear about sex, nor to foster casual, flippant sexual decision-making.

(f) encourage students to abstain from sexual intercourse, without degrading nonvirgins, and taking care not to express a laissez-faire, casual attitude toward teen sexual activity, nor to express a punitive or degrading attitude toward nonvirgin teens.

(g) encourage risk-reduction for teens who do have sex, without condoning their choice, and taking care not to convey a punitive, they-deserve-what-they-get attitude toward these students, nor to suggest that condoms (for HIV protection) or any contraceptives (for pregnancy protection) are 100% safe, easy "excuses" for casual sex.

(h) foster healthy, positive body image, taking care not to promote the attitude that bodies are unclean or embarrassing, nor to infer that modesty or a desire for privacy are unimportant or juvenile.

FIGURE 7.6 *Continued*

-page 2-

(i) express respect for diverse family constellations, teaching that healthy families are those which support their members' physical and emotional well-being, taking care not to assume homogeneity of family constellation or to characterize any one family pattern as the only model of "normalcy," nor to disparage the nuclear family as out-moded

(7) *Address controversial issues* (as opposed to avoiding them). When they do, they take care to:
(a) clearly distinguish facts from beliefs/values.
(b) even-handedly, sensitively describe a full range of community values.
(c) encourage students to find out the beliefs of their families and faiths (if they have one).
(d) teach respect for all families and individuals, and avoid promoting any one value position.
(Any position would offend or hurt some students' families, on these issues.) Thus, for example, they:
(i) dispel sex role stereotyping (substituting accurate information), promoting respect for both males and females and their abilities, taking care not to express judgment of those who do not choose traditional roles, nor to denigrate those who do choose traditional roles.
(ii) dispel sexual orientation stereotyping (substituting accurate information) and support the self-esteem of gay and lesbian students, without sanctioning their becoming sexually active, and taking care not to assume that all students/families are heterosexual, nor to encourage homosexual experimentation.
(iii) discourage teen parenting, and convey the medical, legal and sociological facts, taking care not to express a laissez-faire, casual attitude toward teen parenting, nor to convey a punitive or degrading attitude toward teen parents.
(iv) respect differing beliefs about adult, premarital sex, taking care to convey the risks involved in casual or brief sexual relationships, without implying that premarital sex is wrong or sinful, nor suggesting that it is good, OK, or fine.
(v) respect differing beliefs about contraception and abortion, conveying the medical, legal and sociological facts, without suggesting that everyone should use either or that they are risk-free, always-easy or right, nor suggesting that nobody should use them, or that they are dangerous, always-difficult or wrong.
(vi) respect differing beliefs about masturbation, artificial insemination, in vitro fertilization, conveying the medical, legal and sociological facts about each, without expressing judgment of people who engage in or partake of each, nor expressing judgment of those who choose not to.

(8) *Are "teacher-friendly."* They are well-organized with clear, thorough instructions. They are as self-contained as possible (minimal assembly time). Ideally, they are inexpensive enough that each building, if not each teacher, can have a copy/set.

This non-copyrighted material provided courtesy of ASSET: the Association for Sexuality Education and Training, P.O. Box 668, Oak Harbor, Washington 98277.

may still be cost-effective. On the other hand, a district must decide if a packaged program is worth buying if it only addresses a small part of the comprehensive curriculum.

Policies and Laws Governing Selection of Resources

In general, state and school district policies attempt to help the selection process avoid biases and identify quality in resources. Laws and policies guide the selection process to ensure that resources will be compatible with the philosophy of the community.

Curriculum planners need to be aware of any state laws or school district policies relating to the acquisition of materials. Some state laws may require local school boards to set forth in writing a policy regarding the selection of instructional materials. These laws or policies may provide a procedure for handling complaints against instructional materials. Figure 7.7 shows an example of a form provided by a school district for the purpose of reconsidering instructional material objected to by a parent.

FIGURE 7.7 Request for reconsideration of instructional materials. (Reprinted by permission of the Federal Way School District #210, Federal Way, WA.)

Reconsideration of Instructional Materials — R6132

1.0 Patrons of the Federal Way School District who have concerns regarding instructional materials used by the District may register those concerns with the school principal. The school principal will arrange a meeting with the patron and other building staff within three (3) school days of receiving the concern to review the issue. All attempts will be made to resolve the issue at the building level concerning use of the material. Instructional material may not be removed in this process.

2.0 The principal keeps a record of the recommended solution made at the building meeting and the procedures leading to it. A copy is sent to the Assistant Superintendent of Educational Support Services so that patterns of potential problems may be identified.

3.0 If the patron is dissatisfied with the solution, the principal will provide the patron with Form 6132, Request for Reconsideration of Instructional Materials, which is the formal request for District reconsideration.

4.0 The school principal will send the completed Form 6132 to the Assistant Superintendent for Educational Support Services within three (3) school days after receipt of the concern.

5.0 The Assistant Superintendent or designee will establish a committee to review the request, and will appoint the committee chairperson within eight (8) school days after receipt of Form 6132.

6.0 The review committee will include as a minimum the school principal, a librarian, a department head or teacher from the school, a staff member from another school, and two patrons of the District.

7.0 The committee chairperson will invite the patron filing the request for reconsideration to present his/her concerns of the instructional materials in question to the committee.

8.0 The committee will review the citizen's request and the instructional material in question and submit a written recommendation to the Superintendent within ten (10) school days after the committee chairperson has been appointed.

9.0 The Superintendent will make a decision and notify the patron in writing within five (5) school days after receiving the committee's recommendation.

10.0 The citizen may appeal to the Board if he/she is not satisfied with the Superintendent's decision—within ten (10) school days after receipt of notification.

11.0 If within a three-year period a subsequent Request for Reconsideration of Instructional Materials for the same material is received following the Superintendent's decision, the Superintendent or designee determines whether or not there is sufficient cause to initiate another review.

Adopted: 2/74
Amended: 7/9/90 R6132

FEDERAL WAY SCHOOL DISTRICT #210

FIGURE 7.7 *Continued*

Reconsideration of Instructional Materials (continued) R6132

REQUEST FOR RECONSIDERATION OF INSTRUCTIONAL MATERIALS

Type of Material: ____________________

(textbook, library book, magazine, film, etc.)

Title: ____________________

Author: ____________________

Producer or Publisher: ____________________

Request Initiated By: ____________________

Telephone: ____________________ Address: ____________________

Freedom to read and to have access to a wide variety of materials representing differing points of view is an inherent right of students in a democratic society. The Federal Way School District subscribes to the principles of freedom of information as set forth in the Library Bill of Rights of the American Library Association.

If you represent an organization or group, please indicate the name of the group: ____________________

____

1. Have you discussed the material with the principal and teacher, or person primarily responsible for its use?
   YES ______ NO ______

   If No, please explain: ____________________

   ____

   If Yes, what were the results? ____________________

   ____

2. Are you aware of the teacher's purpose for using the material?

   YES ______ NO ______ If yes, what was the purpose? ____________________

   ____

3. Have you examined (read, viewed, etc.) the material in its entirety?

   YES ______ NO ______ If no, what part did you review? ____________________

   ____

FIGURE 7.7 *Continued*

Reconsideration of Instructional Materials (continued) R6132

Request for Reconsideration of Instructional Materials, continued
Form 6132—Page two

4. Why do you feel the material/book is inappropriate? (Please be specific; cite pages in printed materials.)

____

____

____

____

5. What do you feel might be the result of students' use of this material? ____________

____

____

____

6. For what age group would you recommend this instructional material? ____________

____

7. What do you feel is positive about this instructional material? ____________

____

____

8. What action would you like the District to consider?

   ______ Do not assign the material to my child

   ______ Seek supplementary materials to overcome weaknesses in this material

   ______ Withdraw material from all students as well as from my child

   ______ Reconsider the appropriateness of the material

9. In its place, what other materials would you recommend that would provide adequate information on the subject? ______

____

____

____

____

______________________________ ______________

Signature of Complainant Date

R6132
Page 3

FEDERAL WAY SCHOOL DISTRICT #210

FIGURE 7.7 *Continued*

Reconsideration of Instructional Materials (continued) R6132

Request for Reconsideration of Instructional Materials, continued
Form 6132—Page three

This request should be returned to the school principal or mailed directly to the Assistant Superintendent of Educational Support Services, Federal Way School District, 31405 18th Avenue South, Federal Way, Washington 98003.

Reconsideration Process:

1. Citizen completes Form 6132 and returns to school principal.
2. Principal sends form to Assistant Superintendent for Educational Support Services within three (3) school days of receipt of request.
3. Assistant Superintendent or designee establishes review committee (within eight (8) school days) to include at least:
   School Principal
   Librarian
   Department Head or teacher from the school
   Staff member from another school
   Two District citizens
4. Committee invites citizen filing the request to speak to committee.
5. Committee reviews request and submits written recommendation to the Superintendent within ten (10) school days.
6. Superintendent makes decision and informs citizen in writing within five (5) school days of committee's recommendation.
7. Patrons may appeal to the School Board within ten (10) school days of receipt of notification.

R6132
Page 4

FEDERAL WAY SCHOOL DISTRICT #210

Some states, such as Texas, California, and Oregon, evaluate textbooks and major program materials at the state level. These states approve several textbook series or programs from which local school districts must choose.

Tracking Resources for Screening and Evaluation

Procuring resources for preview is quite a simple idea, but in practice it is a cumbersome process. Many school districts already have a resource-selection process in place that includes monitoring. For instance, requesting resources for preview may need to be done on special forms or through selected departments or people (e.g., librarians). After previewing, resources should be returned in their own cartons. For items not in cartons, a chart such as figure 7.8 can be used to monitor the return of previewed resources. If preview resources are lost or not returned, the district must pay for them.

Such a chart is valuable when the time comes to order selected materials for the curriculum. In some cases the name of the company on the resource may not be the source of the materials, and time may be wasted in tracing this information.

Careful reading of the preview policies of suppliers is necessary. Returning items on time, for example, is a courtesy that program planners should extend. Some suppliers require payment before materials are sent and reimburse schools when they are returned.

Summary

If the curriculum is well planned, from philosophy through teaching activities, resources can make it exciting. Resources help teachers reach all students and help ensure that learning takes place. Selecting a variety of resources demands a great deal of time from many school personnel. First, resources must be located and ordered. Because there are so many, someone must screen out all but the best and then evaluate those on the basis of carefully thought-out criteria. These criteria focus primarily on whether the resources are related to the objectives of the curriculum, to the philosophy of the curriculum, and to the age level, interests, and needs of students. The content must be accurate and free from any bias. Resources must make a difference in the instruction; that is, they must have instructional merit. Finally, they must be cost-effective. Curricula for which resources have been carefully selected and budgeted are curricula to which students respond.

Discussion Questions

1. Discuss the appropriateness of the criteria used for screening materials.
2. Why does the person who selects materials for screening need to be knowledgeable about health education and the quality of sources?
3. Discuss the similarities and differences of these two criteria: *age-appropriate* and *of interest to the intended audience.*

FIGURE 7.8 Resource Tracking Chart

Source of resource (full address)	Item	Date Rec'd	Disposition	Additional Information

Application Activities

1. Develop a form for evaluating resources. Select five resources targeted to a content area and age group, and use your form to evaluate those resources.
2. Obtain either a drug education curriculum or a sexuality education curriculum and assess them, using the criteria in figure 7.5 or figure 7.6.
3. Critique two evaluation forms from the standpoint of ease of use and whether or not sufficient information can be gathered.
4. Compare the criteria for drug education and sexuality education curricula in figures 7.5 and 7.6.

8

Building Partnerships:
Linking Schools with the Community

After reading this chapter and participating in application activities, the student should be able to:

1. Predict the future roles of school health services and a healthful school environment in promoting the health and well-being of young people.
2. Summarize the characteristics of successful partnerships and coalitions.
3. Relate the benefits of linking schools with communities to enhance school health instruction.
4. Identify agencies and organizations that contribute to the school health program.

Good health is too important to be left to schools alone. Good health is influenced by many factors that permeate a person's life. The media, the entertainment world, peers, parents, community recreational pursuits, the health-care system, and the business world all affect the health attitudes, knowledge, and behavior of young people. For example, the number of hours young people spend in school is one-third of the time they spend watching television. Thus, comprehensive school health education cannot be accomplished by schools alone. Health is definitely a community affair!

To promote healthy life-styles and strengthen health education, all facets of the community need to work together to promote a common goal: to promote the health and well-being of young people. Schools simply do not have the time, expertise, or resources to give young people all the tools needed for healthy living. This chapter is about partnerships and the benefits that accrue to collaborating members. A look at the limit of a school's influence on young people's hearts and minds shows the need for linking schools with communities to foster the well-being of young people.

The Future of School Health Partnerships

The school health program traditionally was considered to include health instruction, health services, and a healthful school environment, and as such has been described in most health textbooks. Such a program existed in very few school districts. Ideally, the school health program coordinator supervised health services, environment, and instruction. In reality, several individuals assumed responsibility for different aspects of these programs, if they existed. Yet all of these components are important and probably more necessary now more than ever. Today, health services and a healthful environment are especially in need of school-community collaboration.

While this book does focus on health instruction, other chapters emphasize the need for schools to establish links with communities. Chapter 1 shows the need to involve diverse viewpoints when developing a philosophical focus. Chapter 3 points out the various community members who can influence the curriculum-planning committee. Chapter 6 describes the vast array of resources available from agencies and organizations concerned with health education. Chapter 9 examines concerns that individuals and groups have about topics in school health education curricula, and chapter 10 identifies people and organizations that help to inservice teachers.

Health Services

Health services have traditionally encompassed health appraisals of young people, including at times health examinations; and screenings, and monitoring of students identified as having health problems. These services have included prevention of communicable diseases through the checking of skin for infections and infestations, isolation of those with infectious diseases, and immunizations. Safety regulations such as safety patrols and inspection of playground equipment as well as emergency care for accidents and sudden illness are a part of health services. They also include education for handicapped children and medical and psychosocial assessments, along with health counseling.

Today, most schools still have school nurses, but the nurses are not full-time at any one school. As reported in *Turning Points,* "in many schools today, a school nurse is available to students perhaps once or twice a month. The nurse necessarily concentrates on students needing immediate attention, which leaves little time to identify less obvious conditions that might warrant health care or counseling" (Carnegie Council on Adolescent Development, 1989:62). School nurses may still do immunizations, but usually they do record-keeping of immunizations along with some eye, ear, and skin appraisals, especially in elementary grades. They act as a resource to teachers, now more than ever before. School nurses cover emergency care and sudden illness when in a particular school, but many schools now train specific staff (e.g., secretaries and physical educators) to provide first aid. The availability of the 911 telephone number offers additional emergency service. Few physicians are presently employed in school districts; some are contracted to do physical examinations in their own offices.

It is still important that school personnel (teachers, counselors, and nurses) be responsible for observing the health of young people. Any health problems found should be referred to parents and through parents to health-care providers and community agencies. The problem here is that many teachers are not educated in what to look for or in making referrals to the health-care delivery system.

Code Blue (National Commission on the Role of the School and the Community in Improving Adolescent Health, 1990) states that "many school nurse, counseling, nutrition, health education, and physical education programs are not meeting current adolescent health needs. Significant improvements are required in program content, collaboration with other service providers, professional training, and levels of funding" (p. 10). This is also true for the elementary children.

School children and adolescents need a wide variety of coordinated health and social services that currently are not available to them. "These services should form a continuum of education and care that begins with health promotion and primary prevention and moves on through early problem identification, assessment, secondary prevention, referral, treatment and institutionalization" (The National Commission on the Role of the School and the Community in Improving Adolescent Health, 1990:11). The National Committee felt that the following types of services were especially critical for adolescents: prevention services, including periodic health status assessment; treatment of acute and chronic illness; psychological and mental health care; substance-abuse treatment; social work services; rehabilitative services; family planning; maternity care and related services; vision and dental care; nutritional services; and wellness education.

The *Code Blue* report recommends that health centers be established in schools or other convenient locations. This would not be the responsibility of the school, it would be organized by public health agencies, community health agencies, hospitals, schools, or independent organizations. The cost would be covered by governmental, business, and philanthropic organizations. *Turning Points,* targeted to middle school adolescents, recommends that schools "consider options such as school-based clinics (located on school grounds), school-linked health centers (located off school grounds but joined functionally to the school and perhaps to other area schools), ties to community health centers, and arrangements with adolescent services in hospitals or health maintenance organizations (which might serve both adolescents in schools and those who have dropped out)" (Carnegie Council on Adolescent Development, 1989:62).

The current consensus among those evaluating the status of health among adolescents is that schools should "re-examine their ability to provide students with access to services, paying particular attention to increasing the collaboration of professionals both within schools and with external providers. Many schools already have school nurses, counselors, social workers, psychologists, and outreach workers. Unfortunately, the demands for them to perform administrative tasks have severely restricted the time they have to collaborate and work directly with young people and their families. To give them more time . . . will require additional resources" (National Commission on the Role of the School and Community in Improving Adolescent Health, 1990:36).

Another part of health services in the past was the concern for educating the handicapped youngster. These young people now have a full program administered and provided by staff who have been specially trained to help them. Students, except in rare circumstances, are mainstreamed into the regular classrooms. The classroom teacher is assisted by those who have special training in how to help each youngster.

Healthful School Environment

Traditionally the healthful school environment program has included such things as vermin control, water supply and safety, food service, toilet configuration, illumination, noise control, play areas, fire prevention, location and plan of school buildings, and a mentally healthy atmosphere.

A healthful school environment involves everything from the teacher's creation of a climate that encourages learning to the architects' concern for adequate ventilation. Administrators, school board members, architects, teachers, staff (e.g., custodians, lunchroom personnel, secretaries), and students all have responsibility for a healthful environment. However, in most school districts today, the responsibility for coordinating these efforts does not rest with a school health program coordinator. One or more administrators may be responsible for part of the school environment, and they may or may not be trained in healthful school programs.

The American Association of School Administrators reports that schools have moved from not recognizing the importance of adults as role models to the consideration of adult role models as crucial ingredients in health promotion. Reported in "*Critical Issues Report: Promoting Health Education in Schools—Problems and Solutions*" is the notion that schools have moved from largely ignoring the health conditions of teachers and other school staff to promoting staff wellness (Pine, 1985). And furthermore, whereas schools in the past failed to perceive the school environment as a factor in health education and as a factor in affecting student and staff health, it is now important for buildings and school groups to become cleaner, safer, and freer of toxic agents.

Thus school health services and a healthful school environment are no longer the venue of the school alone. In fact, the recommendations from *Code Blue* and *Turning Points* show why it is vital for schools and communities to form partnerships to promote the health and well-being of young people. The future of the comprehensive school health education program is to connect schools with communities, forming partnerships and other collaborations to ensure students' access to health and social services and to enrich the instructional program.

About Partnerships

By *partnerships,* we mean any cooperative effort on the part of individuals, groups, agencies, or businesses working toward a common goal. It may be a short-term effort focusing on a specific task (e.g., immunization of children against measles) or a long-term relationship focusing on a broader goal (e.g., prevention of substance abuse). Habana-Hafner et al. (1989) suggest that partnerships are defined by the complexity of their purposes and operations, the intensity of the linkages and interaction of members, and the formality of agreements.

At times the name *coalition* is used to depict a partnership. Kahn (1982) defines a coalition as a "group of organizations working together for a common purpose. Some coalitions work on a group of related issues, and some are put together to deal with one issue only. When that issue is resolved, the coalition no longer exists." Successful coalitions share such common characteristics as the following:

- Being formally organized, with governing rules of operation
- Having common goals and shared visions of the future
- Being composed of a broad spectrum of organizations and individuals
- Developing position statements/papers endorsed by members
- Devising action plans and timetables for tending to coalition business
- Documenting endorsements of coalition work
- Having involved and informed volunteer spokespersons (NaSHEC, 1989:1).

Partnerships may be formal or informal in nature and exist at the local, state, and/or national level. A local-level partnership might be an advisory council composed of school and community representatives and having as its main concern the health status of the students. A state-level partnership could exist among health agencies and schools lobbying for smoke-free schools or comprehensive school health instruction. A recent example of a successful partnership activity is the passage of the tobacco initiative in California. The cooperative effort of several parties (e.g., health educators, fire fighters, PTA, health-care providers, insurance companies, maternal and child-care providers, and professional organizations) forged the passing of the initiative by the citizens of California; part of the 50-cent tax per package of cigarettes is now earmarked for school health instruction.

At the national level, the goal of a smoke-free environment has brought together a wide array of interested groups and individuals. Not only have three major voluntary health organizations (American Cancer Society, American Heart Association, and American Lung Association) formed a coalition to promote the "Smoke-Free Class of 2000" and Tobacco Free America Project, but city and county councils, law enforcement, state legislatures, school boards, National Institutes of Health (and other federal agencies), health-care providers, professional health organizations, health insurance companies, and many others are now focusing on a smoke-free environment for all. Through the efforts of coalitions lobbying state legislatures, laws have been passed banning smoking in school buildings, on school grounds, and in school vehicles.

Benefits of School-Community Partnerships

Partners can bring unlimited potential to the collaborative relationship. Program planners should think big and not small when brainstorming possible contributions. As schools confront the urgency of such societal health issues as HIV and AIDS, those with comprehensive health programs in place are in the best position to educate their students. Community partners play active roles in helping comprehensive programs address critical issues regarding the health and well-being of school-age children and adolescents.

Through collaborative relationships, more resources and energy are marshaled toward common goals. Each group in a partnership gains something from the relationship and in turn contributes something to the relationship. Working together can eliminate duplication of efforts and relieve any individual or group from overcommitment of time, energy, and money. Vested interests are less apt to dominate when groups work together. In fact, the identity of individual groups is often sacrificed to promote the common goal of the partnership.

Sensitive health content can be implemented more effectively and with less criticism when community support is first in place. If opposition appears, collaborative relationships may serve to minimize the opposition. "Bringing educators, parents, other community members, and students to the decision-making table results in less blaming and finger-pointing and more genuine problem-solving behavior by all parties" (Jennings, 1989:45).

Significant contributions to health education have been made by voluntary health organizations, nonprofit health agencies, the corporate world, and professional associations. Contributions have been made in the form of curricular materials, audiovisuals, guest speakers, grants, in-service training, and representation on curriculum committees. Agencies have supported state health education conferences through funding, conducting workshops, and providing speakers, and they have helped in lobbying for health education. Specific benefits and contributions are highlighted in the following sections to help the reader understand the value of partnerships.

Financing

Funding has been provided in the form of financial contributions and competitive grant programs by private foundations, state medical associations, insurance companies, the federal government, and other sources to foster and promote successful comprehensive school health education. Grants have been made to individual schools, school districts, and state education departments. Metropolitan Life Foundation's *Healthy Me* (1989) initiative, begun in 1985 with the purpose of encouraging the development, adoption, and implementation of good comprehensive school health education programs, is one example of a successful grant program. From 1985 to 1989, monetary awards were given to stimulate the extension of school health education by "recognizing and rewarding existing exemplary programs that can be replicated to others, to encourage collaborative efforts to introduce innovative new programs or expand existing ones through active promotion by community coalitions, and to enhance professional preparation for the teaching of health education" (Metropolitan Life Foundation, 1989).

Specific health issues funded with federal monies include drug education, nutrition education training (NET), and AIDS education. The latter, funded through the Division for Adolescent and School Health, has been incorporated into comprehensive school health education programs. One such program targeted to deliver specific health information relating to AIDS and HIV infection is *Growing Healthy,* a K–7 school health curriculum.

Expertise

Representatives of agencies and groups lend their expertise in a variety of ways: as speakers to classes, seminars, and conferences; as participants in curriculum-planning groups; as members of advisory councils to schools; as reviewers of curricular materials developed by school personnel; and as providers of workshops on various health topics for the in-service training of teachers. School personnel may in turn serve on advisory councils to agencies or work with agencies in developing curricula or learning materials to help with agency workshops. Experts from the community lend credibility to the need for health education in schools.

Support and Advocacy

Through their contacts in the community, representatives of agencies and organizations can interpret what goes on in school health education, communicate the needs of health education, and, in general, give those not working with schools a greater understanding of the educational world. On the other hand, school personnel can gain an understanding of the agencies and spread the word of their work and goals. For example, a supervisor of health education might speak at a meeting of dairy industry representatives to explain the contributions of the National Dairy Council and explain how a particular state dairy council contributes to the education of young people.

For agencies, another benefit of a collaborative relationship is that the agency has the opportunity to educate young people in large numbers. The agency also receives community recognition and is able to promote its own program.

Curricular Materials

One of the most important contributions made by agencies is their generous sharing of learning materials, lessons, and instructional units. Over the years, curricular projects devoted to specific health topics have been developed—topics such as smoking, genetics, blood and circulation, substance abuse, sexuality, pregnancy, child abuse, birth defects, cardiovascular diseases, and cancer. (See chapters 6 and 7 for further details about resources.)

Instructional units and materials developed by agencies can be worked into a curriculum that is being planned or revised. On the other hand, a school might lend its health educators to agencies to aid them in developing instructional units. The American Lung Association funded a local school district's development of the *Primary Grades Curriculum Project,* which was later joined with a grades 4–6 curriculum to form the *Growing Healthy Curriculum.*

The diverse and numerous instructional materials available from agencies and organizations provide resources for meeting the variety of ways that young people learn. Schools benefit from partnerships because the valuable resources they receive can be woven into the existing health instruction program, thereby enhancing the curriculum. Partners provide expertise, support, and advocacy, which establish a broadbased ownership of comprehensive school health instruction. The result is not only increased support in the community for school health education, but support for schools in general.

Building Partnerships

Various writers (Allensworth and Patton, 1990; Kahn, 1982; Brown, 1984; Weisner, 1983; Feighery and Rogers, 1990) have discussed effective ways of organizing partnerships and coalitions. Feighery and Rogers (1990) pose six questions that should be answered when a group is considering forming a partnership. The answers serve to guide the decision to proceed.

1. Is there an organization already in place that could effectively and more efficiently address this problem?

2. Would the problem be more effectively and permanently solved through the joint ownership and responsibility of others, or can our organization be just as effective working on its own?
3. Are there gaps in community services that would be best met through collaborative relationships?
4. Is this a problem that is perceived as a priority by other organizations?
5. Are we willing to relinquish control of the project to a coalition, or do we just want advice?
6. Do funding sources or our own agency constraints make it impossible to give up or share control of the project?

Communication among members is a key to working partnerships. It is important for each member to be clear about expectations and about what each partner wants and is willing to contribute. "The solution is to work together, sharing problems and solutions while recognizing and supporting each other's best efforts and intentions" (Jennings, 1989:45). This is not the definitive answer to building partnerships, but the guidelines offered may be helpful in establishing cooperative efforts.

Potential Partners for Local Schools

Partnerships with schools exist among private and governmental agencies, institutions such as higher education, local health-care systems (including hospitals), media, law enforcement, business, social services, local health professionals, voluntary health organizations, and city and county governments. Possible relationships between schools and various groups are probably limited only by the imagination. Potential partners may include any of the following:

NonProfit Voluntary Health Organizations Major health-related organizations are the American Lung Association, American Heart Association, American Cancer Society, National Birth Defects Foundation—March of Dimes, Planned Parenthood, Arthritis Foundation, National Mental Health Association, National Dairy Council, National Association for Sickle-Cell Disease, and others.

Local Public Health and Educational Agencies Public health departments (county, city, and state) and state education departments are valuable partners. Some states have regional educational service districts that schools can join as members of a consortium.

City and County Governments Both city and county governments can put forth local legislation (e.g., limiting access of youth to tobacco products) that promote the health and well-being of their youth. Many committees have instituted youth commissions that focus on various health issues concerning children and adolescents. Recreation and parks departments provide many services for promoting the physical fitness of youth.

Federal Health and Education Departments At the federal level, the Division of Adolescent and School Health in the Centers for Disease Control has been a principal contributor of federal monies for drug abuse education and AIDS education. Other federal agencies include the Office of Disease Prevention and Health Promotion, and the National Institutes of Health (in particular, the National Heart, Lung, and Blood Institute; National Cancer Institute; National Institute on Mental Health; and National Institute on Drug Abuse).

Professional Organizations Organizations of medical professionals include the American Medical Association, American Dental Association, American Nurse's Association, American Optometric Association, and American Academy of Pediatrics. Professional organizations such as the National School Board Association and the National Parent-Teacher's Association have shown interest in health education. Professional health education organizations are mentioned in chapter 2.

Community Organizations Each community is unique, but most have churches; police and fire departments; local parent-teacher organizations; fraternal organizations such as Kiwanis, Rotary, Lions, and Soroptimists; and issue-related groups such as Mothers Against Drunk Driving (MADD).

Social Service Organizations Young Women's and Men's Christian Associations (YWCA, YMCA), Young Women's and Men's Hebrew Associations (YWHA, YMHA), the Junior League, Boy and Girl Scouts, Camp Fire, Inc., and Catholic Youth Services are found in many communities. The American Red Cross is highly visible throughout the country.

Health-Care Providers, Hospitals, and Crisis Centers Substance-abuse/chemical dependency centers, rape crisis centers, and mental health centers are funded in many communities. Well-known groups that support school health education include Kaiser Permanente in California, Oregon, and Hawaii; Group Health Cooperative of Puget Sound in Washington; and Harvard Community Health Plan in the Boston area. Local hospitals and health-care providers such as physicians, dentists, nurses, and health counselors are frequent collaborators in intervention programs aimed at improving the health status of school-age children.

Higher Education Institutions Various departments in two- and four-year colleges and universities, especially those with health education programs, are valuable resources.

Corporate/Business Organizations Businesses within each community have vested interests in the health status of the local youth.

Private Foundations Well-known foundations that have funded grants to initiate and promote school health education programs include the Metropolitan Life Foundation, Robert Wood Johnson Foundation, and Kellogg Foundation. For a detailed listing of foundations and other coalition sources, refer to the *Eta Sigma Gamma Monograph Series* on coalition building (Allensworth and Patton, 1990). Local foundations that support programs focused on youth exist in many communities.

Example of a Working Partnership in Health Education

In recent years, schools have been asked by federal and state governments to help solve health problems such as chemical dependency, substance abuse, and HIV transmission. Lacking in funds and expertise, schools have been turning to outside groups and agencies for help.

One small school district in a rural community has become the center of a network to address the prevention of drug and alcohol abuse. This example is typical of how governmental agencies, private groups, and community organizations can work together to solve a health problem of common concern. The program has the following features:

- The school district implemented a drug and alcohol prevention curriculum (*Here's Looking at You, 2000*) in elementary and secondary schools.
- A federal grant pays for instructional materials and part of the in-service training.
- Part of a *Healthy Me* grant from the Metropolitan Life Foundation paid for substitute teachers so that all classroom teachers could attend in-service training.
- The Parent Teacher Organization helps pay for a student peer support program (*Natural Helpers*) in the secondary schools.
- A grant from the state's Department of Social and Health Services provides the salary for a substance-abuse intervention specialist.
- Student government organizes student assembly programs targeted to discuss student issues about chemical use and abuse.
- StraighTalk, a community chemical health organization, and the school district share payment for a series of parent workshops.
- A counselor from a community youth services organization works jointly with school staff to provide group counseling for students from chemically dependent families.
- A sheriff from the county police department comes into the fifth-grade classrooms one hour per week for seventeen weeks to teach the Drug Awareness and Resistance Education (DARE) program.
- Community leaders and service clubs contribute regularly to the school program.

Most important of all, a community-wide chemical health committee with representatives from schools, parents, local businesses, government, and community organizations has been established to help solve the problem. This committee, which meets monthly, is one of the best examples of school-community partnership in action.

National Coalitions That Benefit Schools

Although schools are not a part of national coalitions, they benefit from the activities of these groups.

The National School Health Education Coalition (NaSHEC), founded in May, 1982, is open to national private-sector organizations that have an interest in school health education. Educational professional groups, voluntary health agencies, health-care professional groups, corporations, and business organizations are encouraged to join. Government agencies with an interest in school health education may appoint nonvoting representatives who are invited to participate in a liaison role. In 1990, a new category of membership for state and local coalitions became available. NaSHEC actively promotes comprehensive school health education at the national level.

The Coalition of National Health Education Organizations, formally organized in March, 1972, is composed of eight health education groups from seven national health organizations. The purposes of the Coalition are to:

- Facilitate national-level coordination, collaboration, and communication among the member organizations

- Provide a forum for the identification and discussion of health education issues
- Formulate recommendations and take appropriate action on issues affecting member interests
- Serve as a communication and advisory resource for agencies, organizations, and persons in the public and private sectors concerning health education issues
- Serve as a focus for the collaborative exploration and resolution of issues pertinent to professional health educators (Caufman, 1982)

Two recent position papers developed and widely disseminated by the Coalition focused on strengthening elementary health education ("Incentives for Elementary School Health Education") and supporting AIDS education within comprehensive school health education ("Instruction About AIDS Within the School Curriculum").

Summary

It is easy to recognize that the school health education program is the responsibility of everyone, but it requires planning and diligent networking to get all interested groups to work together to promote the health and health education of America's youth and to prevent common health problems. Forging partnerships among all in our society who have an interest in school health education is not only logical but crucial if we are to be successful in creating a pathway for lifelong health education and health promotion. Comprehensive school health education cannot be accomplished by schools alone.

The long-term goal of comprehensive school health education—to promote the health and well-being of youth—is attained through collaborative relationships among schools, community organizations and businesses, and individuals. These relationships may be formal or informal in nature and involve a wide array of organizations and individuals. The benefits that schools derive from partnerships are numerous. Community representatives and agencies not only lend support and advocacy but also their expertise to school health education.

Discussion Questions

1. Why is school health education a community affair?
2. What are some potential barriers for schools in forming partnerships with community organizations and groups?
3. What issues should be discussed and what information should be exchanged between school personnel and community agencies when they explore a potential partnership?

Application Activities

1. Identify two community coalitions or partnerships operating in your local community. Interview one school member and one community member regarding their decision to participate in the coalition. Ask them to assess the advantages and disadvantages of their membership in the coalition.
2. Design the ideal school-community partnership you would convene to address the addition of AIDS/HIV education to a K–12 school health education program. List the names of the participating agencies as well as the position/job title of the desired partners.

References

Allensworth, D., and Patton, W. 1990. Promoting school health through coalition building. *The Eta Sigma Gamma Monograph Series,* 7(2).

Brown, C. R. 1984. The art of coalition building. New York: The American Jewish Committee.

Carnegie Council on Adolescent Development. 1989. *Turning points: Preparing American youth for the 21st century: The report of the task force on education of young adolescents.* Washington, DC.

Caufman, J. 1982. A history of the coalition of national health education organizations: Its first ten years and future direction. *The Eta Sigma Gamma Monograph Series,* 1(2).

Feighery, E., and Rogers, T. 1990. *Building and maintaining effective coalitions,* Guide No. 12, How-to guides on community health promotion. Stanford: Stanford Center for Research in Disease Prevention.

Habana-Hafner, S.; Reed, H.B.; et al. 1989. *Partnerships for community development: Resources for practitioners and trainers.* Amherst: University of Massachusetts Center for Organizational and Community Development.

Jennings, W. B. 1989. How to organize successful parent advisory committees. *Educational Leadership* 47(2):42–45.

Kahn, S. 1982. *Organizing: A guide for grassroots leaders.* New York: McGraw-Hill.

Metropolitan Life Foundation. 1989. *Healthy me: Metropolitan Life Foundation initiative to promote excellence in school health education.* Metropolitan Life, Health and Safety Education Division, HEALTHY ME, One Madison Avenue, New York, NY 10010–3690.

National Commission on the Role of the School and the Community in Improving Adolescent Health. 1990. *Code blue: Uniting for healthier youth.* Alexandria, VA: National Association of State Boards of Education.

National School Health Education Coalition. 1989. *NaSHEC Newsline.* P.O. Box 515664, Dallas, TX 75251–5664.

Pine, P. 1985. *Critical issues report: Promoting health education in schools—problems and solutions.* Arlington, VA: American Association of School Administrators.

Roberts, Fitzmahan & Associates. 1979. *Natural helpers: A comprehensive program for students to help their friends and themselves.* Seattle, WA: Comprehensive Health Education Foundation.

Roberts, Fitzmahan & Associates. 1986. *Here's Looking at You, 2000.* Seattle, WA: Comprehensive Health Education Foundation.

Weisner, S. 1983. Fighting back: A critical analysis of coalition building in the human services. *Social Service Review* 57, no. 2 (June): 291–306.

9

Identifying Problem Areas:
Staying Out of Trouble

After reading this chapter and participating in application activities, the student should be able to:

1. Identify potentially controversial topics in a school health curriculum.
2. Explain why teacher training in sexuality education is critical.
3. Describe how to prevent controversies in health education from occurring.
4. Summarize laws relating to school health education.

The discipline of health education, like social studies and science, includes some controversial topics. The major causes of controversy are the differences in family value systems and the differences in religious beliefs of various segments of a community. The United States is a pluralistic society with different values, and religious, cultural, and political beliefs. In a democracy, public schools have to reflect the views of the majority without treading on the rights of minorities.

Health education addresses the immediate and future personal health needs and interests of students. Some health-related decisions made by students are difficult. Students have to be given the tools—knowledge, skills, and attitudes—to make difficult choices.

Teachers and administrators must be particularly aware of issues that could polarize a community. School districts are wise to adopt policies and procedures governing the treatment of controversial issues in the classroom. Keeping in mind the composition of the community and the background and needs of the students, administrators, teachers, and parents have to decide among themselves where they stand regarding each of the issues and how they can address them in the classroom.

People have different opinions regarding the proper role of schools and, in particular, of health education. Few people would argue against school health education in general, but some would disagree on which topics should be in the health curriculum and how they should be taught. There are two philosophical camps regarding content in health education. One camp believes that certain health topics should not be taught in the schools because they deal with personal and family matters that should be taught by the family. Another camp believes that schools have the social responsibility to educate all students to lead healthy lives and the curriculum should include all health topics. Controversies arise when people representing two opposing viewpoints try to force a school district to conform to their own beliefs.

Health education is a developing and rapidly changing field in which a variety of controversial issues arise. In public schools, the commonly encountered controversies fall into two categories: (1) issues centering on differences in values and beliefs, and (2) issues arising out of improper implementation of a curriculum. This chapter will focus on the more common issues that have generated debates in schools across the nation in recent years.

Sensitive Issues

The following section identifies some of the potentially controversial topics in school health education curricula. In describing the debates surrounding these issues, the extreme positions of opposing viewpoints are presented. These do not necessarily represent the authors views nor those of health educators in general.

Sexuality Education

In the elementary grades, sexuality education focuses on the reproductive system and the importance of the family. At the secondary level, in addition to reviewing anatomy and physiology, the "curriculum must deal with both feelings and behaviors if it is to be effective. It must address decision making and problem solving in regard to relationship issues, readiness for intercourse, use of contraception, responsibility to one's self and others and society, child rearing, the meaning of becoming an adult, the interaction of sexuality with career and prioritizing one's goals in life" (Hacker, 1981:210). Even the name of this unit of health education is sometimes controversial. Whatever it is called, it should include most of the topics mentioned above. Opponents of sexuality education argue that public schools should not be teaching these topics. Some also believe that schools should teach only the three R's—reading, writing and arithmetic. On the other hand, ample evidence indicates that many parents want help in educating their children in the area of family life. Successful marriages, family planning, healthy newborns, and healthy attitudes toward sexuality can be favorably influenced by well-planned and well-implemented family life/sexuality education programs.

Some people believe that teaching about sexuality causes young people to be sexually promiscuous. They assume that if students are not taught about sexuality, they will not engage in sexual activity. These people want the school to omit sexuality education totally or only teach students to say no. On the other hand, many educators and government officials are advocating sexuality education because they believe it leads to responsible behavior. In addition to these two opposing viewpoints, many other issues related to sexuality education are also controversial. These issues and others are discussed in this chapter.

Contraception

Many people believe that public schools should be responsible for teaching family planning to teenagers to help them avoid unwanted pregnancy. Others believe that contraception should not be taught in the public schools. They believe that if students are told to abstain from premarital sexual activities, learning about contraception will not be necessary. Also, some church doctrines consider procreation as the only reason for sexual intercourse and see no need for contraception even after marriage. Others argue that people are sexual beings and that sexual intercourse between consenting adults is a normal part of life. Planning is a necessary part of giving a newborn the best physical, emotional, and social start in life; every individual should be knowledgeable about family planning.

Prevention of Child Sexual Abuse

In recent years, the publicity and statistics surrounding sexual abuse of children have generated a demand for sexual abuse prevention curricula in the public schools. Some parents object to this because they feel the topic may traumatize their children and cause them to be fearful of adults who are family members. Advocates of prevention curricula believe that public education is one more way to help save children from abuse.

Homosexuality

At the junior high and high school levels, the study of human sexuality usually includes the topic of homosexuality. It is a topic that students will bring up in class regardless of whether it is part of the curriculum. Some people object to schools teaching about homosexuality. Others want the schools to condemn homosexuality in their teaching. Some argue that homosexuality is normal and is a life-style preference that everyone is free to choose. Statistics show that approximately 10 percent of the population is homosexual, and that proportion is most likely represented in the student population.

Alternative Life-Styles

In sexuality education, cohabitation is a subject that interests many high school students. Some parents want the school to tell students that it is wrong to have sexual relations and live together outside of marriage. In today's society, many people form intimate relationships but choose not to get married. The morality of the situation is very personal. In each class, it is likely that some students have parents who are living with others outside of marriage and finding it acceptable.

Masturbation

This is a topic of particular concern to adolescents. Students may bring it up in class when sexuality education is taught. Some people believe that masturbation is wrong and unhealthy and that students should be warned about the consequences of such activity. Others believe that masturbation is natural and is not harmful in any way.

Abortion

The controversy regarding the right of the mother versus the right of the fetus goes beyond public schools. Abortion is hotly debated at almost every level of government, hospital, and church. Advocates who favor choice believe that abortion is a legitimate option for the termination of an unwanted pregnancy. Opponents believe that the right of the fetus from the moment of conception supersedes the right of the mother. Between these two positions lies a spectrum of opinions held by people who believe that under certain circumstances abortion is the best decision.

In 1973, in the landmark case Roe v. Wade, the U.S. Supreme Court ruled that the abortion decision is between the woman and her physician during the first twelve weeks of pregnancy. After the first trimester, the state may regulate the abortion procedure in the interest of the woman's health. The court concluded that the 14th Amendment definition of *person* does not extend to the unborn fetus. This decision is being challenged by some states. The U.S. Supreme Court ruled in 1989 that the state of Missouri has a right to restrict the locations where abortion is performed when public funds are involved. The battle is continuing in the courts and state legislatures.

Death and Dying

Proponents of death education believe that children should be taught the concept that death is a part of the life cycle and that grief associated with death is part of a normal coping process. Opponents believe that death and grief are private family matters and that children should not have to discuss them in the school. They also feel that "morbid" subjects should not be included in a school curriculum.

Drug and Alcohol Education

Most people agree on the need for drug and alcohol education in the public schools, but they may not agree on the approach. Some believe that the only effective way to teach about drugs and alcohol is to cite the dangers of these chemicals and teach students to say "no". Others believe that students ultimately have to make their own decisions and be responsible for the consequences of their actions. Some argue that teaching students to make responsible decisions implies that students can choose to use chemical substances responsibly. Society continues to glamorize drinking alcohol through television and other forms of advertising that give conflicting messages to young people.

A vivid example of a controversy surrounding drug and alcohol education in a school district was an article that appeared on the front page of the *Wall Street Journal* on 10 November 1989. The headline said "*Shunned Lessons*—Even a School That Is a Leader in Drug War Grades Itself a Failure—Students Say Why Bainbridge Hasn't

Stemmed Abuse After 12-Year Effort—Struggling to Interest Parents." The article described a few high school students' attitudes toward alcohol and drug use. Those students who were interviewed gave their reasons why the drug and alcohol education program had not been effective. Several school and community members felt these particular students were not representative of the general student body (Pereira, 1989).

The article generated local and national media attention, and parents and other community members were angry about it. They accused the reporter of irresponsible and sensational reporting and blamed the schools and teachers for not teaching the curriculum. With the exception of a few people, there was general denial that drug and alcohol abuse was prevalent among young people in this upscale suburban community. The district and high school administration estimated that they spent the equivalent of two full weeks in responding to this controversy within the community and in the media.

Looking back, one can see the silver lining in the cloud of controversy that hung over the community for months. Ten months after the *Wall Street Journal* article, parents and teachers were much more aware of chemical abuse by young people. Parents, community members, and the school district are now working closer together to develop strategies to address the problem.

Health education covers many issues that deal with personal life-styles, religious beliefs, and moral values. Because these are emotional issues, they are potentially controversial. Controversies are often beyond the control of schools, as was the one described above. Understanding the issues and dealing with them in a productive manner can sometimes reap unanticipated benefits.

Curriculum Implementation Improprieties

It cannot be overemphasized that proper implementation of a health curriculum, particularly the units on sexuality education, is crucial to a successful and trouble-free program. Administrators and teachers should be aware that mistakes can undermine a curriculum by giving cause for challenges. Mistakes due to poor judgment or lack of experience are not uncommon (Gilbert, 1979). The following section describes some common pitfalls in health instruction and provides some suggestions on how to avoid them.

Inadequate Knowledge and Background

Some teachers are assigned to teach health without the necessary background or training. Health education is an area where teachers must be knowledgeable, especially about potentially controversial issues. Some parents monitor family life and sexuality education very closely. One mistake can lead to trouble for the teacher, the principal, the curriculum, and the school district. Teachers should acquire thorough and current knowledge of the subject by taking university courses, attending available workshops, and reading professional journals and books. Health teachers must be credible to students, parents, and administrators. Some teachers are assigned to teach health education against their wishes; and if a teacher really doesn't want to teach health the quality of the education suffers. Administrators are foolish to give such assignments to reluctant or untrained teachers.

Unrealistic Curriculum Goals

Many curricula have goals and objectives that can never be met. For example, the lowering of the teenage pregnancy rate, the elimination of sexually transmitted diseases, or the production of healthy adults are common objectives of health education. Education can help to achieve these goals, but it cannot counter all the other forces impinging on the behavior of individuals. Goals and objectives should be worded so that the curriculum is not set up for failure. It is natural for educators to be optimistic and hopeful, but reality dictates restraint and modesty in the language that is used. Many critics point to unachievable goal statements as indications of the failure of health education.

Not Being Prepared to Defend the Program

Teachers and principals must anticipate questions and challenges from parents about controversial topics in health education and be prepared to respond to their concerns and to explain the educational basis of the program. Some parents who oppose the program can be hostile and unreasonable and do not deserve a great deal of time and attention because they will never be satisfied. If the questions are sincere, however, parents deserve well-documented answers.

A key to defusing controversy is a clear demonstration of district commitment to the program from the school board/committee, the superintendent, the principal, and the teachers. An unambiguous statement of the program's philosophy and goals is often an effective tool against parental attacks on the program.

Inappropriate Materials or Assignments

Some teachers have made the mistake of giving students poorly drawn diagrams of reproductive organs. Parents are very critical when it comes to teaching human sexuality and reproduction: what may seem innocuous to the educator could be interpreted as pornographic. Teachers have to be thoughtful and purposeful in designing student assignments. A questionnaire on students' sexual experiences or attitudes may seem like a good teaching device, but it may violate the privacy of students, and it is against the law in some states.

Using Materials Without Preview

All audiovisual and printed materials must be previewed by the teacher before use in class. This is a basic rule for all subjects, but it is particularly important in health education. A magazine's review or a friend's recommendation is no substitute for seeing the material personally. Only the teacher knows the level of maturity of the students and the context in which the material will be used. For example, in a ninth-grade health class one teacher did not preview a student-made videotape before showing it to the whole class. The videotape showed stuffed animals using a condom and having sexual intercourse. Needless to say, a couple of parents called the superintendent's office the next day to express concern about the health curriculum and the teacher.

Inappropriate Guest Speakers

Classroom guest speakers must be selected with great care. Most schools have a policy and procedure governing the use of outside speakers in the classroom. Teachers should know in advance what a speaker is going to say in the classroom; before issuing an invitation, they should screen the speaker and give some guidelines. If a school decides to invite someone from a controversial group such as a pro-life organization, it also must be prepared to present the opposing viewpoint from a pro-choice organization. Other groups that generate controversy among parents are homosexual organizations. The principal and district administration should be consulted before speakers from controversial organizations are invited to the school. One has to weigh the benefit to students against potential parental dissension in deciding if a speaker is worth the risk of jeopardizing the whole curriculum.

Another important consideration regarding outside speakers is quality control. Some speakers have hidden agendas and may behave inappropriately in the classroom. If a speaker steps out of line during a class presentation, it is the responsibility of the teacher/host to immediately stop the class or redirect the speaker.

Prior to inviting a guest speaker, the teacher must prepare the students by giving them the necessary background information. Needless to say, the speaker's presentation should be related to the topics being studied.

Personal Bias in Teaching

Everyone has biases toward certain subjects, such as some aspects of nutrition, environmental health, health care, and personal lifestyle, but teachers must not express personal opinions or try to influence students on such matters. Teachers must recognize their own biases so that they can guard against expressing them to the students.

Using Slang

Appropriate terminology should be used in teaching health education. Students may use slang words to describe the gastro-intestinal tract or reproductive anatomy but it is unprofessional for a teacher to use slang terms. The teacher should carefully redirect students to using appropriate terms.

In addition, American classrooms are multi-cultural in nationality and slang words; for example, various parts of the reproductive tract do not mean the same for each student. Cultural diversity warrants the use of appropriate terminology in the classroom.

Personal Sexual Experience

It is difficult to understand why some teachers might discuss their sexual experience with students. It is equally inappropriate for students to be questioned about or encouraged to discuss their sexual experiences.

Behind Closed Doors

Teaching something that is not in the curriculum and then asking students not to tell their parents or the administration is a sure way of getting into trouble. Following the curriculum and keeping the administration informed can prevent trouble.

Steps for Preventing Controversies

In addition to the preceding discussion of improper implementation of a health curriculum and how to avoid them, there are three fundamental steps for preventing controversies in health education: (1) use a systematic curriculum development process involving staff, parents, and health educators; (2) have qualified and well-trained teachers and administrators; and (3) adopt district policies and procedures for handling controversial issues. All three steps are essential.

Step 1: The Process

Avoiding controversy begins with following a systematic curriculum-planning process, such as the one described in chapter 3. This process has proven to be successful because it involves a broad spectrum of people—teachers, administrators, health educators, health-care providers, parents, and community members—to arrive at a consensus on the curriculum. The process gives everyone an opportunity to hear and discuss different points of view and to resolve differences. Condensing the process may save time, but it can lead to trouble later.

A common complaint by those who object to a curriculum is that the planning committee does not represent every different viewpoint. It is difficult to appoint a truly representative committee because no one can know how everyone in the community feels about a particular subject. A committee normally has a limited number of members, and it cannot represent every opinion in the community. However, every attempt must be made to appoint to the committee a balanced cross-section of the community and to include people who are respected in the community.

Regardless of how open and inclusive the process is, some people may not agree with the final decisions on curriculum or materials. They may challenge the curriculum on the basis that it does not represent community values. The Commission on Professional Rights and Responsibilities of the National Education Association has published a booklet describing some of the organizations that oppose sexuality education. Following sound educational principles, being open, and publicizing the process are what most school districts can be expected to do.

Step 2: Training

Readers may wonder why we discuss the qualifications and credibility of teachers here. The reason is that we have seen many good health curricula undermined by controversies generated by teachers' and administrators' mistakes. Sometimes teachers who have little or no professional preparation in health education are assigned to teach health. Without proper training, teachers may use inappropriate materials and learning activities. They may act inappropriately because they do not understand the sensitive nature of the subject or are personally uncomfortable in talking about the subject. School districts that allow unqualified teachers to teach health are inviting controversy.

Students are very astute, even at a young age. They can tell whether a teacher is knowledgeable about a subject or is bluffing. No one expects a teacher to know everything, but being prepared for class is essential. When students raise a question to which the teacher does not know the answer, it is better to admit that and offer to find the answer than to guess and provide misinformation. Knowing one's own limitations and when to say "I don't know" is an important part of being knowledgeable.

In addition to being knowledgeable about the subject, teachers should be especially careful and objective in discussing potentially controversial topics. It is understandable that teachers are human and have personal opinions, but they should refrain from giving their unsolicited personal opinions. Students sometimes complain to their parents that a teacher is proselytizing and that the teacher's view is contrary to their family beliefs. This is how a controversy starts. Teachers should present both sides of issues and discuss them in an objective manner.

After adopting a curriculum, teachers and administrators must be trained in its implementation. In dealing with sensitive topics, it is risky for teachers to be spontaneous, creative, and innovative. Instruction should not deviate from the curriculum or use unapproved materials. An adopted curriculum reflects the wishes of the community. Regardless of whether teachers like the curriculum, they have the responsibility to follow it.

Step 3: Policy and Procedure

Some people will always disagree with parts of a health curriculum, even though it has the support of the staff and community. School districts should be prepared by developing policies and procedures for handling controversies (see the sample policy and procedure in fig. 9.1). Teachers and administrators need direction and guidelines for dealing with controversial issues. Such issues are a normal part of a democratic society, and they can provide stimulation for intellectual inquiry; they should not be avoided in the curriculum.

A companion policy (and procedure) to the one on controversial issues should exist for guest speakers (see fig. 9.2). High school social studies and health courses lend themselves to discussions on controversial topics. Outside speakers who have firsthand knowledge of a subject can provide a powerful educational experience for students. For example, having an AIDS patient talk to students about the disease makes a stronger impression than a teacher's lecture, but some parents may object to bringing an AIDS patient into the school. To guard against inappropriate speakers, most school districts have a policy that guides teachers and administrators.

Laws Relating to School Health Education

There are two categories of laws relating to school health education. One category is *prescriptive:* it includes laws that require schools to teach the subject of health and/or specific topics, such as drug and alcohol education. The second category of law is *protective:* it includes laws that protect the rights of students and parents by requiring schools to invite parents to review the school's curriculum on sexuality and AIDS education.

In 1985, the American School Health Association surveyed the fifty states and the District of Columbia on laws, codes, and policies related to health education in the public schools (American School Health Association, 1987). Thirty-eight states had laws mandating school health education, and seven states had laws encouraging school health education without mandating it. Twenty-seven states required health education for high school graduation, and twenty-seven states (some of them the same) required health education to be taught for a specific number of hours in grades K–12. In addition to these requirements, many states required one or more specific topics to be taught during grades K–12. For example, thirty-four states required education about drugs/alcohol/tobacco, twelve states required nutrition education, and six states required sex education.

Contrary to popular belief, state laws are not static: a law is changed or added when the public recognizes a need. In response to the recent epidemic of Acquired Immune Deficiency Syndrome (AIDS), laws have been enacted in many states to mandate AIDS education in the schools. To comply with such legal requirements, educators must often develop and implement programs on short notice. Teachers and principals need to keep up with new mandates in education and find ways to integrate them into existing school curricula.

Another area of law governing health education is parent participation in planning, developing, selecting materials for, and/or evaluating sexuality education programs. Some states require each school district to establish a committee of parents and community members to preview and help select instructional materials for health or sexuality education. After the materials have been selected and approved by the school board/committee, all parents must be notified of the availability of the materials for their review. These legal requirements must be followed by the school because some parents may not like parts of the adopted curriculum and will use noncompliance with the law as an excuse to remove or replace the curriculum.

FIGURE 9.1 Sample policy and procedure for controversial issues. (From Bainbridge Island School District, Bainbridge Island, WA.)

INSTRUCTION
POLICY 2331

POLICY 2331—CONTROVERSIAL ISSUES

A controversial issue arises when the perspective on a subject is in conflict with the interest, economic, social, or religious beliefs, group affiliations, or political expectations of a segment of the community.

Controversial issues provide stimulation to learning by stirring intellectual excitement and are thus an integral part of the normal classroom environment. Free inquiry in a democratic society requires that controversial issues arising in the normal classroom situation be handled as a regular aspect of instruction and learning in such a way as to not inhibit the dignity, the personality, or the intellectuality of either the teachers or the students.

Controversial issues arising from classroom situations and subject matter must be managed according to established procedure.

ADOPTED 10/2/86

The following procedures shall be in effect:

1. Controversial issues shall be handled as they arise and shall not be avoided in order to restrict or restrain the academic freedom of either the teacher or the student.
2. When handling controversial issues, the teacher may not present his/her own personal position as the only acceptable position on that particular issue nor seek to bring about a single conclusion to which all students must subscribe.
3. Controversial issues shall be studied with as much objectivity as possible. When dealing with a controversial issue, the teacher will provide suggested resource materials or sources of information on different aspects of the issue so that students may pursue individual reading and study in order to arrive at their individual conclusions.
4. Neither the teacher nor the student shall avoid an issue simply because it is of a controversial nature; nor shall an issue be raised merely because it is of a controversial nature.
5. The teacher shall not suppress a student's view on a controversial issue as long as the expression of that view is not derogatory, malicious, or abusive toward other students' views. On the other hand, one student shall not be permitted to dominate the discussion.
6. The handling of controversial issues does not always require an extensive examination, but all the competency of both teacher and student shall be exerted to make a clear definition of the issue.
7. Different sides of a controversial issue shall be explored.
8. In handling controversial issues, both teachers and students shall be encouraged to keep the problem-solving attitude in mind. In other words, rather than determining what is right and what is wrong in certain issues, students shall be encouraged to come to their own conclusions after independent inquiry.

REVIEWED 9/18/86

FIGURE 9.2 Sample policy and procedure on guest speakers. (From Bainbridge Island School District, Bainbridge Island, WA.)

INSTRUCTION

POLICY 2321—GUEST SPEAKERS

POLICY 2321

The Board of Directors encourages the use of guest speakers when such speakers will contribute to the curriculum program for the grade level involved.

INSTRUCTION

PROCEDURE 2321

PROCEDURE 2321—GUEST SPEAKERS

1. When a staff member believes that a guest speaker will contribute to the goals and objectives of the curriculum, the staff member will use the following procedure. At least two weeks before the proposed date for a speaker, the staff member shall submit to the principal the completed form attached. Information on the form shall include the name and affiliation of the speaker, relationship and contribution to the district's curriculum, background of the guest speaker relevant to the curriculum area, and date of the speaker's visit.

   A staff member may request a waiver of the two-week notice period, and a principal may grant such a waiver in order to accommodate the scheduling of a speaker on short notice. However, such a waiver shall be at the sole discretion of the principal, and the previous granting of such waivers shall not obligate any principal to grant a waiver for any future request.
2. Approval of a guest speaker by the principal will be exercised in a manner consistent with the principles of free inquiry and expression. When approved, the guest speaker will be expected to adhere to the purpose of the appearance.
3. If the principal has reason to believe that the appearance of the guest speaker would not contribute to the curriculum or would be harmful to the students, he/she may deny the appearance of the guest speaker. A rationale shall accompany the disapproval.
4. If the staff member and the principal believe the guest speaker's topic is controversial, *Policy and Procedure 2331—Controversial Issues* must be followed.
5. The staff member responsible for inviting the guest speaker shall have the responsibility of interrupting or suspending any proceedings if the presentation of the guest speaker is beyond the purpose of the appearance or is endangering the health and safety of students and/or staff.
6. In the event that the speaker's topic is determined to be controversial, the staff member will notify students beforehand, and any student who wishes not to attend the presentation will be given an alternative assignment.
7. Unless the principal approves otherwise, the staff member will not allow students who are not class members to hear the speaker.
8. The guest speaker will be registered in the office by the staff member on the day he/she speaks.

REVIEWED 10/2/86

FIGURE 9.2 *Continued*

GUEST SPEAKER FORM

Employees wishing to invite guest speakers will fill in the following form and return it to the building principal two weeks prior to the appearance of the guest.

The principal shall return the following form to the employee within one week from the date he/she receives it.

Any employee may request a waiver of the two-week notice period, and any principal may grant such a waiver in order to accommodate the scheduling of a speaker on short notice. However, such a waiver shall be at the sole discretion of the principal, and the previous granting of such waivers shall not obligate any principal to grant a waiver for any future request.

Name of employee ______________________________ Date requested __________

Name of guest ______________________________

Organization or affiliation ______________________________

Date of visit to school ______________________________

Relationship and contribution to the district's curriculum:

Principal approval ______________________________ Date __________

Principal disapproval ______________________________ Date __________

Students who are not class members may attend: Yes ☐ No ☐

Rationale if disapproved:

Another law that exists in many states allows individual students to be exempted from sexuality education. This law allows parents to request that their children be excused from such classes and be given alternate assignments. Teachers and principals may get complaints if they forget to inform parents in advance that a sexuality education unit is being scheduled. Alternative lessons and a system to inform parents can be built into the process of curriculum development and implementation.

The protection of student and family privacy is legislated in some states. Teachers are prohibited by law from using written or oral tests, questionnaires, surveys, or examinations to elicit the personal sexual beliefs or practices of students or their parents.

Unfortunately, some laws are so specific that they do not leave room for teachers and local health educators to exercise their professional judgment. For example, some state laws specify that all AIDS materials must emphasize sexual abstinence outside lawful marriage. This obviates the philosophical focus on decision making as part of health education teaching strategies. Conservative and religious groups who lobbied the legislature for the language regarding abstinence closely monitor the compliance of schools.

From a school district's point of view, state laws relating to health education can be both helpful and troublesome. They can be helpful because they focus attention on a need and make local debate regarding implementation unnecessary. They can be troublesome because compliance is mandatory, and any lapse in compliance can bring complaints and litigation to the teacher, administrator, and/or the school district. To avoid unnecessary controversies, teachers and administrators should make every effort to comply with the letter and intent of the laws.

Summary

This chapter identifies some of the controversial topics found in health education curricula and explains the opposing viewpoints regarding them. Controversies may also arise in schools because of mistakes and poor judgment on the part of teachers or administrators. Three steps for preventing controversies are (1) adhere to a systematic and open curriculum-planning process, (2) assign qualified teachers to teach health and provide them with in-service training in handling sensitive issues, and (3) develop policies and procedures for handling controversial issues. The chapter also discusses laws related to school health education. These can be grouped into two categories: (1) prescriptive laws, which require schools to teach certain topics or courses; and (2) protective laws, which protect the privacy and rights of students.

Discussion Questions

1. Explain why some topics of health education are controversial?
2. What should a school district do to avoid controversy without compromising a good health education program?
3. Discuss the pros and cons of laws governing health education.

Application Activity

A small group of parents complained to the superintendent and school board that a homosexual speaker was invited to talk to health classes at the high school. These parents felt that the health teacher may have been promoting the homosexual life-style. You are the health coordinator of the school district. What would you do? How would you respond to the parents?

References

American School Health Association. 1987. *School health in America: An assessment of state policies to protect and improve the health of students.* 4th ed. Kent, OH.

Gilbert, G. G. 1979. Easy ways of getting into trouble when teaching sex education. *Health Education.* (September/October).

Hacker, S. S. 1981. It isn't sex education unless . . . *Journal of School Health* 51(4):207–10. (Special issue: *Sex education in public schools.*)

Pereira, J. 1989. Shunned lessons. *Wall Street Journal,* 10 November, 1.

10

Curriculum Implementation:
From Plan to Action

After reading this chapter and participating in other application activities, the student should be able to:

1. Identify administrators' roles in successful implementation.
2. Explain the knowledge and skills needed by teachers to be effective health education instructors.
3. Outline an in-service program for implementing a new curriculum.
4. Describe the factors to consider regarding delivery and use of resources when implementing a new curriculum.
5. Suggest factors that may enhance or hinder the implementation of a health curriculum.

Even though implementation begins after curriculum development, it must be an integral part of the initial planning process. Implementation involves the initiation of a program and may include piloting a new curriculum. This chapter discusses the keys to successful implementation and the various facets of curriculum implementation.

The Keys to Successful Implementation

The most important factor for successful curriculum implementation is administrative commitment, which means that the administration is aware of the need for health education and has initiated the steps to a quality program. Administrative commitment is shown through a variety of actions. The first action is to schedule curriculum planning time, including dates for implementation. This includes designating funds in the school budget for both development and implementation. A second action is assigning the responsibility to a specific person for overseeing district-wide implementation. This may be the health education coordinator, if there is one. A third action is to give principals the responsibility for implementing the curriculum within their buildings. To do this, principals need to be involved in the development of the curriculum, so that when the program begins, they can encourage, support, and monitor it. Monitoring insures that the intended curriculum is followed. Principals need to emphasize to their teachers that they must follow a new curriculum to ensure the integrity of subsequent evaluation. A final action that shows administrative commitment is allowing teachers to *buy into* the curriculum. Buying into the curriculum comes about when teachers are involved in the planning and developmental stages. They should assist in presenting the concepts of the curriculum to their own schools, including parents, as the whole building becomes involved. They should also participate in pilot programs, in-service training, and in the evaluation and revision of the curriculum.

Starting the Program

Curriculum implementation starts with determining what is needed to ensure its success. This is done by answering the following questions. Who will hire and/or assign teachers the responsibility for health education? Will in-service programs be needed and what kind? What materials are needed for in-service training and for implementation? What is the best plan for making resources available to the teachers and for monitoring the nature and extent of their use? Is there a need to promote the program to students, to the community, and to the parents? Will there be problems that might hinder implementation?

Assigning Qualified Teachers for Teaching Health

Ideally, all teachers of health education should be qualified, but "there are more unqualified teachers teaching health than any other subject . . . Health education has its own special content that must be treated with care . . . Nonetheless, in many districts, individuals with no training in health stand in front of classes teaching consumer health, environmental health, drug education, disease prevention, nutrition and sex education. This is not the route to quality health education . . ." (Pine, 1985:39).

People professionally prepared in health education understand its wide scope. They recognize how behavior is related to and affects knowledge and attitudes. Teacher competency is required for effective presentation of the health education curriculum and for relating well to students. See appendix 3 for health educators' competencies.

Expertise is attained through university education in professional preparation programs in Health Education. In general, professional preparation programs for school health education include "(1) basic preparation in the social and behavioral sciences, the biomedical sciences, and education; (2) professional preparation in health topics and issues, in processes and methodologies of teaching/learning, and in professional socialization; and (3) familiarity with the field of practice" (NCATE, 1990:19). Expertise can also be attained through in-service training and continuing education programs. When unqualified teachers are assigned to teach health, in-service programs become imperative.

What better way to illustrate the importance of professional preparation in health education than by reporting what students have to say about teachers and how they teach health. Students in grades 4–12 were asked, "Please tell us what you think teachers should do when teaching health?" Their responses included the following:

- Show more than tell, because people seem to be more interested if they can do more.
- Get into it and not just give us a book and give us an assignment.
- Talk to us and tell us things of health so we can understand instead of just reading it out of a book.
- Use current articles about recent discoveries and happenings.
- Classes should include sometimes open discussion, etc., not the old puritanical lecturing by the omniscient teacher where students are empty voids to be filled by the gods of teaching.
- I think the teacher should not just teach the heart, bones; they should teach more about emotions that can affect health.
- Be open and honest.
- Give truthful information.
- Teach us things that we need to know in a way that moves us to concern and keeps us interested. (Trucano, 1984:24–27)

Additionally, unpublished data from the *Students Speak* study revealed what students said teachers should do in health:

- Don't be afraid to teach us what we need to know.
- Ask what the kids want to learn about because a lot of stuff they teach us we already know.
- Teach the things involving our life now and in the future.
- Teach more about things that directly affect people.
- Listen to how we feel because we may have something to contribute.

- Be more friendly to students (than math and science teachers) because in the case of suicide or VD, students should have someone to turn to.

Students do care about the role model the teacher projects. It concerns them whether the teacher is in good health and whether the teacher is well educated in health. Specific student statements from *Students Speak* illustrate this concern:

- Be knowledgeable; have a clue, be a nice person, be competent.
- They should have a good attitude and be willing to take time with students.
- The teacher should be healthy and very open with problems.
- Be prepared—know what they are talking about. (Trucano, 1984:28)

Ann Nolte and William Kane make the following statement: "Just as a teacher of science who does not practice scientific inquiry is a liability to the educational program, a teacher of health who does not practice a healthy life-style is a poor role model for students and thus a liability to the educational program" (1987:3).

Those who guide the development, planning, and implementation of health education curricula and those who instruct within them need expertise in the discipline. They need to keep up-to-date on health information and teaching strategies. They also need to understand the different family and cultural backgrounds that affect how their students process health information. No longer will it suffice for those without professional preparation in health education to be assigned as the school health coordinator or health teacher.

At the lower elementary level, all teachers will be teaching health, but they cannot be expected to be highly trained in health education. Most elementary teachers fulfill the criteria of being able to use a curriculum and being able to relate to their students. The lower elementary grade teachers probably have health background in growth and development, family relationships, health careers, dental health, safety education, and nutrition. They may need in-service training in the areas of human senses, mental health, substance abuse, and disease transmission. At the upper elementary level, teachers who are responsible for health education need background in sexuality education, mental health, substance abuse, consumer health, and anatomy and physiology. They probably will have a background in community health, dental health, disease control, safety education, and family relationships.

At the secondary level, some school districts are recruiting professionally prepared health educators and assigning them to teach comprehensive health education. However, other districts cannot support full-time health educators because of student enrollment and/or budget constraints. Decreasing enrollments in a district may necessitate the use of teachers from other academic fields to teach health. Thus, reality may require school administrators to assign teachers in related fields (e.g., physical education, home and family life, science, social studies) as health instructors. Administrators should be aware that the methods for teaching health and the major health issues confronting young people may not have been part of these teachers' undergraduate and graduate teacher preparation programs. Teachers who are trained in other disciplines have various strengths and weaknesses as health teachers.

Physical educators focus on the physical aspects of well-being. Their undergraduate preparation generally includes courses in anatomy and physiology, cardiovascular fitness, exercise physiology, first aid/CPR, and injuries. They usually lack courses in sexuality education, substance use and abuse, nutrition, consumer health, community health, mental health, disease prevention, and environmental health. They are well prepared to facilitate learning activities in the gymnasium/field environment but lack experience in classroom teaching strategies.

Science educators teach about anatomy and physiology, but very little of what they teach is applied to the human body and specifically to the human being as a whole. They do not focus on life-style and well-being or on decision making to achieve well-being. They too lack courses in sexuality education, substance use and abuse, consumer health, community health, and mental health.

Home and family life educators emphasize marriage and family relationships and the economics of the household. Traditional home and family life educators are hesitant to provide learning experiences for decision-making skills relating to human sexuality and risk-taking health behaviors; contemporary home and family life educators are more apt to include these health issues because they may have preparation in these areas. However, contemporary home and family life educators may lack preparation in physical well-being, disease prevention and health promotion, and substance use and abuse. They usually have a good background in nutrition.

School nurses have a strong background in safety, disease and disease prevention, and the health-care delivery system. They know about prescription drugs but may lack knowledge about illegal drugs and behaviors associated with using them. Unless they have taken special health education courses, they may tend to focus on disease and illness rather than on well-being; they may stress reproductive biology but not the feelings and behaviors youngsters have about growing and developing. Depending also on whether or not they have had special preparation, they may lack knowledge about learning and teaching theories, lesson planning, and the use of instructional materials.

Social studies teachers have preparation in psychology but usually not in mental health and well-being. They lack knowledge about most of the other content areas of health education. Their teaching may not focus on risk-taking behaviors or health behaviors in general.

When teachers are selected from other disciplines to teach health, the choice must be based on the following selection criteria. One criterion is a person's academic background as well as the person's willingness to attend summer school and workshops to learn more about health topics, acquire insights into health teaching strategies, and become familiar with health resources. A second criterion for selecting teachers is that they want to teach health because they value the subject. A third criterion for selecting a health teacher is the ability to relate to young people. Health education touches on issues that are part of young people's everyday lives, and students are aware of whether or not a teacher cares about what they say and do. Furthermore, the teachers chosen should have life-styles that do not conflict with what is taught.

In-service Training and Implementation

In-service activities are almost always a necessity for the users of a new curriculum. These include workshops, courses, and seminars in health education.

As suggested by the American Association of School Administrators survey,

> respondents often reported that they have trouble finding qualified staff. Teachers who are not qualified must be trained for the task. Further, it is often necessary to raise the teachers' appreciation of the importance of health education. Many elementary teachers do not have this appreciation, and their attitudes create a major problem in promoting health. . . .
>
> . . . the amount of time and the type of training teachers need will vary. If a program focuses on behavior change, it may require

> different training methods from those used to impart knowledge . . . If you're going to deal with information, says Tritsch, 'then short one-hour sessions might be fine. If you're going to get into skill development and attitudes . . . you'll have to deal with more than content.' " (Pine, 1985:40–41).

In-service training is crucial for a curriculum to be carried out as planned. It gives teachers a clear understanding of expectations related to the curriculum, and it gives them more confidence. As stated earlier, it also helps them buy into the program. In-service activities reassure parents that the curriculum will be implemented as written. Most important, in-service training makes for better student learning, since teachers are prepared to teach.

Someone needs to be responsible for the overall planning of in-service training. A number of people could do this: the health education coordinator; the administrator who directs curriculum or plans staff development; the health education teacher, if this person has assistance and released time; or even an outside consultant employed by the school district for this purpose. The in-service coordinator may do all the planning and then execute the plan.

The overall tasks in setting up in-service programs center around the following concerns:

- *What kind of training is needed?* For an ongoing curriculum, in-service activity may need to deal only with updating. A new program or an elementary program will require teaching strategies, school district policies, selected resources, and philosophy. As much as possible, the training should simulate actual classroom activity. It should review health needs, interests, and developmental characteristics.
- *Who needs the training?* Teachers definitely will be the focus. In addition, principals, counselors, school nurses, and parents may take part. "In Arkansas, where the state departments of education and health and the University of Central Arkansas are helping teachers get ready for new state health education standards, team training is the rule. Arvil Burks, a health educator at the university in Conway, says that when a new training project begins, superintendents and principals are contacted about attending even before teachers . . . " (Pine, 1985:40)
- *Who provides the training?* Outside consultants can be scheduled to be a part of in-service training. Master teachers within the district may be able to provide some or all of the training. Special training may be available in support of packaged programs selected. Health education faculty from higher education institutions may also provide in-service training.
- *How much time will be needed, and when will individuals attend?* In-service training can take place on a weekend or one or more afternoons after school. It could be done during released time or in the summer. In some school districts, the education association that represents teachers might be involved, especially if conditions of inservice have been negotiated in their contracts.
- *What will be the costs?* In some school districts, participants pay and then receive college credit or an upgrade on the salary schedule; other districts pay teachers to attend. Some districts provide substitutes and release teachers to attend. Other costs may include consultant fees, rental of space and equipment, and snacks.

- *What instructional materials are needed?* Materials identified for the curriculum should be ordered early to be available for the in-service program. As much as possible, teachers need hands-on experience with the materials.
- *What are the logistics?* Will the sessions be held within the district or at a community or university site? The facility and the multimedia resources and equipment must be reserved. Check to see if there are enough outlets and electrical cords, extra bulbs, and batteries, and check to see that everything works. Determine the kind of publicity needed and who will arrange it.
- *Who prepares the evaluation procedures for the in-service sessions?* Decide who will administer, analyze, and evaluate the program and who will use the results.

Resources and Implementation

It is essential that curriculum materials adopted by the district be available for implementation. They should be ordered early enough so that all resources are received and cataloged (accounted for by whatever system a school district uses) and in place when the program begins.

Careful attention must be given to procedures for making materials available to teachers. For example, if a curriculum involves the use of torsos, are they to be housed in each building or at a district office? Because they are expensive, the preference may be to house them at a district distribution center. However, teachers may make more effective use of them if they are housed in each building; the closer the materials are to teachers, the more use the materials get. Materials in a classroom are used more extensively than those in a school library, and much more than those in a central repository.

If packaged curricula have been incorporated in the district's health curriculum, then decisions must be made on how to utilize them. Because they may represent a large expense, procedures for their use by groups, classes, and grades must be considered. In some cases the container tub, which houses the objectives and materials, is kept in a central storage area and checked out for a specific amount of time. Thus, in one school district, three or four elementary schools might use one tub. In another school district, where there may be three or four third grades in one building, a tub for third grade might be stored in the school itself, probably in the school library. Some smaller packaged curricula, such as those available from voluntary health agencies, might be housed in each teacher's room because they are made available free or at nominal costs. Finally, some packaged curricula may be available on loan from agencies or regional educational service districts.

Determining the nature and extent of the use of resources is important, especially in the first months of the new program. How much a resource is used may depend on availability, ease of acquisition, or the lack of alternatives, rather than its quality as a resource. Lack of use may occur because a resource is hard to acquire. Satisfaction with a resource is as important as how well it is used. Monitoring of resources allows for appropriate changes early in the implementation process.

Program Promotion New curricula need promotion in communities to let people know what schools teach about health and how they teach it, to avoid confusion about the health education curriculum. Such promotion also ensures that school personnel see the importance of the program and make it a part of their teaching. This is especially true of elementary school curricula.

Promotion may occur in a variety of ways. Local newspapers and radio and television stations may do stories highlighting selected aspects of the curriculum. Presentations to parent-teacher-student associations and to community groups are excellent ways to promote health curricula. Enlisting the support of health professionals through their professional organizations or by giving presentations to them also promote curricula.

Pilot Programs

Pilot programs can be used to determine what curricula or resources to use. For example, various texts may be piloted to determine whether any or all are acceptable. Two drug curricula might be tried to determine what is more effective. Thus a pilot program tests some or all of the teaching activities and materials. Teachers who do piloting try to determine the effectiveness and appropriateness of teaching activities if these are already written for them, to assess the quality and usefulness of the resources as well as the logistics of resource use, and to determine the appropriateness of objectives. Even a limited pilot provides information to guide any major changes needed in the curriculum design. The decision to pilot is based on how much time and budget the district has allocated.

In piloting a curriculum, several conditions are important; for example, enough time must be available for teachers to have a good chance to use and evaluate the material. Some uniform instrument or system for evaluation must exist so that all people involved can provide the necessary information. One of the best ways to evaluate the pilot curriculum is for teachers to meet together and discuss its strengths, weaknesses, and problems. This is time-consuming but effective.

Administrators, especially principals, must cooperate. They can help by selecting teachers who they feel will give a new program not only a critical look but a good chance to succeed. Principals need to give these teachers additional support because they have taken on additional responsibilities.

Implementation Difficulties

As mentioned earlier, the lack of qualified staff may affect the success of implementation. In-service training may not be enough if the persons assigned to teach health lack specific qualifications. Chapter 5 discussed whether or not teaching activities should be a part of a curriculum. When qualified staff are not available, the authors feel that providing teachers with suggested teaching activities gives a curriculum a better chance of succeeding.

Another potential difficulty comes from special-interest groups, which can sideline an entire program. Careful curriculum design, well-chosen materials, parental involvement, and knowledgeable teachers can prevent such problems. See chapter 9 for more information on sensitive health issues and how to work with them.

Resources have been mentioned already as a contributory factor in successful programs. Lack of resources or resources that are not in place at the beginning of the program can mean the failure of implementation.

Insufficient lead time to plan, develop, and carry out programs; failure to budget enough money; and lack of qualified leadership for planning and implementation all can spell disaster even when there is good curriculum design.

Insufficient instructional time can destroy programs. The old alternating days or rainy-day programs caused health education to become almost nonexistent. In the past, people who provided leadership for school health instruction were not knowledgeable about the academic base and the teaching processes needed to help young people make health decisions. Those in charge would bring in a speaker for an hour-long assembly on drugs and feel the job of educating youth to say no to drugs had been accomplished. Health education requires the same kind of long-term, carefully planned, carefully presented program that any other academic subject requires. Chapter 3 discusses time allocation for the various subjects in a curriculum at the elementary level and course requirements at the secondary level.

Monitoring the Instructional Program

Successful program implementation includes a review after a period of use to determine whether or not the curriculum is being implemented as designed. Other benefits from monitoring a program are to find out what is good about the curriculum and what needs further effort (i.e., more in-service training, different ways to distribute materials, revision of content). Monitoring is a long-term, ongoing process, but it is especially intense in the first couple of years until the program is stabilized.

A system of different kinds of assessment should be devised. For example, secondary students might be asked at the end of a semester program to respond to questions such as these: "Did you feel that the detail of the health education units covered was about right, too superficial, or too detailed?" "What areas of health do you feel you would have liked the course to cover that it did not?" Teachers and parents could be asked to complete a survey or or to come to a meeting to voice their suggestions for improving programs. Principals should be able to suggest improvements as a result of monitoring the program. A more formal evaluation of programs is discussed in chapter 11.

Summary

Without plans for implementation, programs are doomed to failure. Implementation starts with administrative commitment in the form of scheduling, budgeting, and designating someone to be responsible for seeing that all procedures are completed and continued. Implementation involves the selection of qualified teachers and provision of in-service training for teachers and others; the procurement, organization, and delivery of resources; and the promotion of programs.

Discussion Questions

1. Why do you think administrative commitment is essential for successful program implementation?
2. How would you determine the kind of in-service training needed?
3. Some people would rather not promote a program through publicity. Why do you think they would rather not?
4. What are some stumbling blocks to implementation?

Application Activities

1. Suggest how you would monitor the nature and extent of resource usage of a new health curriculum in a school district with four elementary schools and a combined middle-senior high school.
2. Write a short press release for a local newspaper to promote the new health instructional program in the middle school grades.

3. You are the health education coordinator for a school district. Develop a checklist that you will use as you develop an in-service program for a comprehensive health education curriculum for kindergarten through middle school.

References

National Council for Accreditation of Teacher Education (NCATE). 1990. *NCATE approved curriculum guidelines.* Washington, DC.

Nolte, A., and Kane, W. M. 1987. *Health education today: Investing in our children's future.* Reston, VA: Joint Publication of the Association for the Advancement of Health Education and the American College of Preventive Medicine.

Pine, P. 1985. *Critical issues report. Promoting health education in schools—Problems and solutions.* Arlington, VA: American Association of School Administrators.

Trucano, L. 1984. *Students speak.* Seattle: Comprehensive Health Education Foundation.

11

Evaluation:
Determining Curriculum Implementation and Effectiveness

After reading this chapter and participating in application activities, the student should be able to:

1. Distinguish between process and outcome evaluation.
2. Describe the essential components of a process evaluation.
3. Describe the components of an outcome evaluation design.
4. Select appropriate instruments for a process evaluation.

After a health education curriculum has been carefully planned and implemented, we need to ask how well it is working and whether its goals and objectives are being met. A well-designed evaluation should provide answers to these questions. This chapter describes the purposes and importance of curriculum evaluation, different types of evaluation, some unique characteristics of evaluating health education, practical designs for evaluating school health curricula, data-collection tools, and evaluation reports.

Purposes and Importance of Program Evaluation

Without evaluation, how does one know if a curriculum is achieving its goals and objectives? Program evaluation may mean different things to different people; it may be seen as a way to determine the effectiveness of a curriculum, as a management tool, as a way to improve the implementation of the curriculum, or as a way to provide information for policy decisions. In school health the two questions that are most often asked of evaluators are (1) is the curriculum being implemented properly and (2) is the curriculum having an impact on students? Teachers, administrators, students, parents, the school board, and health-care professionals want to know if the school health curriculum really works. If evaluation information is not available, people may draw their own conclusions on the basis of hearsay or personal impressions. School administrators need objective information for making decisions such as discontinuing or expanding a program. For example, if a particular curriculum on AIDS education is being piloted in one school, at the end of a given period of time the administration needs to decide whether to expand the curriculum to other schools or to discontinue it. If an evaluation process has been established during program implementation, data should be readily available for analysis and making the decision. Evaluative information is also helpful in selecting a program.

In the book *Evaluation of Health Promotion and Education Programs,* the following ten major purposes for an evaluation are cited:

1. Determining the rate and level of attainment of program objectives
2. Ascertaining strengths and weaknesses of program elements for decision making and program planning
3. Monitoring standards of performance and establishing quality-assurance and control mechanisms
4. Determining the generalization of an overall program or program elements to other populations
5. Contributing to the base of scientific knowledge
6. Identifying hypotheses for future study
7. Meeting the demand for public or fiscal accountability
8. Improving the professional staff's skills in the performance of program planning, implementation, and evaluation activities

9. Promoting positive public relations and community awareness
10. Fulfilling grant or contract requirements (Windsor et al., 1984:15)

It is impossible for any one evaluation to achieve all these purposes, but an evaluator should consider the importance of each purpose in relation to the situation. A skilled evaluation may be able to accomplish a number of purposes at once.

Types of Evaluation

Related to the different purposes of evaluation are different types and levels of evaluation. The following are common terms that describe different kinds of evaluations of school programs.

Formative evaluation is designed to assess the implementation process. Its goal is to improve the program by determining its strengths and weaknesses as it is being implemented. The evaluator gathers information on the instructional process, teacher training, time allocated for the curriculum, and availability of instructional materials.

Summative evaluation is normally conducted after a curriculum or program has been implemented for at least several years. It determines the effectiveness and impact of the curriculum. Information is used for making funding or policy decisions, such as elimination or continuation of a program. Local school districts rarely conduct summative evaluation unless it is required and paid for by a grant or other outside funding source.

Process evaluation determines to what extent a curriculum is being implemented as designed. Data may be qualitative in nature and include procedures, time allocation, administration, and teacher attitude. Similar to formative evaluation, process evaluation is designed to improve implementation, but it can be conducted at any time.

Outcome evaluation is used to gather information relating to student learning outcomes such as knowledge, skills, and attitudes. It determines short-term results, whereas summative evaluation determines long-term impact.

Uniqueness of Health Education Evaluation

Most health educators would agree that the ultimate goal of school health education is to promote healthy life-styles, "to endow children with an *enduring* sense of the value of health and with the knowledge, attitudes, and motivations that would make them opt for healthful living practices years after they have left school—the rest of their lives" (Hochbaum, 1982:14). This is a laudable and all-encompassing goal, but its achievement is impossible to evaluate. With good intentions, health educators sometimes raise expectations by establishing overly ambitious curriculum goals that cannot be achieved. For example, a two-week unit on sexuality education cannot be expected to reduce significantly the incidence of teenage pregnancy. Because it is very difficult to assess and demonstrate long-term effects of school health education on specific behavior, curriculum developers should write realistic curriculum objectives while keeping long-term goals in mind.

Another unique aspect of school health education is that much of student behavior occurs outside of school. Although research provides much information on factors that promote good health, it cannot be easily determined how frequently students use seat belts, control weight, exercise, abstain from

A giant toothbrush and a large model of teeth, gums, and jaw help students participating in the Growing Healthy curriculum learn about dental health. (Reprinted with permission of the American Lung Association.)

tobacco, and eat proper diets. Therefore in determining if the curriculum objectives have been met, information about some student health habits has to come from self-reporting, the reliability of which depends on trust between the students and the evaluator.

Because affective and psychomotor domains of learning are difficult to evaluate, many evaluations focus only on the cognitive aspect of a curriculum. Some experts believe that objectives in the affective and psychomotor domains, which are very important in health education, are often overlooked in evaluation because they are difficult to measure (Bloom, Madeus, and Hastings, 1981).

Another difficulty in evaluating health education is the determination of long-term effects of health instruction. The outcomes do not become manifest until long after the instructional program has ended. For example, students in fourth grade are taught about the effects of smoking tobacco. Since very few students in fourth grade actually smoke, it is difficult to know if the instruction is effective. The evaluation focuses on the acquisition of knowledge and attitude, not behavior. Determining the effect on behavior of an instructional unit on smoking should be attempted four to eight years after instruction in the fourth grade. In addition, long-term objectives are difficult to measure because students often leave school or move away. The logistics of administering a student questionnaire four or five years after instruction are cumbersome. Even if data are collected, one cannot be sure that the changes observed are the result of instruction rather than other influences such as the media, or state and federal laws. Evaluators have to recognize that establishing a cause-and-effect relationship between a school health education curriculum and the behavior of students is often beyond the scope of program evaluation.

It has been established that students gain knowledge about health through health education, and even though "knowledge does not necessarily translate into desirable attitudes and behavior" (Harris and Associates, 1988:4), there are indications of the positive impact of educational programs.

There are factors other than knowledge that influence health behavior. For example, educators are fighting an uphill battle against the powerful medium of television in promoting sexual abstinence among adolescents. The 1988 Harris survey for the Metropolitan Life Foundation found that comprehensive health education which covers many topics and grades can have a positive impact on student behavior if continued for several years.

- Whereas 43% of students with one year of health education have a drink sometimes or more often, that proportion decreases to 33% for students who have had health education for three years.
- Twenty percent of students with one year of health education smoke a cigarette sometimes or more often, as opposed to 14% among those having had health education for three years.
- In contrast to 13% of students having received health education for one year who have taken drugs a few times or more, only 6% of those with three years of health education have done so.
- The proportion of those who have ridden with a driver who has been drinking decreases from 70% for students with one year of health education to 63% for students with three years of health education. (Harris and Associates, 1988:5).

Even though it is difficult to establish unequivocal effects of health education, survey results indicate that students who have had three or more years of comprehensive health education are more knowledgeable and have better attitudes and health behavior patterns (Harris and Associates, 1988).

The case for school health education is based on the belief that education does make a difference. If educators waited for definitive proof of curriculum effectiveness before implementing a curriculum program, very few subjects would be taught. Social studies education is in a similar dilemma. Although one of the main goals of social studies is better citizenship, no program evaluation has shown a cause-and-effect relationship between social studies learning and good citizenship. Nevertheless, this basic faith in education does not negate the need to determine program effectiveness. Evaluation methodology has improved in recent years as a result of new technology in sampling and data analysis. The issue is the distribution of available resources—how much money and effort should be allocated to program implementation and how much to evaluation?

Evaluation Design

The design for evaluating a health education curriculum is usually dictated by the purpose of the evaluation. A school seeking information for program improvement would be likely to use the process evaluation model. On the other hand, information to prove that a curriculum has had an impact on student behavior would be obtained by using a summative or outcome evaluation model. No single evaluation can address all the different purposes of evaluation—every situation is unique. The evaluator must be flexible and realistic about matching the design to the specific requirements for a particular program. According to the Joint Committee on Standards for Educational Evaluation (1981), evaluations must have utility, feasibility, propriety, and accuracy, which means they must be informative and timely, realistic and practical, discrete and ethical, and sound and valid.

According to Gold and Basch (1986), all evaluations have the following characteristics:

1. *Systematic*—following logical steps designed to lead to a point at which conclusions can be drawn

2. *Empirical*—based on observation
3. *Reductive*—taking large amounts of information and reducing it to summary statements and conclusions
4. *Replicable*—producing similar results if done by others using the same methods.

In other words, evaluation is a scientific process, but it does not have to be experimental.

In school settings, process evaluation and outcome evaluation are the two types commonly used. Therefore, only these two types of evaluation designs are discussed in this section. *Process evaluation* is done for the purpose of improving a program. It can be conducted internally by staff or externally by an outside evaluator or a review panel during or after curriculum implementation. The kinds of information to be gathered may include the following:

1. Curriculum policy and responsibilities
2. Leadership for curriculum development and implementation
3. Input from parents, teachers, administrators, health-care providers
4. Staff qualification and in-service training
5. Instructional delivery system
6. Instructional methods and activities
7. Curriculum content
8. Instructional materials and resources
9. Student learning (Nelson, 1986: ix–xi)

These and other items can be organized into a checklist with descriptors specifying the desired standards (see the Wisconsin Department of Public Instruction checklist, figure 11.1). Information on these items can be gathered through teachers' and administrators' surveys, interviews, and observation.

Outcome evaluation determines the effectiveness of the curriculum at the end of a given period of time. It measures cognitive learning and student attitudinal and behavioral changes as they relate to the goals and objectives of the curriculum. Methods of collecting data may include tests, interviews, questionnaires, observations, and review of student health records and other records.

Short-term cognitive objectives are relatively easy to measure. For example, a paper-and-pencil test can easily determine if students know different nutrients and their value. However, long-term affective domain objectives such as valuing weight maintenance are difficult to measure. An eclectic approach, using a variety of data-gathering methods, may be necessary to obtain evaluative information in the affective domain.

Collecting Data

In evaluating school health education programs, one should gather data from multiple sources. For example, if a school wants to evaluate its health education program in order to make improvements, a checklist such as the one developed by the University of Wisconsin—Madison (figure 11.1) may be used to gather the necessary information. Data from different sources, such as students, teachers, administrators, parents, and health-care providers, would provide the most complete picture of the program.

1. A survey of teachers' opinions on curriculum implementation could include the following questions. Is the amount of time allocated sufficient? Is the material appropriate? Do students achieve the curriculum objectives? What are the strengths and weaknesses of the curriculum? Do you have suggestions for program improvement?
2. An administrator's survey can include questions like the following. In your judgment, has the curriculum been implemented properly? Do teachers have the necessary background and training? Are instructional materials being used appropriately?

FIGURE 11.1 Checklist for evaluating a school health education program. (Reprinted/excerpted from *A Guide to Curriculum Planning in Health Education* with permission from the Wisconsin Department of Public Instruction, 125 South Webster, Madison, WI 33702.)

Checklist for Evaluating a School Health Education Program

KEY: A = COMPLETELY
B = SOMEWHAT
C = NOT AT ALL

Criteria	A	B	C	Recommended Action
A. POLICY AND CURRICULUM The district has a planned health education program with identified goals, objectives, and scope and sequence of instruction for grade levels consistent with the current state curriculum guidelines.				
1. A written statement of the district's policy regarding the health education program is available.				
2. The district has a health education curriculum consistent with the current state health instruction guidelines.				
a. The health education curriculum is up to date.				
b. The health education curriculum includes a statement about health education philosophy, grade-level objectives, and scope and sequence of content.				
3. Responsibilities are defined for all persons involved in the health education program (principals, teachers, school nurses, and others).				
B. STAFF The district has assigned personnel to provide leadership for the implementation and maintenance of a comprehensive health education program and has provided the necessary resources.				
1. A person at the district level has been named health education coordinator with delegated responsibility for providing leadership to the district health education coordinating team.				
a. The district coordinator and coordinating team are provided with time and support to carry out duties.				
2. The person with primary leadership responsibility has interest and professional preparation in health education.				
3. The person with leadership responsibility coordinates school health education activities with community health activities, working with representatives of official and volunteer health agencies, professional health associations, and other groups concerned with health education.				
4. The district provides the resources (funding, personnel, materials) necessary to operate the health education program.				
C. COMMUNITY INPUT AND RESOURCES Health education programs are coordinated with community health programs. Representatives of public and private agencies and organizations, as well as students and parents, are involved in the planning and/or implementation of the program.				

FIGURE 11.1 *Continued*

KEY: A = COMPLETELY
B = SOMEWHAT
C = NOT AT ALL

Criteria	A	B	C	Recommended Action
1. An active school and community health education advisory group is involved in planning, implementing, and/or evaluating the school health education program.				
2. Students are involved in planning, implementing, and/or evaluating the school health education program.				
3. Parents are involved in planning, implementing, and/or evaluating the school health education program.				
4. A guide or directory is available and includes information about community and district resources which support health education.				
5. Community and district resources are screened and evaluated for possible use for inservice training programs in health education.				
6. Teachers are aware of health counseling and health service resources provided by the district and the community.				
7. The community is utilized as a laboratory for student experiences in health education.				
D. STAFF QUALIFICATIONS AND INSERVICE Persons who provide instruction in health education have had professional preparation in health education through preservice or inservice training.				
1. Opportunities for inservice training in health education are available to staff members, support staff, and others.				
2. Teachers are involved in the planning of the inservice training programs.				
3. Inservice training opportunities in health education receive emphasis comparable to that given to inservice training opportunities in other academic subject areas.				
4. Teachers at the elementary and secondary levels other than health instructors have had preservice or inservice preparation in health education.				
5. Those teaching health courses in junior and senior high schools have a major, minor, and/or master's in health education.				
6. The district supports and provides health promotion activities for the staff.				
E. INSTRUCTION ORGANIZATION The educational experience of each student in the elementary school and in the secondary school includes identifiable health instruction.				
1. The philosophy, goals, and objectives for health instruction are consistent with those included in the current state health instruction guidelines.				

FIGURE 11.1 *Continued*

KEY: A = COMPLETELY
B = SOMEWHAT
C = NOT AT ALL

Criteria	A	B	C	Recommended Action
2. Objectives in terms of students' knowledge, attitudes, and behavior related to health have been established at each grade level.				
3. Specific time is allocated for health instruction to achieve stated objectives.				
4. Health instruction is integrated and correlated with other subject areas when such practice will achieve stated health education objectives.				
5. Credit equal to that given for instruction in other academic subjects is given for health instruction.				
6. At the elementary level, the health instruction program is coordinated within the total instructional program.				
7. Students at the junior high school level (except students excused) receive discrete health instruction for at least one semester or the equivalent.				
8. Students at the senior high school (9–12) level (except students excused) receive discrete health instruction as a graduation requirement for at least one semester meeting daily or the equivalent.				
9. Students at the senior high school level have the opportunity to select an elective course in health education.				
F. INSTRUCTION—ACTIVITIES/METHODS Health instruction focuses upon attitudes and problem solving as well as knowledge.				
1. A balance exists between attitude development and cognitive approaches to health education in the classroom.				
2. Instructional activities are planned and developed in such a way as to enable students to: a. grow in self-awareness; that is, develop a positive sense of identity and self-esteem;				
b. develop skills for effective decision-making;				
c. grow in coping skills; that is, apply learning in daily living.				
3. The following methods are used separately or in combination when appropriate. a. Problem solving				
b. Demonstration				
c. Laboratory experimentation				
d. Lecture-discussion				
e. Reading and writing projects				
f. Discussion—large and small group				

FIGURE 11.1 *Continued*

KEY: A = COMPLETELY
B = SOMEWHAT
C = NOT AT ALL

Criteria	A	B	C	Recommended Action
g. Student projects				
h. Research				
i. Community projects				
G. INSTRUCTION CONTENT The content of health education is designed to serve current and future student health needs.				
1. Content centers on health promotion/wellness, prevention, and maintenance of positive health rather than illness, disease, and problems.				
2. The major content includes the following, and the degree of emphasis on each area is based on assessed needs of students. a. Accident prevention and safety				
b. Community health				
c. Consumer health				
d. Environmental health				
e. Family life education				
f. Mental and emotional health				
g. Nutrition				
h. Personal health				
i. Prevention and control of disease				
j. Substance use and abuse				
H. MATERIALS RESOURCES Materials used in health education are current and accurate.				
1. Materials are up to date.				
2. Materials are scientifically accurate.				
3. Materials are selected for their contribution to meeting objectives of the health education program.				
4. Instruction is enriched by the use of materials available from official and volunteer health agencies and professional associations.				
5. Instruction is enriched by the use of current audiovisual materials, such as films, filmstrips, models, charts, radio and TV programs, and tape recordings.				
I. EVALUATION A plan exists for evaluating the health education program.				
1. A planned program of evaluation will appraise the effectiveness of health education in terms of student growth in: a. knowledge related to health,				

FIGURE 11.1 *Continued*

KEY: A = COMPLETELY
B = SOMEWHAT
C = NOT AT ALL

Criteria	A	B	C	Recommended Action
b. attitudes toward health and health practices.				
c. present and future health actions.				
2. The results of evaluations are used to continuously improve the health education programs.				

3. Students' opinions on the instructional program are important, but they can be threatening to the teachers. Evaluators can learn a great deal about the curriculum and its implementation from students, especially at the secondary school level. See figure 11.2 for a sample student questionnaire.

In conducting *outcome evaluation,* the evaluator needs to collect data on student knowledge, attitudes, and behaviors related to the curriculum goals and objectives.

1. Student learning outcomes, showing knowledge and skills attainment, may be obtained through tests, checklists, and work samples (Connell, Turner, and Mason, 1985).
2. Student attitudes toward health education, behavior, and life-styles issues can be measured by questionnaires similar to the one in figure 11.3.
3. A parent survey may be used to determine if students are applying health knowledge and skills outside of school.
4. Health records and other student data such as drug/alcohol use, smoking, and other health habits can be used to assess curriculum effectiveness. One must take care to examine data over time in such areas as teenage pregnancy, sexually transmitted diseases, and the use of chemical substances to determine change.

A written questionnaire is one of the most cost-effective means of gathering information. Questionnaires and surveys must be written carefully, however. Data-gathering instruments must relate to the curriculum being evaluated. They can include either multiple-choice items or open-ended questions. There are many published questionnaires and surveys on health education that can be adapted for an evaluation. Questionnaires can be simplified for younger students. The Louis Harris survey (Harris and Associates, 1988) consists of a student questionnaire for grades 7–12, a parent questionnaire, and a teacher questionnaire. Another national survey, conducted by the IOX Assessment Associates in 1987, provides a pool of questions covering many areas of health for secondary students. The results of these national surveys can be used as baseline data for comparison with local evaluation results.

Evaluators need to be reminded that many states have laws that protect the privacy of students in answering questions relating to sexual behavior (see chapter 9). Parental permission is required before such questionnaires can be administered.

FIGURE 11.2 Sample student questionnaire

HEALTH EDUCATION EVALUATION

DO NOT SIGN YOUR NAME. The purpose of an evaluation is to appraise—good or bad—so that whatever is evaluated may be improved. Be as objective as possible.

1. What is your feeling about the importance of this subject as it relates to essential knowledge needed by you now or in the future?

2. Concerning health education material covered:
   a. Did you feel that the number of units covered was:
   ___ about right ___ insufficient ___ sufficient
   b. Did you feel that the detail of each unit covered was:
   ___ about right ___ too superficial
   ___ too detailed
   c. Check your preference:
   ___ cover more but less detailed
   ___ cover about the same
   ___ cover less but more detailed
   d. Check one or more of the following that you would have liked included this semester *or,* if it was included, that you would have liked more time to study:
   ___ safety education ___ hormones
   ___ first aid ___ civil defense
   ___ body systems ___ ears
   ___ radiation ___ nutrition
   ___ heredity ___ water safety
   ___ eyes ___ communicable diseases
   e. In the first column, star the units from which you feel you received the most worthwhile information for now and the future. In the second column, star the units you feel were of least use to you.

Introduction (value of health, sleep, prevention of fatigue)	___	___
Nutrition	___	___
Sex education	___	___
Alcohol, narcotics, tobacco	___	___
Mental health	___	___
Degenerative diseases (cancer, public health, etc.)	___	___
Communicable diseases (polio, tetanus, V.D., etc.)	___	___
Skin, hair, teeth	___	___

3. Concerning teaching methods:
   a. Which of the following did you feel were *not* effective in teaching you something:
   ___ committee work and reports to class ___ individual oral reports
   ___ lecture by teacher and class discussion ___ lecture by teacher
   ___ read text and write out answers to worksheets ___ movies
   b. Have you any suggestions on methods that could be used that we did not use?
   c. Any comments on the methods that were used:
   d. Did you use the folders at any time in the semester?
   ___ yes ___ no
   e. Approximately how many books or pamphlets did you check out from room 106 during the semester?
   ___ books ___ pamphlets

4. Concerning assignments:
   a. Did you feel that the semester projects (quarter projects; interest area) were worth your time and effort from the standpoint of knowledge acquired in doing them?
   ___ yes ___ no ___ no opinion
   b. Did you feel that there were enough assignments?
   ___ yes ___ no ___ no opinion
   c. Did you feel that the bulletin board assignment added to your knowledge and to the learning atmosphere of the class?
   ___ yes ___ no ___ no opinion
   d. Any comment on assignments:

FIGURE 11.2 *Continued*

5. Concerning grading:
   a. Did you feel that the tests in general were:
      ___ too difficult ___ too easy ___ o.k.
   b. Did you feel that the test questions covered the most important material?
      ___ yes ___ no ___ no opinion
   c. Did you like the number way of grading reports and assignments?
      ___ yes ___ no ___ no opinion
   d. Do you think it fair to require interest-area work for an "A" or "B"?
      ___ yes ___ no ___ no opinion
   e. Did you like the way your quarter and semester grades were arrived at?
      ___ yes ___ no ___ no opinion
   f. Any comment on grading:

6. Concerning teacher:
   a. Did you feel that the teacher was interested in her subject?
      ___ yes ___ no ___ no opinion
   b. Did you feel that the teacher showed some evidence that she "practices what she preaches"?
      ___ yes ___ no ___ no opinion
   c. Did you feel that the teacher showed some evidence that she was interested in you as a person as well as her subject?
      ___ yes ___ no ___ no opinion
   d. Did the teacher have any annoying mannerisms?
   e. Any comments on teacher:

7. Do you have any suggestions for the improvement of this course?

8. Please feel free to write any other comments you wish to make:

FIGURE 11.3 Questionnaire to measure student attitudes toward health education, behavior, and life-styles issues. (Reprinted by permission of John D. Swisher, Ph.D. Data Base, copyright © 1981, form 9a or form 8.)

PRIMARY PREVENTION AWARENESS, ATTITUDE AND USAGE SCALES

Form 9a 1990

DO NOT PUT YOUR NAME ANYWHERE ON THIS QUESTIONNAIRE. This survey asks how you feel about many things, including cigarettes, alcohol and other drugs. Please think about each question and answer truthfully. Your answers will be used only as part of a group pattern. No information about individual students will ever be given to anyone in your school or community.

GENERAL DIRECTIONS: Before each section of this questionnaire, you will find specific directions. Please read them carefully. To give your answer, use a No. 2 pencil and fill in the circle that shows your response. If you want to change your response, please be sure to carefully erase your first answer.

I am a: ○ Male ○ Female

I am in grade: ⑤ ⑥ ⑦ ⑧ ⑨ ⑩ ⑪ ⑫

	EXCELLENT	VERY GOOD	GOOD	AVERAGE	BELOW AVERAGE	POOR
My overall grade average is:	○	○	○	○	○	○

DIRECTIONS: Below are some things that make up how you feel about school. Please fill in the circle that comes closest to showing how you feel about each of them. The higher the number, the more positive you are about each item.

School in general	DISLIKE ←①	②	③	④	⑤	⑥	⑦→ ENJOY
Teachers	NOT HELPFUL ←①	②	③	④	⑤	⑥	⑦→ HELPFUL
Subjects	BORING ←①	②	③	④	⑤	⑥	⑦→ INTERESTING
Classmates	UNFRIENDLY ←①	②	③	④	⑤	⑥	⑦→ VERY FRIENDLY

DIRECTIONS: Below are some things that you may have done or that may have happened to you. For each one, fill in the circle that comes closest to showing how often it has happened to you.

HOW OFTEN HAVE YOU:	Never Happened	Happened More Than a Year Ago	Happens a Few Times a Year	About Once or Twice a Month	About Once or Twice a Week	Happens Almost Every Day
Helped a friend with a problem	○	○	○	○	○	○
Been sent out of the classroom by a teacher	○	○	○	○	○	○
Skipped school without an excuse	○	○	○	○	○	○
Taken money or something from someone	○	○	○	○	○	○
Done volunteer work (school or community)	○	○	○	○	○	○
Taken something from a store	○	○	○	○	○	○
Cheated on a class test	○	○	○	○	○	○
Been drunk	○	○	○	○	○	○
Been high on drugs	○	○	○	○	○	○
Stayed out all night without a parent's permission	○	○	○	○	○	○
Broken or vandalized school property	○	○	○	○	○	○

98048

DO NOT MARK IN THIS AREA

FIGURE 11.3 *Continued*

DIRECTIONS: Several kinds of tobacco, alcohol and other drugs are listed below. This set of questions deals with whether or not you would be willing to try these things or willing to use these things. **These are NOT questions about whether or not you have actually used them.** For each one, fill in the circle that comes closest to showing how you feel about using it. The higher the number, the more willing you would be to use that substance. Here are some examples: If you would never use it or don't know what it is, mark the ⓪;
If you probably wouldn't use it, mark the ①;
If you're not sure whether or not you would try it, mark the ②;
If you would like to try it or would like to use it, mark the ③;
If you would use it any chance you got, or if you use it now, mark the ④.

CIGARETTES	NEVER ←⓪	①	②	③	④→ ANYTIME
CHEWING TOBACCO, SNUFF	NEVER ←⓪	①	②	③	④→ ANYTIME
BEER (beer, ale, malt liquor)	NEVER ←⓪	①	②	③	④→ ANYTIME
WINE (wine, champagne)	NEVER ←⓪	①	②	③	④→ ANYTIME
COOLERS (wine- or alcohol-based)	NEVER ←⓪	①	②	③	④→ ANYTIME
LIQUOR (whiskey, vodka, rum, bourbon)	NEVER ←⓪	①	②	③	④→ ANYTIME
MARIJUANA (grass, pot, hash, weed)	NEVER ←⓪	①	②	③	④→ ANYTIME
INHALANTS (whippets, butane, sniffing glue)	NEVER ←⓪	①	②	③	④→ ANYTIME
MENOTROPINS (rickeys, wagon-wheels)	NEVER ←⓪	①	②	③	④→ ANYTIME
COCAINE (coke, snow, toot, blow)	NEVER ←⓪	①	②	③	④→ ANYTIME
CRACK (rock, fry)	NEVER ←⓪	①	②	③	④→ ANYTIME
HEROIN (smack, skag)	NEVER ←⓪	①	②	③	④→ ANYTIME
HALLUCINOGENS (acid, LSD, trip, shrooms)	NEVER ←⓪	①	②	③	④→ ANYTIME
PRESCRIPTION DRUGS WITHOUT DOCTOR'S ORDERS					
UPPERS (speed, meth, crank, diet pills)	NEVER ←⓪	①	②	③	④→ ANYTIME
DOWNERS (ludes, tranqs, barbs, sedatives)	NEVER ←⓪	①	②	③	④→ ANYTIME
TRAINING DRUGS WITH OR WITHOUT DOCTOR'S ORDERS					
STEROIDS (roids, juice)	NEVER ←⓪	①	②	③	④→ ANYTIME
OVER-THE-COUNTER-DRUGS – TO GET HIGH (cough syrup, robo, antihistamines)	NEVER ←⓪	①	②	③	④→ ANYTIME

DIRECTIONS: Please fill in the circle that comes closest to showing how willing you would be to do the following things.

	Never	Probably No	Probably Yes	Definitely Yes
I would drive a car after drinking alcohol.	○	○	○	○
I would drive a car after smoking marijuana.	○	○	○	○
I would ride with someone who has been drinking alcohol.	○	○	○	○
I would ride with someone who has been smoking marijuana.	○	○	○	○
I would try to stop someone from driving if they had been drinking alcohol or smoking marijuana, or from riding with a driver who had been drinking or smoking pot.	○	○	○	○

DIRECTIONS: If you or a close friend had a problem with tobacco, alcohol or other drugs, who would you be willing to talk to about it? Here is a list of people whom you might consider. For each one, fill in the "YES," "NO" or "MAYBE," as your answer.

WOULD YOU TALK TO:

	YES	NO	MAYBE		YES	NO	MAYBE
A person my age	○	○	○	A parent	○	○	○
A teacher	○	○	○	An adult relative other than a parent	○	○	○
A coach	○	○	○	A counselor in a drug center	○	○	○
An adult friend	○	○	○	A policeman	○	○	○
A person from church	○	○	○	A student support group	○	○	○
A doctor	○	○	○	A school counselor	○	○	○
				The principal or assistant principal	○	○	○

MAKE NO STRAY MARKS

FIGURE 11.3 *Continued*

DIRECTIONS: A few different kinds of activities are listed below. Fill in the circle that comes closest to showing how much time you spend in each type of activity. If you do several things from the same category, simply add their times together for your answer.

HOW OFTEN DO YOU TAKE PART IN:	Never	More Than a Year Ago	A Few Times A Year	About Once or Twice a Month	About Once or Twice a Week	Almost Every Day
Entertainment and Social Activities (going to movies, on a date, to a concert, to a party, etc.)	O	O	O	O	O	O
Academic Activities (doing homework, school projects, research, reading books, etc.)	O	O	O	O	O	O
Sports and Physical Activities (team sports, jogging, swimming, dance class, exercise, etc.)	O	O	O	O	O	O
Religious Activities (going to services, church/synagogue activities, meetings, etc.)	O	O	O	O	O	O
Hobbies and Extracurricular Activities (school clubs, yearbook, student government, band, collecting, sewing, working on cars, etc.)	O	O	O	O	O	O
Work-for-Pay Activities (part-time job, babysitting, mowing lawns, chores at home, etc.)	O	O	O	O	O	O

DIRECTIONS: Below is a list of tobacco, alcohol and other drugs. **Remember that your answers are absolutely confidential and private.** Please fill in the circle that comes closest to showing how often you use (or have used) each one of these things.

	Never Used	Used More Than A Year Ago	A Few Times A Year	About Once or Twice a Month	About Once or Twice a Week	About Once a Day
CIGARETTES	O	O	O	O	O	O
CHEWING TOBACCO, SNUFF	O	O	O	O	O	O
BEER (beer, ale, malt liquor)	O	O	O	O	O	O
WINE (wine, champagne)	O	O	O	O	O	O
COOLERS (wine- or alcohol-based)	O	O	O	O	O	O
LIQUOR (whiskey, vodka, rum, bourbon)	O	O	O	O	O	O
MARIJUANA (grass, pot, hash, weed)	O	O	O	O	O	O
INHALANTS (whippets, butane, sniffing glue)	O	O	O	O	O	O
MENOTROPINS (rickeys, wagon-wheels)	O	O	O	O	O	O
COCAINE (coke, snow, toot, blow)	O	O	O	O	O	O
CRACK (rock, fry)	O	O	O	O	O	O
HEROIN (smack, skag)	O	O	O	O	O	O
HALLUCINOGENS (acid, LSD, trip, shrooms)	O	O	O	O	O	O
PRESCRIPTION DRUGS WITHOUT DOCTOR'S ORDERS						
UPPERS (speed, meth, crank, diet pills)	O	O	O	O	O	O
DOWNERS (ludes, tranqs, barbs, sedatives)	O	O	O	O	O	O
TRAINING DRUGS WITH OR WITHOUT DOCTOR'S ORDERS						
STEROIDS (roids, juice)	O	O	O	O	O	O
OVER-THE-COUNTER-DRUGS – TO GET HIGH (cough syrup, robo, antihistamines)	O	O	O	O	O	O

MAKE NO STRAY MARKS

FIGURE 11.3 *Continued*

DIRECTIONS: Here is a list of reasons that some students give for NOT using tobacco, alcohol and other drugs. Please read each one carefully and fill in the circle that comes closest to showing how important that reason is when you make decisions about drinking, smoking or using other drugs. Take your time to think about each one before you answer.

	Not At All Important	Unimportant	Important	Very Important
Having a clear understanding of the physical and emotional effects of tobacco, alcohol and other drugs.	○	○	○	○
Knowing it is against the law.	○	○	○	○
Feeling self-confident, knowing that I don't need to drink or use drugs in order to like myself.	○	○	○	○
Being able to be involved with interesting and fun things to do.	○	○	○	○
Having close friends who like and accept me as I am.	○	○	○	○
Knowing how to cope with social pressures.	○	○	○	○
Having my academic efforts noticed by my teachers.	○	○	○	○
Knowing my family would be hurt or angry if I were caught.	○	○	○	○
Seeing adults practice what they preach about drinking, smoking and drugs.	○	○	○	○
Having a fair and strict school policy.	○	○	○	○

DIRECTIONS: Below is a list of situations in which you may have found yourself as a driver or a passenger. Please fill in the circle that comes closest to showing how often each of these things has happened to you.

HOW OFTEN HAVE YOU:

	Never Happened	Happened More Than a Year Ago	Happens a Few Times a Year	About Once or Twice a Month	About Once or Twice a Week	Happens Almost Every Day
Been a passenger in a car when the driver had been drinking while driving or drinking shortly before driving?	○	○	○	○	○	○
Been a passenger in a car when the driver had been smoking pot while driving or smoking pot shortly before driving?	○	○	○	○	○	○
Been a passenger in a car when the driver had been drinking AND smoking pot?	○	○	○	○	○	○
Driven a car while or shortly after drinking? ○ I don't drive	○	○	○	○	○	○
Driven a car while or shortly after smoking pot? ○ I don't drive	○	○	○	○	○	○
Driven a car while or shortly after drinking AND smoking? ○ I don't drive	○	○	○	○	○	○

DIRECTIONS: If you have used tobacco, alcohol or other drugs in the last year or so, please fill in the "YES" circle(s) next to the place(s) you usually use (or used) them. If it is a place where you usually don't smoke, drink or use drugs, fill in the "NO." If you do not use tobacco, alcohol or other drugs, please fill in this circle.

→ ○ I do not use tobacco, alcohol or other drugs.

I usually smoke (smoked) or drink (drank) or use (used) tobacco, alcohol or other drugs:

YES	NO	
○	○	In school
○	○	At parties
○	○	At home
○	○	At a friend's house
○	○	In a car
○	○	At a hangout
○	○	Before/after a school activity (sports event, dance, etc.)
○	○	At a public place (mall, etc.)

Please fill in the "YES" or "NO" circle next to each of the following to show whether or not it is a place or person from which you usually get (or got) tobacco, alcohol or other drugs. If you do not use anything, please fill in this circle.

→ ○ I do not use tobacco, alcohol or other drugs.

I usually get (got) tobacco, alcohol or other drugs from:

YES	NO	
○	○	Friends
○	○	Students at school
○	○	A store
○	○	Out-of-school kids
○	○	People at work
○	○	College students
○	○	Adults

DO NOT MARK IN THIS AREA

98048

Dissemination of Evaluation Results

Evaluations are of little use unless the results are disseminated and utilized. While planning an evaluation, one should determine who will receive the program evaluation report and who will be using the results. Different people involved in a school health education program, such as teachers, administrators, parents, students, citizens' advisory committees, school boards, funding agencies, interested community members, and health-care professionals have different reasons for wanting an evaluation. Reports for different groups can be categorized as follows:

1. Teachers and administrators want evaluation for program improvement. They need as much detail as an evaluator can provide, including anecdotal information and relevant observations related to variables in the implementation process.
2. Funding agencies, school boards, and superintendents want evaluation results for accountability or decision making. Because they may not have firsthand knowledge of the program, the report should include program goals and objectives, a program description, the evaluation procedure, results, and a conclusion.
3. Parents, students, and community members often want to know if the curriculum is making a difference. A nontechnical evaluation report, emphasizing the outcome variables, should be written so that the general public can understand it. Often, a summary of the evaluation report will suffice.

In writing an evaluation report, the evaluator should be sensitive to the needs of the target audience and present the kind of information that is needed to make program improvements, to make decisions about program retention or elimination, or to determine program effectiveness. The three levels of evaluation reporting described previously may convey the same basic information, but the details and points of view of the reports will vary with the audience.

Summary

As this chapter has shown, determining the effectiveness of a health education curriculum is not a simple task. Formal process and outcome evaluations take a great deal of time, energy, resources, and expertise. Unless there are questions that affect the continuation of a program, an indepth formal evaluation is probably not necessary. On the other hand, informal process evaluation is an important part of program improvement, and it should be conducted regularly.

Discussion Questions

1. Select one component or strand of a health education program with which you are familiar and outline how you would go about evaluating it.
2. Given the difficulties in linking health behavior to a specific curriculum, discuss why evaluation is an important part of implementation.
3. Why are health education programs more difficult to evaluate than reading or mathematics programs?

Application Activities

1. Two years ago your school started an AIDS education program. As the health coordinator, you are responsible for determining if the program has been implemented properly. Describe an

evaluation design and the data-gathering methods and instruments that you would use.

2. Your high school requires one semester of health education for graduation. Some teachers in other departments are questioning whether the requirement should be dropped, because they believe students do not learn anything in the course. Develop a test and a questionnaire to evaluate student learning outcome at the end of the semester.

References

Bloom, S. B., Madeus, G. F., and Hastings, J. T. 1981. *Evaluation to improve learning.* New York: McGraw-Hill.

Bradley, C. 1986. *A guide to curriculum planning in health education.* Madison, WI: Department of Public Instruction.

Connell, D. B., Turner, R. R., and Mason, E. F. 1985. *School health education evaluation, final report, vol. 1–4.* Washington, DC: Centers for Disease Control and Office of Disease Prevention and Health Promotion, Public Health Service, U.S. Department of Health and Human Services.

Gold, R. S. and Basch, C. E. 1986. Research and evaluation: An overview. *Evaluation and Research in School Health Education.* Second Delbert Oberteuffer Symposium. 13 April 1986. Cincinnati, OH.

Harris, Louis, and Associates, Inc. 1988. *HEALTH—You got to be taught: An evaluation of comprehensive health education in American public schools.* New York: Metropolitan Life Foundation.

Hochbaum, G. M. 1982. Certain problems in evaluating health education. *Health Values: Achieving High Level Wellness,* *6*(1):14–20.

IOX Assessment Associates. 1987. *National adolescent student health survey.* Los Angeles: University of California.

Joint Committee on Standards for Educational Evaluation. 1981. *Standard for evaluation of educational programs, projects, and materials.* New York: McGraw-Hill.

Nelson, S. 1986. *How healthy is your school?* New York: National Center for Health Education.

Pine, P. 1985. *Critical issues report. Promoting health education in schools—Problems and solutions.* Arlington, VA: American Association of School Administrators.

University of Wisconsin—Madison, School Evaluation Services, Room 427, Education Building, Madison, WI.

White, J. S., and Swisher, J. D. 1990, August. *Bainbridge Island school district foundation for prevention: Student perspectives on drug and alcohol abuse, 1989–90 academic year.* State College, PA: Data Base.

Windsor, R. A., Baranowski, T., Clark, N., and Cutter, G. 1984. *Evaluation of health promotion and education programs.* Palo Alto, CA: Mayfield.

12

Maintaining Programs:
Fine-Tuning, Updating, and Revising

After reading this chapter and participating in application activities, the student should be able to:

1. Distinguish between fine-tuning a curriculum and maintaining a curriculum.
2. Describe ways to keep current as a health educator.
3. Distinguish between an interim review and a full curriculum review.

It is not enough to develop and implement a program; it must be fine-tuned, revised, maintained, and kept updated. These activities, which must be scheduled and budgeted, must also be assigned to someone who is responsible for seeing that it happens. Remember that curriculum development is a gradual process; a program develops over two or three years before becoming fully implemented and institutionalized. The task then is to keep the curriculum vibrant.

Fine-Tuning

Fine-tuning means uncovering weaknesses in a curriculum and overcoming them. Here are some examples of program weaknesses and suggested ways to overcome them.

- Elementary teachers find that the four food groups are taught for several years in a row, and students become disinterested. The curriculum is changed to apply the information in different ways after the first year; for example, the students plan a morning meal using the four food groups.
- Information on puberty was not included until sixth grade. Students and teachers alike complained that this was too late. The unit on puberty was moved partly to the fourth grade and partly to the fifth grade.
- The curriculum committee feels that death and dying should not be taught to young children. A shooting tragedy in a neighboring school district creates a need to have at least some lessons in death education available to teachers for elementary students.
- An inexpensive booklet on mental health for middle school youngsters was provided as a supplementary resource. It was found to be too difficult for students to read. One of the teachers suggested another booklet at the same cost and at a better reading level.

Assessing a program is another way of fine-tuning. This is not the formal assessment discussed in the chapter on evaluation, but the teachers' assessment of the curriculum and their instruction. A discussion or simple questionnaire can be used to ascertain students' concerns about the health education curriculum and instruction. At the secondary level, students can be asked the following questions: Do you feel the course, as structured, covered knowledge needed by you now or in the future? Are there health topics not now included that you feel should be included in a semester of health? Do you feel that the grading system used is fair? If not, why not? See figure 11.2 for additional questions.

Fine-tuning should occur throughout the years of a program's use, but it is especially necessary in the first year of implementation. Through close monitoring and evaluation, changes needed in content, resources, objectives, placement of content, and in-service training are determined. The data collected during process and outcome evaluations provide important information that assists in fine-tuning.

Keeping Current

Keeping people current in the field of health education, as well as maintaining and updating resources and programs, is a challenge. Teachers need help in keeping current on health information, resources, and teaching strategies. It is important that school districts budget for a variety of opportunities to provide their personnel with current information as well as for the inclusion of health education in the curriculum revision cycle.

A number of avenues for staying current are available to health teachers. In some cases, individuals must use their own time, effort and/or money; in other cases, the district assists outright by providing stipends or release time, or at least encourages ongoing staff development. We suggest several ways for school personnel to stay current in the following sections.

Reading Professional Literature

Professional health education journals, such as the *Journal of Health Education* and *Journal of School Health,* provide current data and teaching ideas relevant to the school setting. Teachers and curriculum coordinators may receive these journals as a result of membership in professional organizations (e.g., AAHE and ASHA), or district librarians may subscribe to the journals. Other health-related journals, magazines, and newsletters can also be made available at school libraries (e.g., *Health Values: Achieving High Level Wellness, Hippocrates, Health and Medicine, Wellness Newsletter, Tufts Nutrition Newsletter, Nutrition Forum,* and *NCAHF Newsletter*). See chapter 6 on locating resources and for more suggestions on periodicals and newsletters.

Attendance at Professional Meetings

Teachers may attend meetings of professional organizations, school district in-service programs, and college and university seminars. Summer health education conferences help teachers both personally and professionally. Washington's Fort Worden Conference, Oregon's Seaside Conference, and Wisconsin's Lakeside Conference send participants back to their teaching and supervisory positions filled with enthusiasm. At the 1990 Fort Worden Conference, the first three days focused solely on healthy living ideas. "Personal Wellness Profiles were conducted and sessions presented on stress management, physical fitness, weight management, self-esteem, cancer education, heart-healthy nutrition education, and more! The goal was to provide participants with ideas, tools, and motivation to begin to make health changes in their life-styles" (*Washington, A State of Wellness,* 1990). As participants became more knowledgeable about their own health, the conference began to focus on ways they could implement healthy living concepts in their school districts. Over thirty sessions were presented to offer ideas, materials, and resources for use in the schools and classrooms. Examples of sessions included "When the Tooth Fairy Talks, the Wisdom Tooth Listens," "Prevention—Focus on Special Populations," "Working with Angry Youth," "Fun, Creative Ways to Teach K–6 Health Education," and "Strategies for Enhancing the Self Esteem of Students."

Figure 12.1 shows the mission statement and goals of a summer institute that was the combined effort of a health education foundation and a university. The week-long institute gave participants the opportunity to engage in learning activities to enhance their own self-esteem and to acquire information and resources for improving their professional skills.

Extending Extra Effort

One of the best ways to keep current is to peruse resources that come from reliable sources. In addition to helping themselves stay informed in this way, teachers or health education coordinators may help the district by

FIGURE 12.1 Mission statement and goals of a summer institute. (From the Health Education program, Western Washington University, Bellingham, WA.)

The Comprehensive Health Education Foundation's
First Annual
Experienced Health Educator Fellowship
Summer Institute

August 12–17, 1990
Western Washington University
Bellingham, WA

MISSION STATEMENT

The mission of the Experienced Health Educator Fellowship's first Summer Institute is to empower participants with the knowledge, attitudes and skills to teach about the interrelationship between self-esteem and health. Participants will also understand the primary purpose of health education is to help people achieve optimal well-being through individual and/or cooperative actions and efforts. This will be accomplished by:

- providing current, accurate information about self-esteem and its link to health.
- instilling confidence in each participant's ability to make a difference in the lives of their students.
- involving participants in examining creative approaches to enhancing their own as well as their students' self-esteem.
- exploring a variety of health concepts through learning activities that will enhance each student's self-esteem.
- motivating participants to try new ideas and ways of looking at how their students can learn cooperatively.
- creating awareness of new and innovative resources for improving the quality and quantity of health education.
- facilitating successful completion of requirements for university credit applicable for a health endorsement.
- encouraging the development of new professional and personal friendships.
- demonstrating that health education is basic to the success and self-esteem of all students.
- acknowledging similarities and differences in learning styles among students from various cultural/ethnic backgrounds.

recommending resources for classroom use and for the library collection. The health educator can watch health-related television programs and newscasts for relevant subject matter. Health hotlines are also helpful. Teachers who help with the evaluation of new materials can benefit both themselves and the district. The health education coordinator can keep teachers informed about coming media events, supply them with current health-related hotline telephone numbers, and send them copies of current articles, brochures, and pamphlets.

Revision

The curriculum revision schedule is a responsibility of the school district's administration. Each district should have a schedule indicating when revision is to take place for each subject area in the school's curriculum. A commonly recommended time for revisions is every five years. It may be necessary and prudent, however, to revise the health education curriculum every three years because of rapid changes in content that occur as a result of research findings and societal needs.

Revision can be of two kinds: an interim review or a full revision. An interim review may involve only teachers and not a fully constituted committee, as described in chapter 3. Those involved with such a review would look at whether or not content is still accurate and current and if there is a need to replace or renew resources.

An interim review of a curriculum may result from pressure from health professionals, parents, or other community groups who wish to add or eliminate something. This pressure is often created by events such as the drug crisis, HIV infection and the AIDS epidemic, and suicide among teenagers. The criteria used in considering the inclusion of new content are the same as those used in the original selection of curriculum content (see chapter 2). Is the proposed content of interest to students? Is it something they need? Is it for the appropriate grade level? What is its priority in relationship to other topics? (Adding something generally means that something else must be deleted!) Does it relate to the philosophy?

Full revision is similar to the planning process explained in chapter 3. When health education is scheduled for in-depth revision, a district administrator or a health education director convenes a new curriculum committee using the criteria previously outlined, and any new materials would be ordered for preview. A consultant could be employed if local personnel do not have the time or are not qualified to identify new resources. The curriculum committee would review new materials; read any new local, state, or national studies on health needs and interests; and investigate any new laws and policies that affect school curricula. The members of the committee may want to survey teachers and parents to ask what is lacking in the program and what strong points should be retained. Principals should be able to suggest improvements as a result of monitoring the curriculum.

The curriculum committee would analyze the philosophy, goals, scope and sequence, and curriculum objectives in light of the information gathered in the review process. After additions, deletions, and other modifications, any new resources would be added. New materials must go through the same process outlined earlier. After the materials are screened to be sure they are in line with the philosophical intent and that they relate to the objectives, they are evaluated on the same merits as the original resources. (see chapter 7).

The final step in the revision process is in-service training. This provides a review of old content, an in-depth look at new content, and familiarization with new teaching strategies and resources. A good in-service program leads to renewed enthusiasm for the program.

Summary

Fine-tuning requires careful and ongoing attention to a new program to see if anything must be changed, added, or deleted. As teachers use any program, it becomes clear where changes are needed in content, resources, or teaching opportunities. Someone must be responsible for receiving and coordinating the information that teachers gather.

Updating is the effort to be sure that all aspects of a program keep pace with what is current in the field of health and education. This refers to content, resources, and teaching strategies and is the responsibility of teachers, supervisors, media personnel, and administrators.

School districts should have regularly scheduled revision cycles. Interim reviews may take place between the longer, more thorough revisions. Full revision closely resembles the original curriculum-planning process and should occur every five years, if not sooner, for health education.

During the time period between the development of a health education curriculum and each revision, school districts need to budget for basic program maintenance. A basic maintenance budget includes provisions for new materials, for new editions of existing materials, and for replacement of lost and damaged materials. Nothing is so discouraging to a good teacher as not being able to replace good resources that are worn out or lost, or not being able to add new resources as the years go by. Basic maintenance also includes staff development, especially for teachers new to the program and for those having difficulty teaching the curriculum.

Discussion Questions

1. What are the strengths and weaknesses of various ways to keep current in health education?
2. What avenues are open to teachers and principals to communicate to a curriculum coordinator the weaknesses in a program?
3. What are some recognizable conditions that indicate the need for revision?

Application Activities

1. Design a system that you can use to keep current on health information and teaching strategies.
2. Outline the steps of a full curriculum revision. Mark the steps that would be part of an interim review.

References

Washington: A state of wellness. 1990. From the Fort Worden XI Agenda, 17–22 June 1990. Fort Worden Conference, Port Townsend, WA. Conference coordinated by RF & A, Inc.

Appendix

Developmental Characteristics
of Students Ages Five to Eighteen:
Health Education Implications

Health Education Implications of Young People 5 to 9 Years of Age

Relating to Program Goal I: The Student Practices Behaviors Which Promote and Maintain Mental Health

Selected developmental characteristics, health interests, and health needs:	Desired health knowledges, attitudes or behaviors
• is aware of attitudes and opinions of others; begins to be influenced by individual and societal expectations	• discusses feelings resulting from helping others; is pleased with self
• feels urge to be friendly but focuses on two or three best friends, which change frequently	• describes how it feels to be included and excluded from a group
• exhibits openly feelings of anger, fear, joy, hate, jealousy	• learns that feelings are normal and can be expressed in positive ways; understands that feelings affect behavior
• may fear making mistakes; needs opportunities to try independence	• realizes that everyone makes mistakes and making a mistake can be a learning process; seeks help of others; learns to predict consequences

---

Superintendent of Public Instruction, *Health Education Framework: Supplemental Material* (Olympia, WA. 1980).

Health Education Implications of Young People 5 to 9 Years of Age (*Continued*)

Relating to Program Goal I: The Student Practices Behaviors Which Promote and Maintain Mental Health

Selected developmental characteristics, health interests, and health needs:	**Desired health knowledges, attitudes or behaviors**
• may have disturbing dreams, fears, anxieties	• understands reason for dreaming and that dreams are just dreams; talks out fears and anxieties
• gives up easily when task is difficult	• recognizes that learning sometimes takes effort
• accepts ideas of others at times and yet may want own way too often	• shares and takes turns; realizes how one's actions affect others
• may have difficulty accepting differences in others	• learns that both similarities and differences can be good
• may tattle, invent stories, say cruel things	• knows when to report actions; learns that thoughtfulness brings happiness to self and others
• needs frequent assurance of love and approval; self-concept not always strong	• feels loved and feels secure; identifies actions that make one feel good about self
• works well in groups; may be preoccupied with acceptance by groups	• shares and cooperates; respects rights of others; recognizes power to influence others and be influenced; develops comfort with being alone at times

Health Education Implications of Young People 5 to 9 Years of Age

Relating to Program Goal II: The Student Practices Behaviors Which Promote and Maintain Physical Well-Being

Selected developmental characteristics, health interests, and health needs:	**Desired health knowledges, attitudes or behaviors**
• wants to grow/learn	• learns relationship of growth/learning to health habits; identifies activities which deter growth/learning
• needs adequate amounts of nutrients and minimum amounts of sweets and soft drinks	• eats food served; knows value of and eats breakfast; tries healthful snacks; knows effect of sugar on teeth
• may need encouragement to try new foods	• tries new foods; knows value of and eats a variety of foods
• participates in scheduled time for eating	• chews well; eats slowly; makes mealtimes pleasant
• may not be aware of effect of unsanitary practices	• washes hands before eating and after using bathroom; correctly uses toilets, toilet paper, drinking fountains

Health Education Implications of Young People 5 to 9 Years of Age (*Continued*)

Relating to Program Goal II: The Student Practices Behaviors Which Promote and Maintain Physical Well-Being

Selected developmental characteristics, health interests, and health needs:	**Desired health knowledges, attitudes or behaviors**
• has a high level of energy; tires easily	• understands value of rest, relaxation and exercise; participates in big muscle activities; takes responsibility for own bedtime
• experiences eruption of all primary teeth, six-year molars and anterior permanent teeth; is forming foundation and calcification of permanent teeth	• brushes teeth and visits dentist; understands why first teeth need to be kept in good condition; learns importance of six-year molars
• poor posture may develop	• responds to encouragement for improvement in posture

Health Education Implications of Young People 5 to 9 Years of Age

Relating to Program Goal III: The Student Knows the Structure and Function of the Human Body and Patterns of Healthy Growth and Development

Selected developmental characteristics, health interests, and health needs:	**Desired health knowledges, attitudes or behaviors**
• is curious about the human body, but may not know correct names; can draw human body	• learns correct names and functions of parts of body
• high interest in growth	• learns ways individuals grow and what affects growth; accepts that individuals grow in different and similar ways
• eyes and ears not yet fully mature and may present some problems	• learns importance of ears and eyes; understands the importance of glasses; takes care of eyes and ears
• is curious about the birth of animals and humans and the phenomenon of growth	• understands the concept "like begets like"

Health Education Implications of Young People 5 to 9 Years of Age

Relating to Program Goal IV: The Student Understands Personal, Social, Economic, Cultural, and Ethnic Factors Which Influence Personal and Family Relationships

Selected developmental characteristics, health interests, and health needs:	**Desired health knowledges, attitudes or behaviors**
• needs security of family	• knows that families take care of young people and young people need a lot of care
• likes to be helpful	• demonstrates ways to help at home
• shows interest in different types of family configurations	• appreciates families

Health Education Implications of Young People 5 to 9 Years of Age

Relating to Program Goal V: The Student Contributes to Community Health and Effectively Uses the Health Care System

Selected developmental characteristics, health interests, and health needs:	Desired health knowledges, attitudes or behaviors
• may ingest harmful substances	• recognizes importance of medicine; knows who should give a person medicine
• may need encouragement to visit medical advisor, dentist, nurse	• understands what health professionals do; learns importance of physical and dental examinations; asks questions of health-care professionals
• is curious about hospitals, fire departments, etc.	• learns place of community agencies in keeping people safe and healthy and in caring for the ill
• may not be aware of where to go for help	• knows and seeks help from reliable adults
• associates self with school community	• learns about a wider community; is aware of how community and self affect each other
• needs immunizations	• accepts immunizations

Health Education Implications of Young People 5 to 9 Years of Age

Relating to Program Goal VI: The Student Practices Principles of Safe Living and is Able to Utilize Emergency Procedures in Case of Accidents

Selected developmental characteristics, health interests, and health needs:	Desired health knowledges, attitudes or behaviors
• likes to play with abandon	• consciously uses rules of safety on playground, in gymnasium, on bicycles, when skating, etc.
• relates cause to effect	• assesses situations as safe or hazardous
• may not know or practice safety rules in cars and buses	• learns and practices safe travel rules including use of seat belts
• is involved in accidents to and from school	• takes safest route to school; respects safety patrol; does not play in streets
• may take unfamiliar paths	• avoids strangers offering rides or candy; learns what to do if lost
• may "show off"	• assesses relationship of "showing off" to accidents; knows why people "show off"
• avoids dangerous situations when reminded	• begins to take responsibility for own safety, i.e., uses drinking fountains safely, picks up objects from floor, cleans spilled liquids
• may be victims of sexual abuse	• learns what is acceptable behavior by others
• sometimes samples contents of bottles	• avoids ingesting unknown substances; does a home check with parents on storing cleaning supplies and medicines; begins to watch out for younger children ingesting substances

Health Education Implications of Young People 5 to 9 Years of Age (*Continued*)

Relating to Program Goal VI: The Student Practices Principles of Safe Living and is Able to Utilize Emergency Procedures in Case of Accidents

Selected developmental characteristics, health interests, and health needs:	**Desired health knowledges, attitudes or behaviors**
• may forget rules and safeguards when on vacation	• learns to swim and practices safety in and on the water; learns camping safety; identifies common poisonous plants
• is serious about fire and earthquake drills	• practices fire and earthquake drills
• is concerned about small cuts and bruises	• learns how to care for minor injuries to self

Health Education Implications of Young People 5 to 9 Years of Age

Relating to Program Goal VII: The Student Applies Principles of Disease Prevention, Where Possible, to Avoid Health Problems

Selected developmental characteristics, health interests, and health needs:	**Desired health knowledges, attitudes or behaviors**
• experiences periods of great susceptibility to communicable diseases; comes to school when ill	• understands how germs travel; covers sneezes and coughs, does not share personal objects; learns activities to stay well
• may fear immunizations	• learns reasons for and importance of immunizations
• exhibits interest in what is eaten or drunk	• learns where food comes from and how it is safeguarded; knows medicine may help individuals get well if taken properly
• is curious about diseases friends or family have	• knows what causes disease and health problems; investigates selected diseases and health problems; learns that flies carry disease germs

Health Education Implications of Young People 9 to 12 Years of Age

Relating to Program Goal I: The Student Practices Behaviors Which Promote and Maintain Mental Health

Selected developmental characteristics, health interests, and health needs:	**Desired health knowledges, attitudes or behaviors**
• wants independence but needs to know that help is nearby when wanted	• values seeking help from reliable adults
• wants adult approval but not at the expense of own group relationship	• identifies ways to feel good; explains reasons behind rules; identifies reasons adults may be concerned

Health Education Implications of Young People 5 to 9 Years of Age (*Continued*)

Relating to Program Goal V: The Student Contributes to Community Health and Effectively Uses the Health Care System

Selected developmental characteristics, health interests, and health needs:	**Desired health knowledges, attitudes or behaviors**
• feels considerable peer-group influence; becomes overly concerned with peer-imposed rules	• receives parent or guardian involvement; explores ways to cope with peer pressure; assesses why others can influence; shows increasing independence
• enjoys satisfaction of achievement; likes hard work; desires to be helpful	• accepts challenges of new experiences; is challenged intellectually; needs opportunities to plan, lead, and execute
• forms cliques to the exclusion of others; wants to make friends; is aware of importance of belonging	• learns all people need friends; learns to show concern for others; seeks groups through interests; identifies and practices qualities of good friendship
• occasional emotional outbursts	• learns to release built-up emotion in acceptable ways
• has tendency to carry stories about others; engages in considerable competition and boasting	• appreciates importance of truth; learns how stories hurt self-image of self and others; needs to know failure can be a learning situation; learns to appreciate differences in individuals' abilities
• wants to impress friends and be attractive to others; worries about lack of popularity or achievement	• strengthens habits of personal cleanliness, good grooming; develops communication skills; recognizes positive traits in self; learns empathy skills
• feels peer criticism if deviation from stereotype of sex roles	• values individual differences; becomes aware of changes in role expectations in today's society
• tends to want things own way; develops strong concepts of right and wrong	• practices reasoning with contingencies; considers alternative solutions; assesses effect on total group or on individual
• is capable of planning	• is able to set goals and show movement toward reaching goals
• sees cause-effect relationship	• understands motivation for using and understands effects of use of caffeine, alcohol, tobacco and drugs; understands role habit plays
• becomes sensitive to criticism	• develops self-confidence; learns how to give and take positive criticism
• worries	• gains understanding of such problems as death, disease, divorce, and financial problems of parents; learns skills for dealing with stress.

Health Education Implications of Young People 9 to 12 Years of Age

Relating to Program Goal II: The Student Practices Behaviors Which Promote and Maintain Physical Well-Being

Selected developmental characteristics, health interests, and health needs:	**Desired health knowledges, attitudes or behaviors**
• constantly active or wants to be busy; shows tendency to over-exert and become fatigued	• plans for well-balanced days; knows own physical limitations; is physically fit
• has a great amount of energy that needs to be channeled; becomes over-stimulated easily	• develops healthy hobbies and interests, some of which may be quiet activities; recognizes need for relaxation; learns relaxation techniques
• shows increasingly poor posture	• investigates aesthetic, social and physical value of good posture; practices good posture
• may have ear infections or problems	• knows relationship of ear infections to loss of hearing; selects actions not injurious to ears
• eyes are not fully mature; views television frequently	• responds to need for eye examinations; wears glasses, if needed; practices eye care
• wants to stay up late	• recognizes the need for sufficient sleep; discovers amount of sleep needed
• values fitness	• relates health habits to fitness; knows effect of drugs on fitness
• may not take time to eat leisurely; may begin to miss meals, especially breakfast	• learns to relax at mealtime; has regular time for meals; knows value of and eats breakfast
• may be selective in what is eaten	• knows what constitutes a well-balanced diet; tries new foods; knows effect of sugar on teeth and general health
• is interested in what happens to food eaten	• understands that food is needed for energy, building new tissue, and for maintenance of health
• shows concern about overweight and underweight; most are unceasingly hungry	• calculates input and output of energy
• questions need for personal hygiene, but is interested in appearance	• investigates hygiene's effect on personal relationships and health and energy
• permanent teeth appearing; may need orthodontic care	• relates structure and health of teeth to dental care; responds to need for dental check-ups and care

Health Education Implications of Young People 9 to 12 Years of Age

Relating to Program Goal III: The Student Knows the Structure and Function of the Human Body and Patterns of Healthy Growth and Development

Selected developmental characteristics, health interests, and health needs:	**Desired health knowledges, attitudes or behaviors**
• high interest in human body; concern with body image	• learns structure and function of human body; relates health habits to body image
• shows interest in human growth and development	• acquires basic and accurate information on how one grows and develops mentally, physically, intellectually, and socially
• concerned with differences in growth patterns; may be embarrassed about own and others' physical development	• understands normalcy of differences in growth patterns and cycles
• high interest in growth and development of embryos and fetuses	• appreciates the process of healthy growth and development
• tends to fear any differences in sexual orientation	• explores accurate information on differences in sexual preferences

Health Education Implications of Young People 9 to 12 Years of Age

Relating to Program Goal IV: The Student Understands Personal, Social, Economic, Cultural, and Ethnic Factors Which Influence Personal and Family Relationships

Selected developmental characteristics, health interests, and health needs:	**Desired health knowledges, attitudes or behaviors**
• shares sexuality misinformation	• seeks sources of and acquires reliable information
• ambivalent toward need of family	• contributes to family harmony; knows needs of all people; knows importance of family on individual development
• has "crushes"	• examines factors which help to identify "love"; contrasts qualities inherent in successful dating, friendship, and marriage relationships
• girls ahead of boys in wish to date	• analyzes pressures in society which influence dating; develops friendships with both boys and girls; sees individuals as people first and then as sexual beings

Health Education Implications of Young People 9 to 12 Years of Age

Relating to Program Goal V: The Student Contributes to Community Health and Effectively Uses the Health Care System

Selected developmental characteristics, health interests, and health needs:	Desired health knowledges, attitudes or behaviors
• does some of own shopping	• evaluates advertising and its effect on purchasing food and personal products; establishes criteria for purchasing
• has feeling of pride in own town	• determines activities to contribute to making town better; predicts effect of community problems on health of people
• interested in stories of great people	• learns about people who have contributed to health advances; studies health careers
• may experiment with drugs	• identifies drugs and their effects on the body and behavior

Health Education Implications of Young People 9 to 12 Years of Age

Relating to Program Goal VI: The Student Practices Principles of Safe Living and is Able to Utilize Emergency Procedures in Case of Accidents

Selected developmental characteristics, health interests, and health needs:	Desired health knowledges, attitudes or behaviors
• accidents are leading causes of death and injury	• develops behavior patterns which contribute to personal and group safety; analyzes relationship of accidents and behavior
• is interested in fires and fire hazards	• learns principles of fire control; learns what to do in case of fire
• uses electricity and stoves at home and tools at school	• learns safety in use and care of tools, pans, electrical devices, and stoves
• is interested in first aid	• demonstrates stoppage of bleeding, mouth-to-mouth resuscitation, care of minor wounds and reporting injuries; knows when not to move victims; learns about explosives, electrical accidents, and poisonous substances
• spends much time bicycling and skating	• understands and obeys traffic signs and regulations relating to cycling and skating
• dares and accepts risks	• understands motivation behind daring and risking; predicts consequences of risking
• may spend much time swimming, boating, and fishing	• learns how to swim and what to do and not to do when others are in trouble in the water; learns boating safety

Health Education Implications of Young People 9 to 12 Years of Age

Relating to Program Goal VII: The Student Applies Principles of Disease Prevention, Where Possible, to Avoid Health Problems

Selected developmental characteristics, health interests, and health needs:	Desired health knowledges, attitudes or behaviors
• is interested in disease; may show signs of hypochondria	• learns about disease prevention and the body's defenses
• is curious about health-related problems in the world	• understands sanitation, water purification, and health laws and regulations
• identifies with "ideal" men and women and imitates actions; period of hero worship	• studies about people who have contributed to health and medical advances
• period of good health generally	• takes responsibility for preventing illness, especially in avoiding behavior that may be detrimental
• is curious about disabilities	• understands physical, social, emotional implications of having a disability

Health Education Implications of Young People 12 to 15 Years of Age

Relating to Program Goal I: The Student Practices Behaviors Which Promote and Maintain Mental Health

Selected developmental characteristics, health interests, and health needs:	Desired health knowledges, attitudes or behaviors
• needs to belong to a group or groups	• explores groups, related to own interests, values, hobbies
• ambivalent between independence and need for adults; self-identity strong at times to a point of rebellion	• strengthens self-concept and self-understanding; explores effect of selected situations; assesses own feelings about selected risk behavior
• easily upset with self and others	• practices coping skills; knows needs of people; assesses positive qualities about self; infers why each person must set own standards; discusses fairness in judging others
• questions values, beliefs and rules	• needs strong parental or other adult role models about acceptable behavior; understands need for rules; understands relationship of values and behavior
• concerned with group opinions and yet is beginning to assert and develop own value system; sometimes intolerant of others' apparent differences because of importance of conformity	• knows own values, where they come from and how they influence; parental or other adult influence important; develops appreciation of the value of differences; understands social, emotional, physical implications of disabilities

Health Education Implications of Young People 12 to 15 Years of Age (*Continued*)

Relating to Program Goal I: The Student Practices Behaviors Which Promote and Maintain Mental Health

Selected developmental characteristics, health interests, and health needs:	Desired health knowledges, attitudes or behaviors
• needs practice in making decisions; can apply logic and can consider alternatives	• explores decision-making process; applies process to a variety of health problems; explores consequences of hypothetical decisions
• may lack self-confidence and may be self-conscious, shy and worry about popularity	• assesses strengths; develops interests and hobbies; relates good physical and mental health to attractiveness; practices communication skills; learns qualities of good friendship
• sometimes moody and unpredictable, but emotional outbursts less frequent; needs to be aware that suicides are a leading cause of death in this age group	• understands emotions and positive ways of expressing them; participates in mental health practices

Health Education Implications of Young People 12 to 15 Years of Age

Relating to Program Goal II: The Student Practices Behaviors Which Promote and Maintain Physical Well-Being

Selected developmental characteristics, health interests, and health needs:	Desired health knowledges, attitudes or behaviors
• may make poor selection of food; may avoid breakfast	• applies knowledge of nutrition to food selection; understands relationship of nutrition to appearances and health; examines research on value of breakfast; understands relationship of food selection to dental health
• may have concern with underweight or overweight	• knows principles of weight maintenance; stabilizes weight
• postural difficulties increase with body changes	• brings good-posture feel into consciousness; practices good posture
• spends many hours in recreational activities	• participates in a variety of activities which contribute to fitness, some of which can be lifetime activities
• may practice extremes in grooming	• develops criteria and assesses health products related to grooming; considers effects of grooming on health and interpersonal relationships
• may have skin problems	• assesses value of and practices good health habits; visits dermatologist if necessary

Health Education Implications of Young People 12 to 15 Years of Age (*Continued*)

Relating to Program Goal II: The Student Practices Behaviors Which Promote and Maintain Physical Well-Being

Selected developmental characteristics, health interests, and health needs:	Desired health knowledges, attitudes or behaviors
• tires easily	• determines relationship of nutrition, exercise, balanced day, sleep, and stress to fatigue
• vision and hearing defects increase	• responds to need for ear and eye checks; assesses effects of noise pollution, respiratory infections, etc. on ears; wears glasses if necessary; evaluates how eyes are used
• personal appearance important	• determines what good personal appearance is; selects behavior which contributes to good personal appearance
• may have dental problems	• understands effect of good dental health practices on health of teeth and mouth

Health Education Implications of Young People 12 to 15 Years of Age

Relating to Program Goal III: The Student Knows the Structure and Function of the Human Body and Patterns of Healthy Growth and Development

Selected developmental characteristics, health interests, and health needs:	Desired health knowledges, attitudes or behaviors
• concerned with body image	• knows relationship of exercise, food selection, metabolism, physical activity, heredity, environment, attitude, and grooming on body image
• has interest in structure and function if related to immediate concerns	• reviews systems of body as they relate to use of drugs, appearance, illness, etc.
• high interest in continued changes in body at puberty	• understands how heredity and the endocrine system affect body changes
• ambivalent feelings about dependence and independence	• investigates possible interrelationship of physical, emotional, and social growth
• high interest in embryonic and fetal growth	• understands mother's ability to affect healthy embryonic and fetal development
• tends to fear differences in sexual orientation	• explores accurate information on differences in sexual preferences
• menstrual disorders may occur	• explores relationship of good health to normal menstrual periods; accepts medical assistance if necessary

Health Education Implications of Young People 12 to 15 Years of Age

Relating to Progam Goal IV: The Student Understands Personal, Social, Economic, Cultural, and Ethnic Factors Which Influence Personal and Family Relationships

Selected developmental characteristics, health interests, and health needs:	Desired health knowledges, attitudes or behaviors
• influence by parents on young person's behavior diminishing outside the home but needs adult affection even if reaction is rejection or ambivalence	• continued communication from and involvement with parents important even if there is rejection; understands parents' concerns; knows where reliable help is available
• physical changes may result in emotional stress; changes may not be easily accepted	• understands normalcy of maturation and especially differences in rate of change; explores changes in roles and responsibilities as age levels change
• interested in opposite sex, although girls may be more interested than boys	• explores similar and different factors in friendships and dating; seeks a variety of friends of both sexes
• crushes and hero worship common for same and opposite sex	• explores "in love" phenomenon; explores patterns of growth and development
• unwanted pregnancies may occur	• knows functioning of the reproductive system; knows types of correct use of contraceptives; assesses impact of early unwanted pregnancies on mother, infant, father, family, society; explores ways to enhance relationships other than sexually; analyzes pressures which influence men-women relationships
• one's sexual role is a concern and information from peers, especially, is actively sought	• develops a code of behavior self consistent with value system

Health Education Implications of Young People 12 to 15 Years of Age

Relating to Program Goal V: The Student Contributes to Community Health and Effectively Uses the Health Care System

Selected developmental characteristics, health interests, and health needs:	Desired health knowledges, attitudes or behaviors
• is faced with decisions regarding use of drugs, including alcohol and tobacco, foods, and health products	• acquires accurate information on products; evaluates information against one's own established criteria; understands motivation behind abuse and misuse
• sometimes seeks assistance for health problems on one's own	• knows community resources; evaluates resources against one's own established criteria; asks questions of health-care professionals
• gets involved in solutions to community problems	• investigates and utilizes good problem-solving techniques for community health problems

Health Education Implications of Young People 12 to 15 Years of Age

Relating to Program Goal VI: The Student Practices Principles of Safe Living and is Able to Utilize Emergency Procedures in Case of Accidents

Selected developmental characteristics, health interests, and health needs:	Desired health knowledges, attitudes or behaviors
• accidents are the leading cause of death in this age group	• investigates causes and preventions of accidents related to this age group; suggests reasons for high accident rate in this age level
• is interested in emergency procedures, but tends to panic in emergencies	• demonstrates basic first aid

Health Education Implications of Young People 12 to 15 Years of Age

Relating to Program Goal VII: The Student Applies Principles of Disease Prevention, Where Possible, to Avoid Health Problems

Selected developmental characteristics, health interests, and health needs:	Desired health knowledges, attitudes or behaviors
• shows interest in sickness and disease	• explores diseases, their causes and preventions; assumes personal responsibility in controlling selected disease and health problems
• beginning increase of sexually transmitted diseases	• learns about transmission, dangers, and prevention of STD
• has empathy for disabled	• investigates emotional, physical, and social implications of disabilities
• may pretend illness	• understands relationship of physical and mental health; explores coping mechanisms

Health Education Implications of Young People 14 to 18 Years of Age

Relating to Program Goal I: The Student Practices Behaviors Which Promote and Maintain Mental Health

Selected developmental characteristics, health interests, and health needs:	Desired health knowledges, attitudes or behaviors
• may aspire to more than is possible	• assesses own strengths and weaknesses in determining capabilities
• fluctuates between following own beliefs and being influenced by groups	• understands influence; knows own beliefs (values); compares own beliefs to groups with which one is involved
• makes independent judgments regarding drugs, including alcohol and tobacco	• understands decision-making process; understands factors which influence behavior; makes responsible judgments

Health Education Implications of Young People 14 to 18 Years of Age (*Continued*)

Relating to Program Goal I: The Student Practices Behaviors Which Promote and Maintain Mental Health

Selected developmental characteristics, health interests, and health needs:	**Desired health knowledges, attitudes or behaviors**
• needs communication skills and group activities	• uses communication skills in work, home, play; explores and participates in group activities related to interests; develops and uses coping skills
• may leave home for extended periods; enjoys freedom but may feel uncertain	• understands ambivalent feelings; accepts parental advice and support during transition period into adulthood
• experiences stress	• develops a variety of coping skills such as hobbies and sports and utilizes them
• does not always comprehend ramifications of risk-taking	• theorizes consequences of selected behavior and utilizes this information when making decisions
• needs to integrate values into a personal philosophy which includes ethical and moral values to be used throughout adult life	• establishes relationship of individual's values to societal values; knows own values
• independently judges matters despite tendency to conform	• explores consequences of decisions based on own values and compares to consequences of others' values; develops confidence in self as a unique person; increasingly is less influenced by others
• may have extreme emotional states	• explores mental health practices and utilizes those best suited to self
• shows concern for interpersonal problems	• understands possible causes and preventions of abusive behavior; formulates plan for maintaining mental health

Health Education Implications of Young People 14 to 18 Years of Age

Relating to Program Goal II: The Student Practices Behaviors Which Promote and Maintain Physical Well-Being

Selected developmental characteristics, health interests, and health needs:	**Desired health knowledges, attitudes or behaviors**
• may worry about physical appearance, attractiveness, and physical development	• understands relationship of exercise, nutrition, attitude, and grooming to appearance and development and utilizes this information
• may have obesity problem	• understands and practices principles of weight maintenance; determines dangers of fad diets and schemes; loses weight slowly and with safe methods

Health Education Implications of Young People 14 to 18 Years of Age (*Continued*)

Relating to Program Goal II: The Student Practices Behaviors Which Promote and Maintain Physical Well-Being

Selected developmental characteristics, health interests, and health needs:	Desired health knowledges, attitudes or behaviors
• may indulge in bizarre health behavior; may need more sleep than one is getting	• knows when and how to exercise; eats a variety of foods; critiques information on food; knows need for sleep; organizes life-style to get more sleep
• has all permanent teeth except third molar	• uses good dental health practices to preserve teeth and gums
• may not be living at home so no longer has parental concern for health	• acquires and uses knowledge about low-cost good nutrition, physical check-ups, etc.; projects relationship of well-being to achievement of goals

Health Education Implications of Young People 14 to 18 Years of Age

Relating to Program Goal III: The Student Knows the Structure and Function of the Human Body and Patterns of Healthy Growth and Development

Selected developmental characteristics, health interests, and health needs:	Desired health knowledges, attitudes or behaviors
• develops fully physically	• understands and appreciates growth and development, especially variances
• shows concern for healthy children	• understands factors involved in healthy embryonic and fetal development, especially effects of nutrition; knows that mothers can affect development
• may be impatient with other age groups	• cites major growth and developmental characteristics of people at selected ages

Health Education Implications of Young People 14 to 18 Years of Age

Relating to Program Goal IV: The Student Understands Personal, Social, Economic, Cultural, and Ethnic Factors Which Influence Personal and Family Relationships

Selected developmental characteristics, health interests, and health needs:	Desired health knowledges, attitudes or behaviors
• struggles to learn socially approved outlets for sex drive; may experiment with intimate and casual sexual activity	• relates goals and values to sexual behavior, to type of relationships into which one enters, and to responsibilities toward children; shows respect for individuals as individuals and not just sexual beings

Health Education Implications of Young People 14 to 18 Years of Age (*Continued*)

Relating to Progam Goal IV: The Student Understands Personal, Social, Economic, Cultural, and Ethnic Factors Which Influence Personal and Family Relationships

Selected developmental characteristics, health interests, and health needs:	Desired health knowledges, attitudes or behaviors
• usually has great concern for children	• understands and appreciates effect of family on the development of individuals; needs to develop parenting skills for food selection, caring for a sick child, nurturing a child physically and emotionally, etc.
• is aware of risks to child and mother of early unwanted pregnancy	• relates life goals and values to sexual activity; knows ways to prevent conception if involved in sexual activity until one is able to meet a child's physical, emotional, and social needs
• shows high interest in the birth process	• knows the normal activities of birth; critiques literature on differing viewpoints on birth; knows father's role
• anxious about formation and continuation of relationships; looks for permanence in relationships	• assesses own values and goals and their relationships to mate selection; explores factors in successful relationships; needs to know self in relationship to capabilities of sustaining relationships
• concerned with alternative forms of sexual preference	• takes opportunities to understand all forms of sexual preference; establishes own sexual preference

Health Education Implications of Young People 14 to 18 Years of Age

Relating to Program Goal V: The Student Contributes to Community Health and Effectively Uses the Health Care System

Selected developmental characteristics, health interests, and health needs:	Desired health knowledges, attitudes or behaviors
• begins development of socially responsible behavior	• assesses individual's and society's responsibility for certain community health problems; contributes to the maintenance and improvement of health of friends, neighbors, family; recognizes the emotional health value of consideration toward others; asks questions of health-care professionals
• utilizes more drugs, independent of family	• acquires accurate information about drugs and regulations concerning their use; purchases, uses and stores drugs correctly
• formulates and tests hypotheses to solve problems	• assesses community health problems and possible solutions; evaluates world food shortage

Health Education Implications of Young People 14 to 18 Years of Age (*Continued*)

Relating to Program Goal V: The Student Contributes to Community Health and Effectively Uses the Health Care System

Selected developmental characteristics, health interests, and health needs:	**Desired health knowledges, attitudes or behaviors**
• is concerned with the hypothetical and the future	• explores possible health decisions that may arise from research and technology
• worries about career choice	• assesses self in relation to selected health careers; understands change as an acceptable factor throughout life
• chooses occupations suited to individual's capacities	• identifies potential and health assets and liabilities in choosing a career

Health Education Implications of Young People 14 to 18 Years of Age

Relating to Program Goal VI: The Student Practices Principles of Safe Living and is Able to Utilize Emergency Procedures in Case of Accidents

Selected developmental characteristics, health interests, and health needs:	**Desired health knowledges, attitudes or behaviors**
• accidents are the leading cause of death in this age group	• assesses situations as safe or hazardous; explores safety problems of young children; assesses own attitudes, values, skills, and knowledge in preventing accidents
• may resent limitations imposed on driving	• explores reasons for limitations
• has opportunities to use first aid	• completes American Red Cross first-aid courses

Health Education Implications of Young People 14 to 18 Years of Age

Relating to Program Goal VII: The Student Applies Principles of Disease Prevention, Where Possible, to Avoid Health Problems

Selected developmental characteristics, health interests, and health needs:	**Desired health knowledges, attitudes or behaviors**
• shows selected interest in disease prevention	• understands relationship of life-style and disease; is able to care for self for minor problems; investigates the epidemiology of selected diseases
• shows much interest in health problems	• explores physical, emotional, and economic costs of handicapping conditions and chronic illness; explores preventative measures; assesses personal and societal responsibility for health problems

Appendix

Report of the 1990 Joint Committee
on Health Education Terminology

NOVEMBER 1, 1990

Joint Committee on Health Education Terminology 1990 Committee Members

Evelyn E. Ames, Ph.D., CHES
Western Washington University
(American Public Health Association, School Health Education and Services Section)

Harriet H. Barr, M.P.H., CHES, Committee Co-Chair
University of North Carolina at Chapel Hill, School of Public Health
(American Public Health Association, Public Health Education and Health Promotion Section)

Bradley J. Bradford, M.D.
Pediatrician
(American Academy of Pediatrics)

Chet E. Bradley, M.S., CHES
Wisconsin Department of Public Instruction
(Society of State Directors of Health, Physical Education, and Recreation)

Peter A. Cortese, Dr. P.H., CHES, Committee Co-Chair
California State University, Long Beach
(Association for the Advancement of Health Education)

Karen A. Gordon, M.P.H.
Princeton University
(American College Health Association, Health Education Section)

This report was received and acknowledged in November 1990 by the Board of Directors of the Association for the Advancement of Health Education

(Permission granted for publication by the Association for the Advancement of Health Education/American Alliance for Health, Physical Education, Recreation and Dance.)

Marian V. Hamburg, Ed.D., CHES
Professor Emeritus, New York University
(Society for Public Health Education)

Cheryl C. Lackey, M.P.H., CHES
Texas Department of Health
(Association of State and Territorial Directors of Public Health Education)

Paul Mico, M.P.H., CHES
(Attended the August meeting as alternate delegate for Dr. Hamburg)
Third Party Associates, Inc.
(Society for Public Health Education)

John Seffrin, Ph.D., CHES
Indiana University
(American School Health Association)

Report of the 1990 Joint Committee on Health Education Terminology

One of the essential underpinnings of any profession is a body of well-defined terms used to enable members to communicate easily and with the clarity necessary for understanding among themselves and with others. The field of health education has changed dramatically in the past two decades. The definitions in this report provide a common interpretation of terms frequently used by health educators in a variety of settings. Therefore, the terms presented here are defined for use by the professional health educator as well as by other individuals and groups.

The Committee recognized that other health professionals (e.g., physicians, nurses, etc.) are concerned with and involved in health education as a part of their professional role and that they may have a different orientation. Consequently, they may use different terminology from that contained in this report. It is hoped, however, that the terms defined will be of help to these groups to clarify terminology used by health education professionals.

Words referring to health service and related personnel (e.g., patient educator, health counselor) or words which are in general use and understood by a variety of professionals (e.g., mass communication, objectives, self-help, self-care, evaluation) are not included. The Committee chose to define community and school health education and associated terminology, because degrees are offered in these areas. Other areas (e.g., patient and worksite health education) were omitted because they tend to be areas of emphasis rather than degrees.

There may be other interpretations of the words defined; however, those presented in this report are as many health educators view them today. The terms included reflect trends, concepts, and practices. They help to explain what the profession is, who its practitioners are and how they function. Additional uses might include the following:

- articulating the health education professional preparation program to other units on college and university campuses.
- assisting governmental agencies in planning effective health education policies and programs.
- assisting editorial boards in determining appropriate health education word usage.
- guiding accrediting and credentialing agencies.
- explaining the field of practice to other professionals.
- establishing a basis for consistency of language usage in the professional literature and in research endeavors and grantsmanship.

Historically, the Public Health Education Section of the American Public Health Association (APHA) developed a statement of terminology about 1927 (1). The first committee report on terminology was published by the American Physical Education Association in 1934 (2). The American Association for Health, Physical Education, and Recreation (AAHPER) presented a report on health and physical education terminology in 1950–51 (3). Another AAHPER joint committee was appointed in 1962 to foster and improve understanding on the part of school and public health educators (4). After nine years, AAHPER again took the lead which resulted in a 1973 joint committee terminology report (5). In 1990, the Association for the Advancement of Health Education (AAHE), an Association of the American Alliance for Health, Physical Education, Recreation and Dance, continued this leadership by convening a joint committee of delegates of the Coalition of National Health Education Organizations (CNHEO)* and a representative from the American Academy of Pediatrics to update the earlier terms and to add relevant new definitions.

The Association for the Advancement of Health Education provided staff support as well as funding for the Terminology Committee meeting. Additional financial support for dissemination of the report was contributed by the majority of organizations represented. The meeting was convened at the AAHE/AAHPERD headquarters in Reston, VA. August 2–5, 1990.

Process of Formulating the Definitions

The charge to the Committee was to review the 1973 Report of the Joint Committee on Health Education Terminology, to determine which terms are still relevant, to delete those considered outdated, to revise as deemed appropriate, and to add new terms currently used in the health education field. Individual members came with reference documents to be used in the process. AAHE library materials also were available. The committee was co-chaired by the coordinator of the Coalition and the AAHE delegate to the Coalition.

A draft document was completed during the meeting and subsequently circulated to a select number of outside reviewers for comment. The final document was presented as a Committee Report to the AAHE Board of Directors.

After acceptance by the AAHE Board of Directors, the Report was published in the *Journal of Health Education* and copies were provided to organizations whose delegates served on the Joint Committee. Each organization was encouraged to disseminate the final report to a wide audience.

---

*The Coalition was established in 1973 to provide a vehicle for collaboration of all major national health education organizations. Its primary mission is to mobilize the resources of the Health Education profession in order to expand and improve health education, regardless of the setting. Each member organization appoints one delegate and one alternate. The following organizations are members: American Public Health Association, School Health Education and Services Section and the Public Health Education and Health Promotion Section; American College Health Association; American School Health Association; Association for the Advancement of Health Education, American Alliance for Health, Physical Education, Recreation and Dance; Association of State and Territorial Directors of Public Health Education; Society for Public Health Education, Inc.; and the Society of State Directors of Health, Physical Education and Recreation.
The Coalition facilitates national level communication, collaboration and coordination among the member organizations; provides a forum for the identification and discussion of health education issues; formulates recommendations and takes appropriate action on issues affecting member interests; serves as a communication and advisory resource for agencies, organizations and persons in the public and private sectors on health education issues; and serves as a focus for the exploration and resolution of issues pertinent to professional health educators.

Criteria

The 1973 report was reviewed carefully. Some terms from this report were excluded, some repeated verbatim, some revised, and new terms were added based upon the criteria listed below.

Essentialness is basic to the field of health education and necessary for communication.

Authoritativeness is recognized or accepted by the profession as official language.

Significance is so important in communication within and among groups that its use requires common interpretation.

Encompassment is sufficiently broad and inclusive to eliminate unnecessary additional definitions but is restrictive enough to have clear meaning.

Usage occurs frequently enough to affect and effect communications.

Adaptability can be used effectively by various health professions and other individuals and groups.

Clarity definition is necessary to maintain consistency of use among disciplines.

A. Contextual Definitions

Health education takes place within the broad context of health. Certain health terms are defined to clarify how health education functions. These are:

Health

There are many definitions written for the word "HEALTH." Three examples are provided.

> "A state of complete physical, mental, and social well-being, and not merely the absence of disease and infirmity." (6)

> "A quality of life involving dynamic interaction and independence among the individual's physical well-being, his (sic) mental and emotional reactions, and the social complex in which he (sic) exists." (7)

> "An integrated method of functioning which is oriented toward maximizing the potential of which the individual is capable. It requires that the individual maintain a continuum of balance and purposeful direction with the environment where he (sic) is functioning." (8)

Health Promotion and Disease Prevention

Health promotion and disease prevention is the aggregate of all purposeful activities designed to improve personal and public health through a combination of strategies, including the competent implementation of behavioral change strategies, health education, health protection measures, risk factor detection, health enhancement and health maintenance.

Healthy Lifestyle

A healthy lifestyle is a set of health-enhancing behaviors, shaped by internally consistent values, attitudes, beliefs and external social and cultural forces.

Official Health Agency

An official health agency is a publicly supported governmental organization mandated by law and/or regulation for the protection and improvement of the health of the public.

Voluntary Health Organization

A voluntary health organization is a non-profit association supported by contributions dedicated to conducting research and providing education and/or services related to particular health problems or concerns.

(Note: Private voluntary organization—PVO is the term used outside the U.S.A. to denote a voluntary health organization; in some countries and in connection with the United Nations, the term non-governmental organization—NGO—is used.)

Private Health Agency

A private health agency is a profit or non-profit organization devoted to providing primary, secondary, and/or tertiary health services which may include health education.

B. Primary Health Education Definitions

Certain health education terms are generic and are defined here, as follows:

Health Education Field

The health education field is that multidisciplinary practice, which is concerned with designing, implementing, and evaluating educational programs that enable individuals, families, groups, organizations, and communities to play active roles in achieving, protecting, and sustaining health.

Health Education Process

The health education process is that continuum of learning which enables people, as individuals and as members of social structures, to voluntarily make decisions, modify behaviors, and change social conditions in ways which are health enhancing.

Health Education Program

A health education program is a planned combination of activities developed with the involvement of specific populations and based on a needs assessment, sound principles of education, and periodic evaluation using a clear set of goals and objectives.

Health Educator

A health educator is a practitioner who is professionally prepared in the field of health education, who demonstrates competence in both theory and practice, and who accepts responsibility to advance the aims of the health education profession.

Examples of settings for health educators and the application of health education include, but are not limited to, the following:

- Schools
- Communities
- Post-secondary educational institutions
- Medical care institutions
- Voluntary health organizations
- Worksites (business and industry)
- Rehabilitation centers
- Professional associations
- Governmental agencies
- Public health agencies
- Environmental agencies
- Mental health agencies

Certified Health Education Specialist (CHES)

A Certified Health Education Specialist (CHES) is an individual who is credentialed as a result of demonstrating competency based on criteria established by the National Commission for Health Education Credentialing, Inc. (NCHEC).

Health Education Coordinator

A health education coordinator is a professional educator who is responsible for the management and coordination of all health education policies, activities, and resources within a particular setting or circumstance.

Health Education Administrator

A health education administrator is a professional health educator who has the authority and responsibility for the management and coordination of all health education policies, activities, and resources within a particular setting or circumstance.

Health Information

Health information is the content of communications based on data derived from systematic and scientific methods as they relate to health issues, policies, programs, services, and other aspects of individual and public health, which can be used for informing various populations and in planning health education activities.

Health Literacy

Health literacy is the capacity of an individual to obtain, interpret, and understand basic health information and services and the competence to use such information and services in ways which are health enhancing.

Health Advising**

Health advising is a process of informing and assisting individuals or groups in making decisions and solving problems related to health.

C. Definitions Related to Community Settings

The terms that relate more specifically to community or public health education are defined here, as follows:

**The Committee believes that Health Counseling is a term that should be defined by the health counseling profession.

Community Health Education

Community health education is the application of a variety of methods that result in the education and mobilization of community members in actions for resolving health issues and problems which affect the community. These methods include, but are not limited to, group process, mass media, communication, community organization, organization development, strategic planning, skills training, legislation, policy making, and advocacy.

Community Health Educator

A community health educator is a practitioner who is professionally prepared in the field of community/public health education who demonstrates competence in the planning, implementation, and evaluation of a broad range of health promoting or health enhancing programs for community groups.

D. Definitions Related to Educational Settings

The terms that relate more specifically to school health education are defined here, as follows:

Comprehensive School Health Program

A comprehensive school health program is an organized set of policies, procedures, and activities designed to protect and promote the health and well-being of students and staff which has traditionally included health services, healthful school environment, and health education. It should also include, but not be limited to, guidance, counseling, physical education, food service, social work, psychological services, and employee health promotion.

School Health Education

School health education is one component of the comprehensive school health program which includes the development, delivery, and evaluation of a planned instructional program and other activities for students pre-school through grade 12, for parents and for school staff, and is designed to positively influence the health knowledge, attitudes, and skills of individuals.

School Health Services

School health services are that part of the school health program provided by physicians, nurses, dentists, health educators, other allied health personnel, social workers, teachers, and others to appraise, protect and promote the health of students and school personnel. These services are designed to insure access to and the appropriate use of primary health care services, prevent and control communicable disease, provide emergency care for injury or sudden illness, promote and provide optimum sanitary conditions in a safe school facility and environment, and provide concurrent learning opportunities which are conducive to the maintenance and promotion of individual and community health.

School Health Educator

A school health educator is a practitioner who is professionally prepared in the field of school health education, meets state teaching requirements, and demonstrates competence in the development, delivery, and evaluation of curricula for students and adults in the school setting that enhance health knowledge, attitudes, and problem-solving skills.

Comprehensive School Health Instruction

Comprehensive school health instruction refers to the development, delivery and evaluation of a planned curriculum, pre-school through 12, with goals, objectives, content sequence, and specific classroom lessons which includes, but is not limited to the following major content areas:

- Community health
- Consumer health
- Environmental health
- Family life
- Mental and emotional health
- Injury prevention and safety
- Nutrition
- Personal health
- Prevention and control of disease
- Substance use and abuse

Post-Secondary Health Education Program

A post-secondary health education program is a planned set of health education policies, procedures, activities, and services that are directed to students, faculty and/or staff of colleges, universities, and other higher education institutions. This includes, but is not limited to:

- general health courses for students
- employee and student health promotion activities
- health services
- professional preparation of health educators and other professionals
- self-help groups
- student life

Errata

References for the Report of the 1991 Joint Committee on Health Education Terminology

1. Mabel Rugen. (1972). *A fifty year history of the public health section of the American Public Health Association, 1922–1972.* American Public Health Association, Inc. Washington, DC, p. 9.
2. Jesse Feiring Williams (Chair). (1934, Dec. 10). Report of the Health Education Section of the American Physical Education Association. Definitions of terms in health education, *Journal of Health and Physical Education,* 5(16–17), 50–51.
3. Bernice Moss (Chair). (1950). Joint Committee on Health Education Terminology. *Journal of Health and Physical Education,* 21(41).
4. Robert Yoho (Chair). (1962, Nov). Joint Committee on Health Education Terminology. Health education terminology, *Journal of Health, Physical Education, Recreation,* 33(27–28).
5. Edward B. Johns (Chair). (1973, Nov/Dec). Joint Committee on Health Education Terminology. Report of the Joint Committee on Health Education Terminology, *Health Education,* 4(6), p. 25.
6. World Health Organization. (1946). *Constitution of the World Health Organization.* Geneva, World Health Organization.
7. *Health education: A conceptual approach to curriculum design, school health education study.* Washington, DC: 3M Education Press, p. 10.
8. Halbert Dunn. (1967). *High level wellness.* Virginia: R. W. Beatty, 4–5.

Appendix

Responsibilities and Competencies for Entry-Level Health Educators

Responsibility I—Assessing Individual and Community Needs for Health Education

Competency A: Obtain health-related data about social and cultural environments, growth and development factors, needs, and interests.

Sub-Competencies:

1. Select valid sources of information about health needs and interests.
2. Utilize computerized sources of health-related information.
3. Employ or develop appropriate data-gathering instruments.
4. Apply survey techniques to acquire health data.

Competency B: Distinguish between behaviors that foster, and those that hinder, well-being.

Sub-Competencies:

1. Investigate physical, social, emotional, and intellectual factors influencing health behaviors.
2. Identify behaviors that tend to promote or compromise health.
3. Recognize the role of learning and affective experience in shaping patterns of health behavior.

Competency C: Infer needs for health education on the basis of obtained data.

Sub-Competencies:

1. Analyze needs-assessment data.
2. Determine priority areas of need for health education.

From National Task Force for the Preparation and Practice of Health Educators, *A Framework for the Development of Competency-based Curricula for Entry Level Health Educators* (1985). Used by permission of the National Commission for Health Education Credentialing, Inc., which now holds the copyright.

Responsibility II—Planning Effective Health Education Programs

Competency A: Recruit community organizations, resource people, and potential participants for support and assistance in program planning.

Sub-Competencies:

1. Communicate need for the program to those who will be involved.
2. Obtain commitments from personnel and decision makers who will be involved in the program.
3. Seek ideas and opinions of those who will affect, or be affected by, the program.
4. Incorporate feasible ideas and recommendations into the planning process.

Competency B: Develop a logical scope and sequence plan for a health education program.

Sub-Competencies:

1. Determine the range of health information requisite to a given program of instruction.
2. Organize the subject areas comprising the scope of a program in logical sequence.

Competency C: Formulate appropriate and measurable program objectives.

Sub-Competencies:

1. Infer educational objectives facilitative of achievement of specified competencies.
2. Develop a framework of broadly stated, operational objectives relevant to a proposed health education program.

Competency D: Design educational programs consistent with specified program objectives.

Sub-Competencies:

1. Match proposed learning activities with those implicit in the stated objectives.
2. Formulate a wide variety of alternative educational methods.
3. Select strategies best suited to implementation of educational objectives in a given setting.
4. Plan a sequence of learning opportunities building upon, and reinforcing mastery of, preceding objectives.

Responsibility III—Implementing Health Education Programs

Competency A: Exhibit competence in carrying out planned educational programs.

Sub-Competencies:

1. Employ a wide range of educational methods and techniques.
2. Apply individual or group process methods as appropriate to given learning situations.
3. Utilize instructional equipment and other instructional media effectively.
4. Select methods that best facilitate practice of program objectives.

Competency B: Infer enabling objectives as needed to implement instructional programs in specified settings.

Sub-Competencies:

1. Pretest learners to ascertain present abilities and knowledge relative to proposed program objectives.
2. Develop subordinate measurable objectives as needed for instruction.

Competency C: Select methods and media best suited to implement program plans for specific learners.

Sub-Competencies:

1. Analyze learner characteristics, legal aspects, feasibility, and other considerations influencing choices among methods.
2. Evaluate the efficacy of alternative methods and techniques capable of facilitating program objectives.
3. Determine the availability of information, personnel, time, and equipment needed to implement the program for a given audience.

Competency D: Monitor educational programs, adjusting objectives and activities as necessary.

Sub-Competencies:

1. Compare actual program activities with the stated objectives.
2. Assess the relevance of existing program objectives to current needs.
3. Revise program activities and objectives as necessitated by changes in learner needs.
4. Appraise applicability of resources and materials relative to given educational objectives.

Responsibility IV—Evaluating Effectiveness of Health Education Programs

Competency A: Develop plans to assess achievement of program objectives.

Sub-Competencies:

1. Determine standards of performance to be applied as criteria of effectiveness.
2. Establish a realistic scope of evaluation efforts.
3. Develop an inventory of existing valid and reliable tests and survey instruments.
4. Select appropriate methods for evaluating program effectiveness.

Competency B: Carry out evaluation plans.

Sub-Competencies:

1. Facilitate administration of the tests and activities specified in the plan.
2. Utilize data-collecting methods appropriate to the objectives.
3. Analyze resulting evaluation data.

Competency C: Interpret results of program evaluation.

Sub-Competencies:

1. Apply criteria of effectiveness to obtained results of a program.
2. Translate evaluation results into terms easily understood by others.
3. Report effectiveness of educational programs in achieving proposed objectives.

Competency D: Infer implications from findings for future program planning.

Sub-Competencies:

1. Explore possible explanations for important evaluation findings.
2. Recommend strategies for implementing results of evaluation.

Responsibility V—Coordinating Provisions of Health Education Services

Competency A: Develop a plan for coordinating health education services.

Sub-Competencies:

1. Determine the extent of available health education services.
2. Match health education services to proposed program activities.
3. Identify gaps and overlaps in the provision of collaborative health services.

Competency B: Facilitate cooperation between and among levels of program personnel.

Sub-Competencies:

1. Promote cooperation and feedback among personnel related to the program.
2. Apply various methods of conflict reduction as needed.
3. Analyze the role of health educator as liaison between program staff and outside groups and organizations.

Competency C: Formulate practical modes of collaboration among health agencies and organizations.

Sub-Competencies:

1. Stimulate development of cooperation among personnel responsible for community health education program.
2. Suggest approaches for integrating health education within existing health programs.
3. Develop plans for promoting collaborative efforts among health agencies and organizations with mutual interests.

Competency D: Organize in-service training programs for teachers, volunteers, and other interested personnel.

Sub-Competencies:

1. Plan an operational, competency-oriented training program.
2. Utilize instructional resources that meet a variety of in-service training needs.
3. Demonstrate a wide range of strategies for conducting in-service training programs.

Responsibility VI—Acting as a Resource Person in Health Education

Competency A: Utilize computerized health information retrieval systems effectively.

Sub-Competencies:

1. Match an information need with the appropriate retrieval system.
2. Access principal on-line and other database health information resources.

Competency B: Establish effective consultative relationships with those requesting assistance in solving health-related problems.

Sub-Competencies:

1. Analyze parameters of effective consultative relationships.
2. Describe special skills and abilities needed by health educators for consultation activities.
3. Formulate a plan for providing consultation to other health professionals.
4. Explain the process of marketing health education consultative services.

Competency C: Interpret and respond to requests for health information.

Sub-Competencies:

1. Analyze general processes for identifying the information needed to satisfy a request.
2. Employ a wide range of approaches in referring requesters to valid sources of health information.

Competency D: Select effective educational resource materials for dissemination.

Sub-Competencies:

1. Assemble educational material of value to the health of individuals and community groups.
2. Evaluate the worth and applicability of resource materials for given audiences.
3. Apply various processes in the acquisition of resource materials.
4. Compare different methods for distributing educational materials.

Responsibility VII—Communicating Health and Health Education Needs, Concerns, and Resources

Competency A: Interpret concepts, purposes, and theories of health education.

Sub-Competencies:

1. Evaluate the state of the art of health education.
2. Analyze the foundations of the discipline of health education.
3. Describe major responsibilities of the health educator in the practice of health education.

Competency B: Predict the impact of societal value systems on health education programs.

Sub-Competencies:

1. Investigate social forces causing opposing viewpoints regarding health education needs and concerns.
2. Employ a wide range of strategies for dealing with controversial health issues.

Competency C: Select a variety of communication methods and techniques in providing health information.

Sub-Competencies:

1. Utilize a wide range of techniques for communicating health and health education information.
2. Demonstrate proficiency in communicating health information and health education needs.

Competency D: Foster communication between health-care providers and consumers.

Sub-Competencies:

1. Interpret the significance and implications of health-care providers' messages to consumers.
2. Act as liaison between consumer groups and individuals and health-care provider organizations.

Author Index

(Publications are in italics)

D

E